er: A roast leg of lamb, its surface seared by an
al blast of high heat, its interior pink and juicy, is carved
thin slices. Before the leg was roasted, the shank
e was cut short to leave a straight shaft of bone to
h a clamp — a *manche à gigot* — could be screwed.
lamp serves as a handle to steady the joint while it is
carved *(pages 32-33)*.

Books Inc.
ly owned subsidiary of
CORPORATED
Henry R. Luce 1898-1967
Chief: Henry Anatole Grunwald
J. Richard Munro
of the Board: Ralph P. Davidson
ice President: Clifford J. Grum
Executive Committee: James R. Shepley
rector: Ralph Graves
President, Books: Joan D. Manley
an: Arthur Temple

BOOKS INC.
tor: Jerry Korn; *Executive Editor:* David Maness;
aging Editors: Dale M. Brown (planning),
stable, Martin Mann, John Paul Porter, Gerry
ny), Art Director: Tom Suzuki; *Chief of
id L. Harrison; *Director of Photography:* Robert
istant Art Director: Arnold C. Holeywell;
of Research: Carolyn L. Sackett; *Assistant
tography: Dolores A. Littles; *Production Editor:*
ham; Operations manager: Gennaro C.
n E. Buck (assistant); *Assistant Production
Madrid; Quality Control: Robert L. Young
s J. Cox (assistant), Daniel J. McSweeney;
t (associates); *Art Coordinator:* Anne B.
aff: Susan B. Galloway (chief), Nancy
Gibert, Celia Beattie; *Picture Department:*
fic: Kimberly K. Lewis

McSweeney; President: Carl G. Jaeger;
idents. John Steven Maxwell, David J.
ents: George Artandi (comptroller);
al counsel); Peter G. Barnes; Nicholas
tions); John L. Canova; Beatrice T.
*Carol Flaumenhaft (consumer affairs);
urope/South Pacific); Herbert Sorkin
*Stewart (marketing)

of this book was created in London for
*I (Nederland) B.V.
an Tulleken; Design Director: Louis
rector: Pamela Marke; *Planning
Chief of Research: Vanessa Kramer;
Gray; Production Editor: Ellen Brush;
*as Whitworth

ditor: Gillian Boucher; *Series
y; Text Editor: Josephine Christian;
e Benet; Staff Writers: Alexandra
llen Galford, Thom Henvey;
Researchers: Krystyna Davidson,
Litton; Sub-Editors: Sally Rowland,
an; Design Assistant: Sally
ment: Steven Ayckbourn, Kate
Garner, Theresa John, Lesley
nda Mallett, Molly Sutherland,
orn, Sylvia Wilson

Editor: Ellen Phillips (acting);
ief Researcher: Barbara Fleming;
huyler; Text Editor: Mark Steele;
ll, Fran Moshos; *Researchers:*
*Pamela Gould (anthology),
ner: Peg Schreiber; *Art
ditorial Assistants: Brenda
Special Contributor: Christine

CHIEF SERIES CONSULTANT

Richard Olney, an American, has lived and worked for some three decades in France, where he is highly regarded as an authority on food and wine. Author of *The French Menu Cookbook* and of the award-winning *Simple French Food,* he has also contributed to numerous gastronomic magazines in France and the United States, including the influential journals *Cuisine et Vins de France* and *La Revue du Vin de France.* He is a member of several distinguished gastronomic societies, including L'Académie Internationale du Vin, La Confrérie des Chevaliers du Tastevin and La Commanderie du Bontemps de Médoc et des Graves. Working in London with the series editorial staff, he has been basically responsible for the planning of this volume, and has supervised the final selection of recipes submitted by other consultants. The United States edition of The Good Cook has been revised by the Editors of Time-Life Books to bring it into complete accord with American customs and usage.

CHIEF AMERICAN CONSULTANT

Carol Cutler is the author of a number of cookbooks, including the award-winning *The Six-Minute Soufflé and Other Culinary Delights.* During the 12 years she lived in France, she studied at the Cordon Bleu and the École des Trois Gourmandes, and with private chefs. She is a member of the Cercle des Gourmettes, a long-established French food society limited to just 50 members, and is also a charter member of Les Dames d'Escoffier, Washington Chapter.

SPECIAL CONSULTANT

Richard Sax, who was responsible for many of the step-by-step demonstrations in this volume, was for two years Chef-Director of the test kitchens for *The International Review of Food and Wine.* Trained in New York and in Paris, where he served an apprenticeship at the Hotel Plaza-Athénée, he has run a restaurant on Martha's Vineyard, written articles for a number of publications and conducted cooking courses.

PHOTOGRAPHER

John Cook, born in London, was trained as a photographer with the Royal Air Force and with the Regent Street Polytechnic in London. He specializes in food and still-life photography for both advertising and editorial use.

INTERNATIONAL CONSULTANTS

GREAT BRITAIN: *Jane Grigson* has written a number of books about food and has been a cookery correspondent for the London *Observer* since 1968. Alan Davidson, a former member of the British Diplomatic Service, is the author of several cookbooks and the founder of Prospect Books, which specializes in scholarly publications about food and cookery. FRANCE: *Michel Lemonnier,* the cofounder and vice president of Les Amitiés Gastronomiques Internationales, is a frequent lecturer on wine and vineyards. GERMANY: *Jochen Kuchenbecker* trained as a chef, but worked for 10 years as a food photographer in several European countries before opening his own restaurant in Hamburg. *Anne Brakemeier* is the co-author of a number of cookbooks. ITALY: *Massimo Alberini* is a well-known food writer and journalist, with a particular interest in culinary history. His many books include *Storia del Pranzo all'Italiana, 4000 Anni a Tavola* and *100 Ricette Storiche.* THE NETHERLANDS: *Hugh Jans* has published cookbooks and his recipes have appeared in several Dutch magazines. THE UNITED STATES: *François Dionot,* a graduate of L'École des Hôteliers de Lausanne in Switzerland, has worked as a chef, hotel general manager and restaurant manager in the United States and in France. He conducts his own cooking school in Maryland. He has been responsible for many of the step-by-step photographic sequences in this volume. *Judith Olney,* author of *Comforting Food* and *Summer Food,* received her culinary training in England and France. In addition to conducting cooking classes, she regularly writes articles for gastronomic magazines.

Correspondents: Elisabeth Kraemer (Bonn); Margot Hapgood, Dorothy Bacon, Lesley Coleman (London); Susan Jonas, Lucy T. Voulgaris (New York); Maria Vincenza Aloisi, Josephine du Brusle (Paris); Ann Natanson (Rome).
Valuable assistance was also provided by: Janny Hovin (Amsterdam); Judy Aspinall, Karin B. Pearce (London); Bona Schmid (Milan); Carolyn T. Chubet, Miriam Hsia, Christina Lieberman (New York); Mimi Murphy (Rome).

For information about any Time-Life book, please write:
Reader Information, Time-Life Books
541 North Fairbanks Court, Chicago, Illinois 60611

Library of Congress CIP data, page 176.

THE GOOD COOK
TECHNIQUES & RECIPES

Lamb

BY
THE EDITORS OF TIME-LIFE BOOKS

CONTENTS

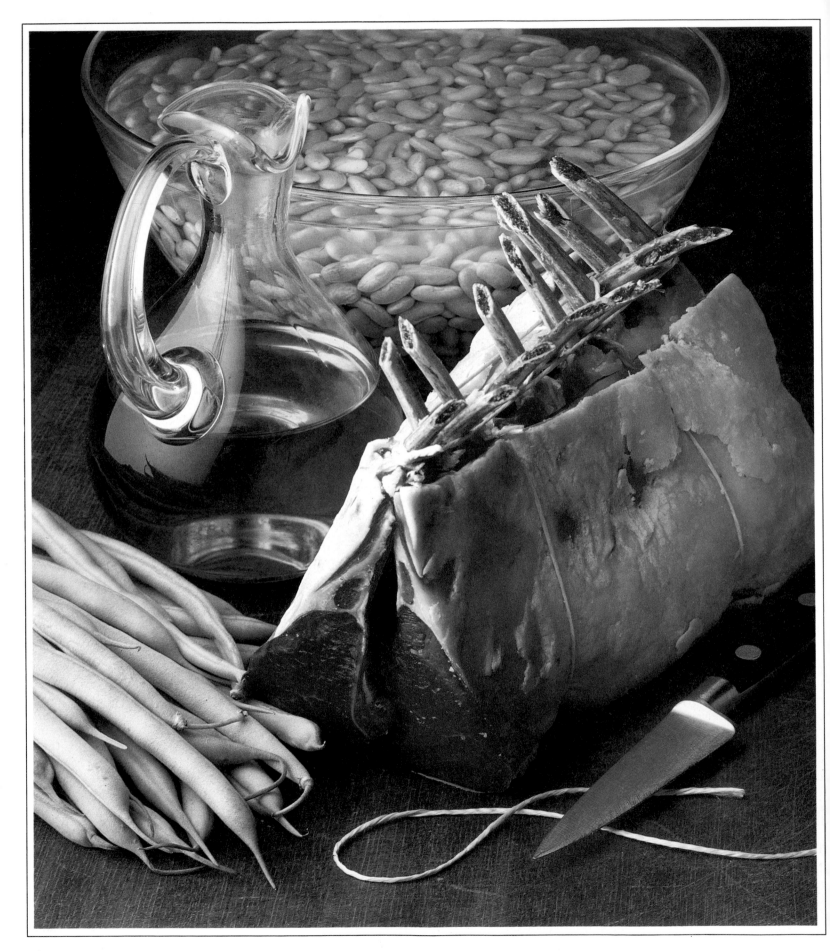

A Meat for All Seasonings

The virtue of lamb lies in the complexity of its flavor. At once delicate and rich, with faintly musky undertones, the meat lends itself to a remarkable variety of seasoning, cooking and garnishing treatments. In the sheep-raising areas of the Mediterranean — Southern France, Italy, Greece and Spain — the robust qualities of lamb are emphasized with olive oil, garlic and such assertive herbs as rosemary and tarragon. Many Middle Eastern, North African and Indian lamb dishes, on the other hand, concentrate on lamb's sweetness: A Moroccan lamb stew may well contain such fruits as dates, apricots and oranges. And lamb can also be treated with elemental simplicity: Small chops or large legs, innocent of any flavoring save salt and pepper, may be roasted or grilled to pink perfection, then served accompanied with foods that, like the meat itself, are the fruits of spring — fragile young lettuces, tender asparagus tips or diminutive new peas.

This book is an exploration of these and many other ways of cooking and serving lamb. The first half of the volume begins with an introductory section that explains how to recognize the different cuts of lamb and how to choose among them to make particular dishes. Also in this section are demonstrations of procedures fundamental to lamb cookery: the techniques for removing unwieldy bones from various large cuts so that the meat can be formed into regular shapes convenient for cooking and carving, and the methods of mixing marinades and combining ingredients for stuffings.

Three succeeding chapters offer step-by-step instructions for the different methods of cooking lamb — grilling, broiling, frying, roasting, poaching and braising — and outline the principles of garnishing and seasoning the meat. The final chapter shows how to combine preparatory and cooking techniques to create some of the most interesting and renowned of lamb dishes — Greek moussaka and Indian curry, for example — and also demonstrates appetizing assemblies that make inventive use of different cuts of leftover meat.

Armed with all of these skills, you will be ready to use the second half of the book — an anthology of 200 recipes gathered from cookbooks of many centuries and many cultures.

The festive animal

No meat-producing animals have had as long and profound an association with civilized man as sheep and their offspring. Curly-horned wild sheep called mouflons, whose descendants still exist on the relatively isolated islands of Sardinia and Corsica, were domesticated tens of thousands of years ago in what is now Kurdistan, a cool, hilly region that spreads through the countries of Iraq, Iran and Turkey.

As agricultural civilizations sprang up around the Mediterranean, in India and elsewhere in Asia, sheep — which could survive almost anywhere and produced wool for clothing as well as meat for food — remained the principal source of meat. Even today, the word "meat" in almost any Middle Eastern recipe means the flesh of sheep. One indication of the animals' importance to ancient civilizations is found in the language of the kingdom of Sumer, which flourished in present-day Iran 3,000 years before Christ: The Sumerian vocabulary contained more than 200 words to use in describing the characteristics of various breeds of sheep.

The strongest testament to the importance of these animals, however, is their role in religious ceremonies. In early religions, the primary sacrificial animal — and the one therefore most valuable to man — was the lamb. This role is echoed today in the festivals of the major Western religions. In Muslim countries, lambs are roasted whole to celebrate the New Year and other important rites of passage — weddings and the birth of children, for example. Lamb — served, as specified in the Old Testament, with unleavened bread and bitter herbs — is also the prescribed food for the Jewish Passover feast in the spring. And lamb, significant as the symbol of Christ, is the traditional Easter meat for Christians, particularly in Italy, Greece and other countries where the pastoral tradition is strong.

Developing tender meat

Laborious tenderizing instructions in recipes surviving from medieval times and earlier indicate that the meat supplied by the flocks of those eras was rather tough. In imperial Rome, for example, whole lambs were wrapped in caul — a fatty membrane that covers animals' stomachs and intestines — and then stewed for hours in milk and honey. Persians of the Seventh Century A.D., like their Arab neighbors then and now, marinated lamb in such acidic ingredients as pomegranate juice or yogurt before cooking, or else they ground the meat. The cooks for medieval European courts first pounded lamb meat to a purée, then combined it with eggs, spices and marrow, or they stewed it in wine or ale.

One reason for the necessity of such tenderizing is that the animals were bred as much for their wool — a prime source of income — as for the food they provided. In addition, the flocks were often driven long distances in search of pasturage. In Spain, for instance, medieval shepherds took their flocks each year all the way from the Pyrenees, where they summered on the French border, to winter feeding grounds in the southern part of the Iberian Peninsula, a distance of more than 500 miles. Such strenuous exercise naturally made the animals muscular and their flesh stringy.

During the late Renaissance, however, some farmers began experimenting with crossbreeding and improved feeding methods for sheep, all with an eye to obtaining tender and abundant meat along with a good yield of wool. By the 18th Century, the practice had become widespread, and even King Louis XV of France had an experimental flock. His son referred to the animals as "walking cutlets."

The most serious and productive experimentation in crossbreeding and feeding took place in 18th Century England, led

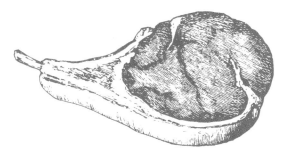

by a breeder named Robert Bakewell. "Symmetry, well rounded" was Bakewell's motto, and thanks to his work, English sheep developed into chunky, compact animals that provided a plenitude of flavorful meat.

Lamb in America

Most of the lamb meat sold in American markets comes from English breeds—descendants of Robert Bakewell's flocks. The sheep are raised in every state, but the vast majority originate in the West, where sheep have long been bred on a grand scale.

The first sheep in the West were hardy little *churros*, left there in the 16th Century by Coronado and other Spanish explorers, who had carried the animals on their ships for food. These sheep multiplied into the huge flocks—some as large as two million animals—that populated the ranches of 17th and 18th Century Spanish dons in the Southwest. Although *churros* were raised chiefly for their wool, they proved an invaluable food source for the armies of newcomers who flooded into California and other parts of the West when gold and silver were discovered in the mid-19th Century. At about the same period, flocks of larger, finer sheep, such as Spanish merinos and Bakewell's English breeds, were driven across the continent by pioneering settlers. Careful crossbreeding in the succeeding decades eventually produced the meaty animals that still supply American markets.

Texas, California and Wyoming support the largest flocks of sheep in the United States. Fittingly enough, most of these flocks are herded by men from Spain—the Basques of the Pyr-

enees, who have been emigrating to America for more than a century to earn their fortunes by following their traditional shepherd's calling.

Choosing the meat

As sheep age, their meat becomes stronger in taste and firmer in texture. Of the lamb available on the market, the type considered most delicate in flavor and tender in flesh is baby lamb, also known as milk lamb or hothouse lamb. These animals, produced all year round by controlled breeding, are slaughtered when they are six to 10 weeks old, before weaning. They are sold in specialty stores in larger cities and are expensive. (Infant goat, or kid, is equally tender, rare and expensive and also can be found in specialty markets in the winter months. It is cooked in the same ways as baby lamb.)

The largest supply of meat by far comes from animals dropped in the spring lambing season, which may be as early as January in the warm states of the Southwest and as late as May in colder northern areas. These lambs are slaughtered when they are between the ages of six months and one year. After that age, physiological changes occur that intensify the flavor of their flesh. Meat from a lamb older than one year cannot legally be labeled "genuine lamb." Animals that are slaughtered between the ages of a year and 20 months are sometimes called "yearling lamb"; the meat they produce is firmer in texture and stronger in flavor. For culinary purposes, that meat should be considered mutton rather than lamb.

Mutton—meat from older animals—is undeservedly unpopular and is rarely found in American markets. But it has figured prominently in the cooking of all sheep-raising countries, and is well worth experimenting with when it is available. It has a strong, rich flavor (enthusiasts claim that not even the best beef can match fine mutton) that marries well with the intense seasonings that are found in Middle Eastern, Indian and Chinese dishes.

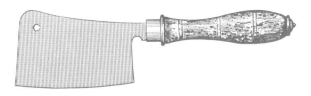

The care and cooking of lamb

Lamb will be freshest in taste if it is cooked on the same day it is purchased. Whole cuts may, however, be kept for up to four days in the refrigerator if they are securely enclosed in plastic wrap or aluminum foil. Ground lamb has a greater area of exposed surfaces and hence is more vulnerable to contamination; it should not be kept for more than two days.

Carefully wrapped lamb may also be frozen; whole cuts will keep for up to nine months at temperatures of 0° F. [−18° C.] or lower. Ground lamb will last only four months in a freezer. Any frozen meat should be defrosted in the refrigerator so that the ice crystals formed by the meat juices melt slowly, allowing the meat to reabsorb its juices instead of drying out. Allow four to seven hours per pound for defrosting.

Prepare the meat carefully for cooking. If you happen to find baby lamb or kid, you will have to add fat to the meat; otherwise, the lean flesh of these young animals will dry out during cooking. The meat may be larded with pork fat, available from butchers. Or, for a particularly delicious flavor, wrap the baby lamb or kid in caul, as demonstrated on page 47. All other lamb or mutton must be carefully trimmed of fat before cooking: Lamb fat has a waxy flavor, and too much of it will give the meat a disagreeable tang.

Lamb meat is covered by a papery surface membrane called the fell. This membrane, which lies between the skin and flesh of live animals, is left on large cuts by most butchers as a protective covering for the tender meat. Do not remove the fell from such large cuts as legs: It helps them retain their shape and juiciness during cooking. Any fell found on small cuts of lamb such as chops should be removed: The membrane shrinks somewhat during the cooking period and could distort the shape of the small meat pieces.

Because the lamb sold today comes from young animals bred for tenderness, most cuts may be cooked by the so-called dry-heat cooking methods—roasting, grilling, broiling and frying, all of which apply heat in the absence (or near absence) of liquid. The shape and thickness of a particular cut should determine which cooking approach you choose. Large cuts such as rib roasts, loins and legs are best roasted: The enveloping heat penetrates their irregular shapes most evenly. Smaller cuts such as steaks or chops can be grilled, broiled or fried.

These methods produce delectable results when the meat is discreetly perfumed with herbs, especially those of the labiate family, so called because their leaves are thought to resemble lips. The group includes thyme, savory, marjoram and oregano. The pungent flavors of rosemary and dill, used with restraint, also combine happily with the richness of roast lamb.

Large cuts such as boned legs and foresaddles can be stuffed, offering wide opportunities for imaginative flavoring. Stuffings may be based on sweet ingredients such as fruit or chestnuts, on aromatic ones such as garlic and onion, or they can be hearty mixtures containing meats such as pork and ham.

Whether the meat is roasted, grilled, broiled or fried, it will be at its succulent best when it is still pink, or rare. With a longer cooking time, the meat becomes drier and a good deal of its flavor vanishes.

As a general rule, the moist-heat cooking methods, poaching and braising, are best suited to firmer cuts of lamb—breast, shank and shoulder. These cuts profit from the tenderizing action of long, slow simmering. As a bonus, lamb braises and stews permit the blending of the meat's flavor with those of other ingredients for rich and subtle effects. Lamb braises frequently include aromatic vegetables such as carrots, onions and turnips, for instance, but they can also be given unusual, spicy accents by seasonings such as cloves, cinnamon and ginger, as in classic Indian curries. Another traditional approach is to include bland, starchy ingredients—beans in France, potatoes in Ireland—which acquire distinction as they absorb the meat juices and flavors.

Wine with lamb

The wines most often chosen to accompany lamb are red. But which red wine is best depends on how the meat is seasoned, cooked and garnished. As a general rule, serve the finest and most complex wines with simple dishes, which will not distract the palate from the subtleties of the wine; serve complex lamb dishes with uncomplicated wines. Any honest red wine serves as a good complement to roast lamb, but nothing softens the

reserve of a great Burgundy or relaxes the austerity of a fine, aged Bordeaux so auspiciously as a discreetly seasoned leg, saddle or rack of lamb.

Many red wines of considerable finesse make milder demands than particularly fine Burgundies or Bordeaux. American examples include Zinfandels and Cabernet Sauvignons from California. French candidates are the red Cornas and Saint-Joseph from the Côtes du Rhône, the various growths from the Beaujolais, and Chinons from Touraine. These wines are perfect with stews and braised dishes; a *navarin* with spring vegetables *(pages 61-62)* is the paradigm. Perhaps with the intensity of flavor to be found in a daube—lamb braised for hours with aromatic vegetables and salt pork *(pages 58-59)*—a rougher, more muscular red wine such as a Barolo from Italy or a Châteauneuf-du-Pape would be well chosen.

The spicy, exuberantly flavored lamb dishes of the Middle East and North Africa demand robust, even coarse wines. An earthy white or a rosé, drunk cool or chilled, can often support the presence of strong flavorings better than red wine. Highly seasoned dishes such as the lemon-scented Moroccan *tajine* demonstrated on pages 56-57 would be well served by a Roman Frascati, by white wines from Southern Italy and Sicily, by most Greek wines or by white cassis or rosé from Southern France. A particularly appropriate choice would be an Algerian red, white or rosé wine: The best of these are the Coteaux de Mascara.

Baby lamb is customarily accompanied by red wine, but it can very happily share honors at the table with a fine white—a Meursault or Puligny-Montrachet from France, perhaps, or a Chardonnay from California. Whatever the age of the lamb, there are no fixed rules for serving wine. As in cooking, there are only guidelines that may well be altered in the interest of new experiences and new pleasures.

A Guide to Lamb Cuts

Knowing which part of the carcass a cut of lamb or mutton comes from can help you gauge how tender it will be: Meat from the back, where the muscles are little worked, will be meltingly tender; meat from other parts of the animal that are harder worked will be less tender—although rarely tough.

The usual first divisions of a lamb carcass—or mutton, when it is available—are shown in the center diagram at right. Before sale, these divisions—called primal sections—are generally subdivided into the smaller retail cuts shown surrounding the central diagram. On request, however, butchers will divide the animal differently to make double cuts: Among them are such lavish pieces as the foresaddle, which includes the entire front section of the animal, or the baron of lamb, which includes the entire hind section. Or these sections can be cut to make double-loin roasts or chops.

All lamb is stamped with the round seals used by state or federal inspectors to indicate that the meat is wholesome. Additionally, about two thirds of all carcasses are graded for quality. Cuts graded "prime" are the most tender and have generous marbling—or streaks of fat—within the lean to enhance their flavor and succulence. "Choice" lamb, which is the grade most often available at retail markets, has less marbling but is still tender and juicy. "Good" grade lamb is tougher and has little marbling.

When buying lamb, make your own inspection to be certain that it has not suffered from improper handling or storage: Fresh, young lamb should have firm flesh and white fat, and the ends of its bones should be red, moist and porous. In mature lamb or in mutton, the meat is darker and the bones are whiter and drier. The fat of any cut should be dry and firm to the touch.

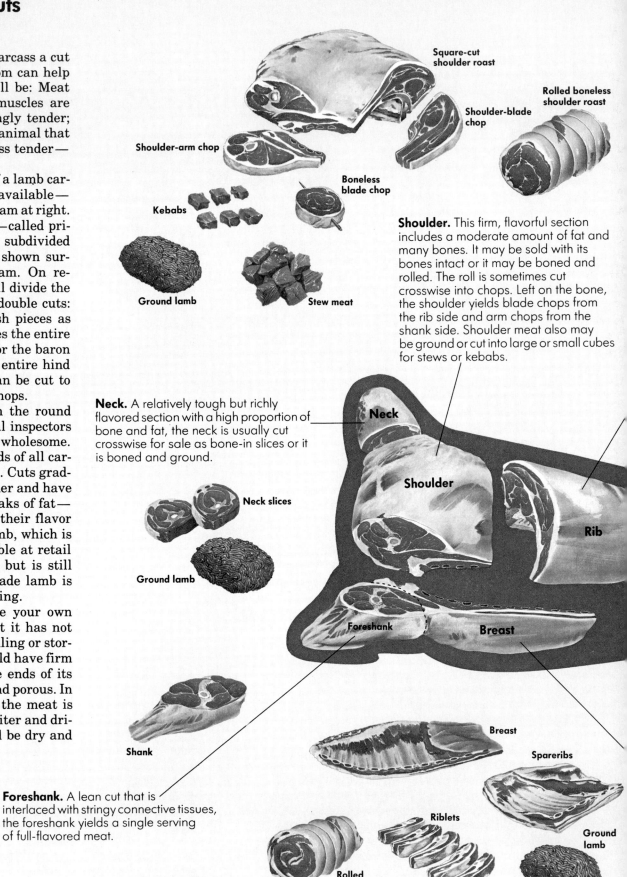

Square-cut shoulder roast

Rolled boneless shoulder roast

Shoulder-blade chop

Shoulder-arm chop

Boneless blade chop

Kebabs

Ground lamb

Stew meat

Shoulder. This firm, flavorful section includes a moderate amount of fat and many bones. It may be sold with its bones intact or it may be boned and rolled. The roll is sometimes cut crosswise into chops. Left on the bone, the shoulder yields blade chops from the rib side and arm chops from the shank side. Shoulder meat also may be ground or cut into large or small cubes for stews or kebabs.

Neck. A relatively tough but richly flavored section with a high proportion of bone and fat, the neck is usually cut crosswise for sale as bone-in slices or it is boned and ground.

Neck

Shoulder

Rib

Neck slices

Ground lamb

Foreshank

Breast

Shank

Breast

Spareribs

Foreshank. A lean cut that is interlaced with stringy connective tissues, the foreshank yields a single serving of full-flavored meat.

Riblets

Ground lamb

Rolled boneless breast

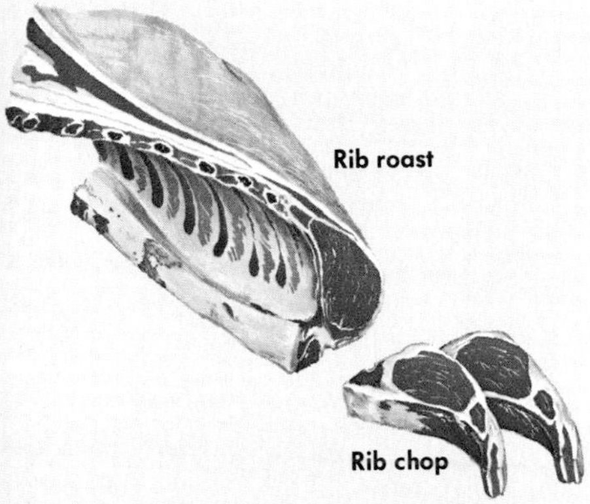

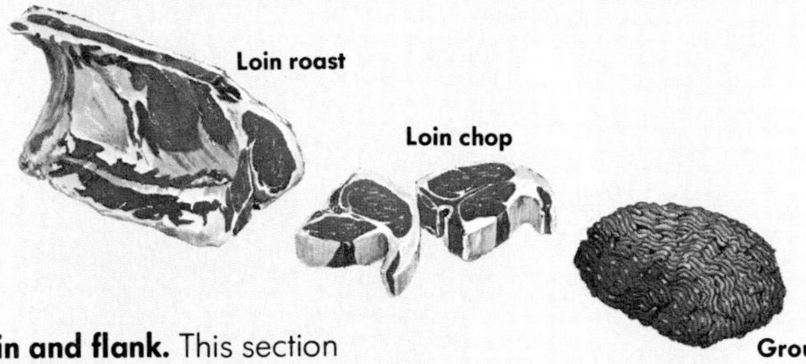

Loin roast

Loin chop

Ground lamb

Rib roast

Rib chop

Loin and flank. This section contains the lamb's tenderest and toughest meat. Tenderest are the eye of loin and the tenderloin, which, left whole along with the T-bone, make up the loin roast. Divided crosswise, the section yields chops. The toughest lamb is the meat from the flank, or apron. It is usually cut off and ground.

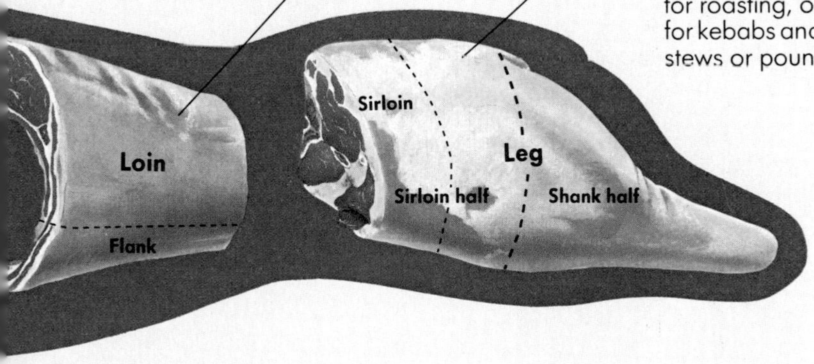

Rib. This expensive section includes a lode of tender, richly marbled meat along the backbone and a thick, outer layer of fat that melts and bastes the meat during roasting. A whole rib roast — also known as a rack — usually contains seven ribs; it may be divided into smaller roasts, containing fewer ribs, or into one- or two-rib chops.

Leg. The leg offers both the tender, marbled meat of the upper, or sirloin, end and the firmer meat of the shank end. With the bone in, it may be sold whole, cut into large sirloin-half and shank-half roasts or divided into smaller sirloin and center roasts, sirloin chops and leg steaks. A boned leg may be rolled whole for roasting, or the sirloin portion cubed for kebabs and the shank meat cut up for stews or pounded for cubed steak.

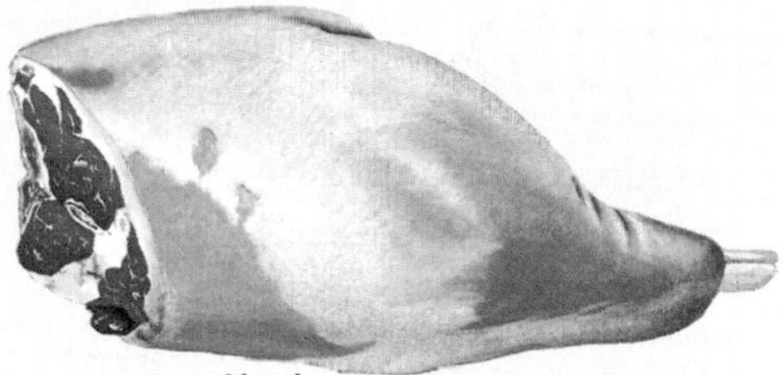

Leg of lamb

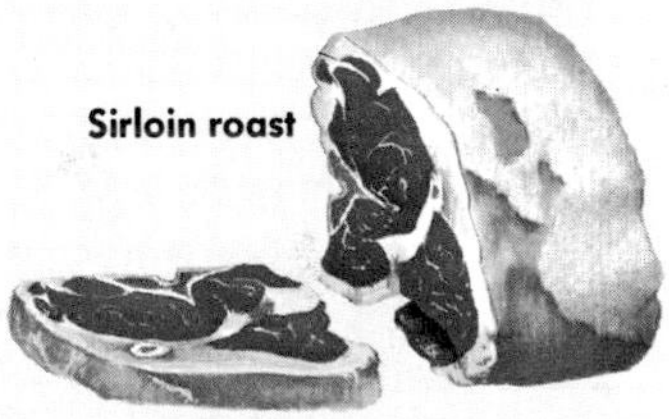

Sirloin

Loin

Leg

Sirloin half

Shank half

Flank

Sirloin roast

Sirloin chop

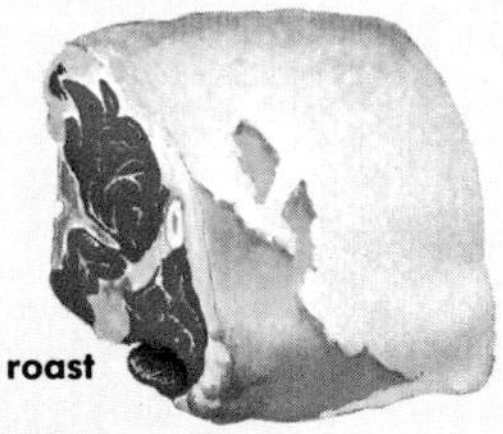

Sirloin-half roast

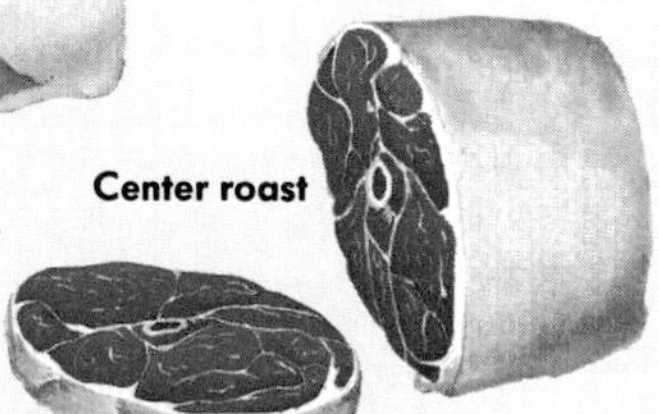

Center roast

Rolled boneless leg

Kebabs

Leg steak

Cubed steak

Breast. A fatty but full-flavored section, breast is sold whole with bones intact or is boned and rolled. It may also be divided into four- to 12-rib slabs of spareribs or split between every rib for riblets. The breast section also yields ground lamb for patties.

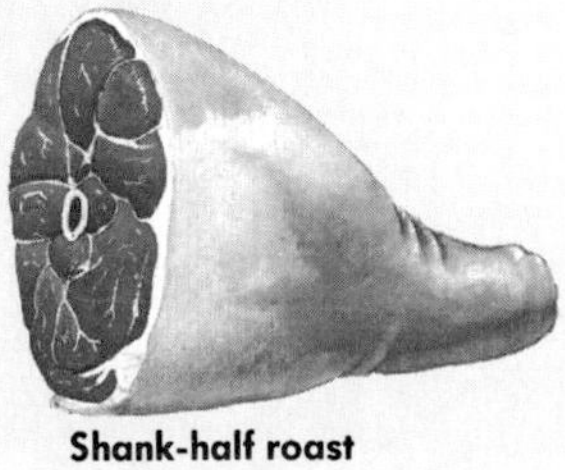

Stew meat

Shank-half roast

Boning Large Cuts for Carving or Stuffing

Removing bones from large cuts of lamb (*right and following pages*) is a straightforward operation that needs little more than a sharp knife and patience. However, the rewards are many. Partially boned, a leg of lamb can be easily carved into neat slices (*pages 32-33*). With all of the bones taken out, a breast yields a meaty slab to enfold stuffing (*pages 40-41*), and a shoulder becomes a compact roast suitable for rolling (*pages 36-37*). Furthermore, the bones can be put to use in stock-making (*page 52*) and any meat trimmings can be incorporated into a stuffing (*page 15*).

When preparing a leg for carving (*top demonstration*), begin by severing the tough Achilles tendon at its shank end and pushing the tendon and surrounding flesh away from the end of the bone. The shaft of bone can then be used as a handle while the leg is being sliced. Or, for surer control and a more elegant presentation, you can saw off the knobby end of the shank and fit the shaft with a *manche à gigot* — the carving handle shown on the cover of this book.

Removing the pelvic bone at the rounded end of the leg—the sirloin end—will make the meat easier to carve into neat slices. The amount of pelvic bone in a leg varies according to the proportion of sirloin the butcher has cut off to sell as sirloin roast or chops: A long leg, such as the one shown here, may contain the entire bone; a shorter leg may hold only a piece.

The breast is simpler in structure, although its bones are more numerous: It contains a breastbone and, in most cases, 10 or 11 ribs, depending on how the butcher has divided the carcass. By working methodically, you can detach all the bones in a single piece (*bottom demonstration*).

Any boning job will be simplified if you firm the meat by chilling it for about three hours in the coldest part of the refrigerator—or for about 15 minutes in the freezer. To avoid wasting meat when you cut around bones, use a small, sharp knife that has a fairly flexible, narrow blade. To shorten the shaft of the leg shank, you will also need a butcher's saw, which can be obtained from a kitchen-supply store, or a hacksaw, obtainable from a hardware store.

Partial Boning of a Leg

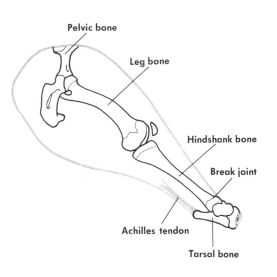

Leg bones. The pelvic bone lies crosswise in the rounded end of the leg. A ball-and-socket joint connects it to the leg bone, which meets the hindshank bone about halfway down the leg. A small knob, which butchers call the break joint, joins the shank to the tarsal bone. The Achilles tendon connects the tarsal bone to the muscles of the upper leg.

Exposing the shank bone. Sever the Achilles tendon about 1½ inches [4 cm.] above the break joint. Expose the lower 2 to 3 inches [5 to 8 cm.] of the shank bone by loosening the meat around it with a knife (*above*). Push the meat and the severed tendon aside.

Simple Tactics for a Breast

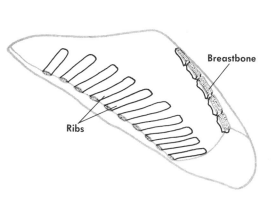

Breastbone. The breastbone runs the length of the thick side of the breast. Ribs extend across it from the opposite side. A strong band of cartilage — not shown here — runs through the meat to connect the ribs to the breastbone.

Making a pocket. Place the breast bony side up, with the rib tips pointing toward you. Lift the flap of meat at the thin end of the breast. Slip a knife under the flap and cut horizontally to separate the meat from the ridge of cartilage underneath (*above*). Push the meat away from the cartilage to open up a pocket.

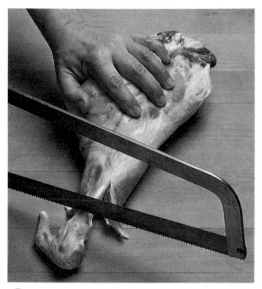

2 **Sawing the shank bone.** Using your free hand to steady the leg, saw off the hindshank bone just above the break joint with a butcher's saw, as shown here, or with a hacksaw.

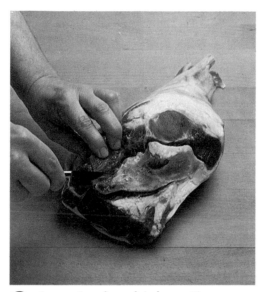

3 **Loosening the pelvic bone.** Place the leg with its rounded end toward you, and cut around the exposed edges of the pelvic bone. Then gradually work the knife deeper into the flesh, following the contours of the bone.

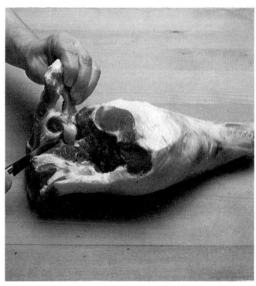

4 **Removing the pelvic bone.** When you have exposed the ball-and-socket joint, sever the ligaments joining the pelvic bone to the leg bone. Finally, scrape any last bits of flesh from the pelvic bone and pull it free.

2 **Freeing the breastbone.** Starting at one end of the breastbone, insert the knife between the bone and the thick layer of flesh underneath it. Using short, up-and-down sawing strokes, work the knife blade along the entire length of the bone (above).

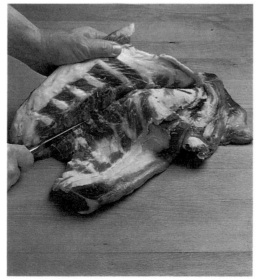

3 **Detaching the ribs.** Position the breast so that the thick end is closest to you. Grasp the breastbone and pull it — and the ribs attached to it — away from the meat. In places where the ribs do not easily pull free, scrape along the bones with your knife.

4 **Cutting away rib tips.** As you work, the bones will fall to one side of the knife blade and the meat to the other. When all of the bones are cut free, lift off the breastbone and rib assembly. Cut away any tiny rib tips attached to the meat.

Freeing Bones from the Cumbersome Shoulder

A shoulder, one of the largest cuts available and one with an especially complex bone structure, is easy to handle—and carve—once the bones have been removed. Although lamb shoulder is sold already boned, doing the job yourself can save money and ensure that the cut will exactly suit your needs.

To speed the work, familiarize yourself with the anatomy of the cut (diagram, below). In addition to detaching the rib, back and neck assembly, which lies on the surface, you must remove two internal bones—the blade and the arm. Taking out the surface bones is relatively simple, but removing the internal bones requires meticulous work to avoid cutting through the shoulder—thus spoiling its appearance.

Because boning a shoulder involves cutting close to irregularly shaped bones, the best implement is a boning knife. Its narrow blade can be maneuvered around knobby vertebrae, and its razor-sharp tip slices cleanly through the meat, keeping waste to a minimum. Hold the edge of the blade pressed against the bones, using your free hand to pull the loosened meat aside. Take care, however, to keep your free hand out of the path of the blade.

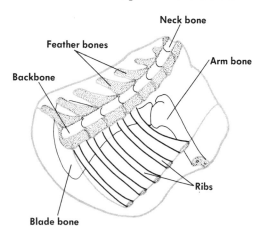

Shoulder bones. The vertebrae of the backbone and neck bone lie along the thick side of the shoulder. Ribs and short feather bones arch out from the back vertebrae; only feather bones protrude from the neck. Beneath the ribs and not visible on the surface are the blade bone and the arm bone, which connect as a ball-and-socket joint.

1 **Freeing the ribs.** Lay the shoulder bony side upward, with the end of the backbone closest to you. Starting at the exposed ends of the ribs and working toward the backbone, cut along the underside of the rib assembly. Work with short strokes, made as close to the bones as possible, and lift up the ribs as you free them from the meat.

2 **Freeing the neck.** After freeing all of the ribs from the underlying meat, turn the shoulder so that the backbone and neck bone are away from you. Lift the loosened rib assembly. Angling the knife to follow the knobby contours of the vertebrae, cut as close to the neck bone as possible to free it from the meat.

6 **Exposing the blade bone.** Bend the shoulder back and forth to locate the joint between the blade and arm bones. Starting over this joint, make a long incision along the inner edge of the blade bone. Cut along the contours of the upper side of the blade bone, folding back the meat covering the bone as you free it (above).

7 **Freeing the blade bone.** With the meat above the bone still folded back, cut underneath the blade bone, lifting it gently as you free it. Follow the contours of the bone closely; the long ridge on its underside necessitates cutting with care to avoid splitting the shoulder.

3 **Freeing the feather bones.** Turn the shoulder around and pull back the freed ribs. Working along the backbone, cut underneath the feather bones to separate them from the meat.

4 **Removing the rib assembly.** Fold the entire rib, back and neck assembly — which includes the feather bones — away from the meat while you sever any bits of cartilage that still attach it to the shoulder. Save the assembly for a stock or braise.

5 **Removing the tendon.** Use the knife to pry out and cut away the long, yellow ligament exposed by the removal of the backbone and neck bone. Trim away any cartilage or excess fat from the channel that held the bones.

8 **Removing the blade bone.** When you have freed all of the surfaces of the blade bone, lift it and cut through the ligament at the joint that attaches it to the arm bone. Grasp one end of the blade bone and pull firmly to remove the bone completely.

9 **Removing the arm bone.** Make an incision along the length of the arm bone to expose it. Then carefully cut along both sides and beneath the bone until it can be pulled free.

10 **Removing excess fat.** Turn the shoulder around so that the fatty side is facing you. From its center, cut out the large clod of fat. Discard the fat and the grayish, harmless gland it contains.

Marinades and Stuffings to Enhance Flavor

Marinades and stuffings both give extra flavor to lamb, but in quite different ways. A marinade is a fragrant mixture in which the meat is steeped before cooking. A stuffing exchanges flavor with the meat during the cooking, and is then served as a garnish to the meat.

Marinades *(right)* usually contain aromatic vegetables and herbs. Oil, which lubricates the surface of the meat and helps to distribute flavors, is often added, as is an acidic liquid such as wine.

Marinades come in two basic forms, called (somewhat misleadingly) dry and wet. A dry marinade contains oil, but no more than a few spoonfuls of any water-based liquid. It is used principally before meat is roasted or grilled to lubricate the surface of the meat so that it will sear without drying. A wet marinade usually employs enough liquid to cover the meat and is valuable in braising; when the meat is cooked, the marinade can serve as part of the braising liquid.

Both types of marinade need time to permeate the meat. For small cuts, allow one hour per inch [2½ cm.] of thickness if marinated at room temperature, three hours in the refrigerator. For large cuts, refrigerate for at least 24 hours; turn the meat over occasionally if it is not completely submerged in a wet marinade.

Stuffings *(opposite)* are usually associated with large, boned cuts: A bulky mixture is stuffed into the space left by the bones, and the meat is then sewed or tied around it. A lighter mixture can be spread on meat before rolling it *(pages 36-37)* or placed between the flesh of a leg of lamb and its membrane *(pages 44-45)*.

Persillade—a combination of crushed garlic and chopped parsley *(right, bottom)*—may be used as a light stuffing on its own or serve as a flavoring in a bulky stuffing. Other substantial flavorings include chopped, parboiled leaf vegetables; raw or sautéed mushrooms or onions; or chopped or ground meat. For a bulky stuffing, add the flavorings to starchy ingredients such as bread crumbs or cooked rice. Fatty elements—soft, fresh cheese or butter among them—will moisten the stuffing; eggs will bind the ingredients. The stuffings on the opposite page show some possibilities *(recipe, page 166)*.

A Coating of Oil and Herbs

A dry marinade. Place the meat — in this instance, leg steaks — in a dish just large enough to hold it easily. Slather the surfaces of the meat with a mixture of oil, lemon juice, dried or freshly chopped herbs such as thyme, rosemary or the dill shown here, and seasonings such as salt, pepper or dry mustard. Strew sprigs of fresh herbs over the top. Cover the meat and let it absorb the flavors of the marinade. Before cooking, brush off the herb sprigs.

An Aromatic Wine Bath

A wet marinade. Place meat — in this case, lamb shoulder — in a bowl with all of the marinade ingredients: here, thin slices of onion and carrots, unpeeled crushed garlic cloves, a bay leaf and sprigs of rosemary, thyme and oregano. Pour in a spoonful or two of oil and enough wine to submerge the meat. Cover the meat and let it marinate. Before cooking, drain the meat and — if you plan to sear it — pat the surfaces dry with paper towels.

Persillade: A Versatile Stuffing Element

Combining parsley and garlic. Thump garlic cloves lightly with a mallet or the flat of a knife to split the skins. Peel the cloves and put them in a mortar with some coarse salt — the salt will help you grind the garlic to a paste. Pound with a pestle until the garlic is puréed *(above, left)*. Chop flat-leafed parsley fine and blend it into the garlic purée with your fingers *(right)*.

Ham Allied with Cheese

1 **Preparing ingredients.** Cut boiled ham into small cubes. Make a *persillade (opposite, bottom)*. Put these ingredients into a bowl together with ricotta cheese, eggs and fresh bread crumbs.

2 **Seasoning the mixture.** Add some softened butter. Season with salt, freshly ground black pepper and mixed dried herbs. If you like, grate in some nutmeg *(above)*.

3 **Mixing the stuffing.** With your hands, knead the ingredients together lightly until they are amalgamated. The stuffing should be firm; if it is soft or wet, knead in additional bread crumbs.

A Seasoned Pork Mixture

1 **Grinding meat.** Cut lean and fat pork — leg and belly are used here — into cubes and push the meat twice through the medium disk of a food grinder, then once through the fine disk.

2 **Assembling ingredients.** Chop parsley and garlic fine. Place them in a bowl with the ground meat, bread crumbs, an egg and herbs. Chop an onion fine, sauté it until soft and add it to the mixture.

3 **Mixing the stuffing.** Season the mixture with salt and pepper. Work the ingredients together until the seasonings, egg and meat are evenly distributed. The mixture should be moist but firm.

An Eclectic Blend

1 **Chopping ingredients.** Chop scallions, mushrooms, fresh herbs and lamb trimmings fine. Put them in a bowl with salt and butter. Remove the rind from lean salt pork; chop the pork.

2 **Combining ingredients.** Add the salt pork to the mixture; season to taste with ground spices such as mace, nutmeg and allspice. Mix the ingredients together with your hands.

3 **Kneading.** Thoroughly amalgamate all of the ingredients to make a loose, fairly light mixture. If you want a heavier stuffing, knead in fresh bread crumbs and bind the mixture with an egg.

1
Grilling, Broiling and Frying
Swift Cooking for Tender Cuts

A barbecuing trick for thick chops
A touch test for doneness
Juxtaposing flavors on a skewer
Capturing the savory residue of a sauté
A crisp envelope of bread crumbs

When lamb or mutton is cooked by dry heat, the surfaces turn crisp and brown while the interior remains juicy and pink. Roasting produces this delicious contrast for large cuts of meat *(pages 29-46);* for smaller ones, it can be achieved by any of three cooking methods: grilling, broiling or frying. All three methods apply dry heat from a single direction, either above or below the meat.

In grilling, the meat is cooked on a rack set directly over charcoal embers. Broiling usually is done on a rack or pan set under an oven broiler, although a ridged-griddle pan *(opposite)* can be used to accomplish the same results on the stove top. Before meat can be grilled or broiled, it must be slathered with oil or bathed in an oil-based marinade *(page 14)* to prevent it from sticking to the rack or pan. Before frying, oil or a fat such as butter is heated in a skillet or sauté pan instead of being applied to the meat; because the meat is then cooked without water, wine, stock or other liquid, frying is technically a dry-heat rather than moist-heat method.

With any dry-heat method, the meat is seared quickly at high temperatures to brown the surfaces. For pieces no more than 1 inch [2½ cm.] thick, searing on both sides may be sufficient to cook the interiors to pink perfection. For pieces from 1 to 3 inches [2½ to 8 cm.] thick, additional cooking at a lower temperature is necessary.

In all cases, cooking must be kept as brief as possible to retain the meat's natural juices. For this reason, direct dry-heat methods are best suited to tender lamb and mutton cuts of uniform thickness: loin, rib, sirloin or leg steaks and chops, and the cubes used for kebabs. Unless ground and formed into sausage shapes *(pages 22-23)* or hamburger-like patties, tougher cuts would not soften and become succulent in the time allowed; bulky or irregularly shaped cuts would burn before their interiors were cooked.

Any cut will take longer to cook through if the meat is chilled; it should therefore be removed from the refrigerator and brought to room temperature (about 70° F. [20° C.]) in advance. The time required for warming it will vary with the thickness of the cut and the heat of the kitchen: As a rule, the process will take from 15 to 30 minutes in a warm kitchen, about an hour in a cool one.

As three sirloin chops sizzle, a fourth is speared at the edge by one tine of a kitchen fork and turned over to expose its unseared surface to the direct heat of a ridged-griddle pan *(box, page 20).* The raised ridges simulate the bars of a grill or barbecue and imprint the meat with sear marks while supporting it well above the fat that is accumulating in the bottom of the pan.

Grilling Each Part of a Chop to Perfection

Grilled over the glowing embers of a wood or charcoal fire, lamb chops and steaks become suffused with the aroma of smoke. The lamb must be cut at least 1½ inches [4 cm.] thick to remain pink inside while the surface sears. However, if it is to cook through without burning, the lamb should not be more than 3 inches [8 cm.] thick—the thickness of the loin chops shown here.

Before the lamb is grilled, all fat must be trimmed off: The fat would drip onto the embers, bursting into flames that would char the meat. For extra flavor, the lamb may be steeped in a marinade made with oil to lubricate its surfaces; lamb that is not marinated should be rubbed with oil to keep it from sticking to the hot rack of the grill.

Preparing loin chops poses a challenge. On opposite sides of the T-shaped finger bone are the tender eye and the smaller, still more delicate tenderloin; both taste best served rare or medium rare. However, the attached length of flank, or "apron," is best well done, even slightly crisped. To address these different cooking requirements, order chops with long aprons, then wind the apron around the triangle comprising the eye and tenderloin. Secure the apron with a wooden skewer or rosemary twig that has been soaked in water for 10 minutes to keep it from burning. The apron will protect the tender parts from overcooking as each surface is subjected, in turn, to the heat.

For searing any chop or steak, the grill heat should be intense enough to brown all of the cut surfaces in about 10 minutes. To ensure this, set the grill rack about 3 inches from the fire and allow at least half an hour for the fire to burn down to ash-covered coals.

After searing, the heat must be reduced so that the surfaces do not burn while the meat cooks through. Raise the rack 2 inches [5 cm.] farther from the fire if the rack is adjustable; otherwise, spread out the coals or move the meat to a cooler part of the rack. Thin cuts will need just a few minutes' additional cooking; thick cuts may need 20 minutes. To check for doneness, press the meat with a finger. If the lamb is soft, it is rare; if just firm to the touch, it is medium rare; if it feels very firm, the lamb is well done.

1 **Trimming the chops.** Ask the butcher to cut loin chops about 3 inches [8 cm.] thick and to leave the aprons long. Cut away the fat from the angle between the apron and the body of each chop *(above, left)*. Turn the chop over and, with your knife, loosen the fat from the back of the chop, starting at the thick end *(right)*. Pull the loosened fat away from the meat with your fingers.

4 **Grilling the meat.** Place the chops over the high heat of a thoroughly preheated grill. Using the rosemary twig or tongs to turn each chop, sear the two flat sides *(above, left)* for about 10 minutes in all; then sear the curved, apron-wrapped sides. Reduce the heat and grill the chops, apron sides down, turning them regularly to expose all parts of their aprons to the heat again *(right)*. Baste the chops occasionally with oil from the marinade.

2 **Trimming the aprons.** Loosen, pull away and cut off the surface fat from the apron of each chop. Then, to remove the fat embedded between the layers of lean meat in the apron, cut into the apron and pull apart the layers of lean. Strip away the exposed layers of fat with your fingers *(above)*.

3 **Skewering the chops.** Trim most of the leaves from rosemary twigs, leaving a flourish of leaves at one end. Cut the other end of each twig to a point. Soak the twigs in water for 10 minutes or so. Rub oil and dried herbs — in this case, thyme, savory, marjoram and oregano — into the chops and set them side by side in a dish. Roll the apron around each chop and secure it with a sharpened rosemary twig. Cover the dish with foil or plastic wrap, and let the chops marinate for three hours at room temperature or at least nine hours in the refrigerator.

5 **Serving the chops.** When the chops are rare — after about 10 minutes — turn each one so that a flat side is exposed to the grill. Turning them once, grill the chops for five to 10 minutes more, or until they reach the desired degree of doneness. Remove them from the rack, season, and serve at once — garnished, if you like, with sprigs of watercress.

The Basics of Broiling

Broiling, either in an oven or in a ridged, cast-iron pan, produces succulent lamb chops and steaks—brown outside and pink at the center—in a matter of minutes. The procedure is basically the same as for grilling: Meat is placed on a preheated rack or ridged-griddle pan and seared at high temperature on both sides. Then, if the meat is thick enough to require additional cooking, it is broiled to doneness at reduced heat.

Because the heat of an oven broiler or griddle pan is less intense than that of charcoal embers, the chops or steaks can be a mere 1 inch [2½ cm.] thick. They should not exceed 2 inches [5 cm.], for heftier cuts would char before they had time to cook through.

To avoid spattering and smoking, the meat should be trimmed of all but a ¼-inch [6-mm.] border of fat. The flat surfaces should then be oiled lightly to prevent the meat from sticking to the hot rack or pan. In the demonstration at right, lamb center-cut leg steaks are steeped in a blend of dill, olive oil and lemon juice before broiling; the marinade enhances their flavor as well as lubricating their surfaces. The sirloin chops in the box at bottom are simply rubbed with garlic and brushed with oil.

For oven broiling, the pan and rack should be positioned so that the top surface of the meat will be about 1 inch below the flame or heating element while it is being seared. To reduce the heat for continued cooking, lower the rack so that the meat surface is 3 inches [8 cm.] from the heat source.

For pan broiling, simply set the pan over high heat for about three minutes to let it heat through before you use it to sear the meat. Keep the heat high for searing, then adjust the temperature to medium low for additional cooking.

1 Marinating. In a bowl, mix oil with lemon juice and chopped fresh dill. Season with dry mustard, salt and pepper. Pour a thin layer of this marinade into a large, flat dish. Place the meat — here, leg steaks — in the dish and spoon in the remaining marinade *(above, left)*. Strew dill sprigs over the steaks *(right)*, cover, and let the lamb marinate for one hour per inch [2½ cm.] of thickness at room temperature or three times as long in the refrigerator.

A Pan That Imitates a Grill

1 Preparing chops. Trim excess fat from the meat; sirloin chops are used here. Slice a garlic clove in half and rub the cut sides over the flat surfaces of the meat. Brush olive oil on the chops.

2 Grilling the chops. Preheat a cast-iron ridged-griddle pan until water dripped into it sizzles immediately. Sear the chops on both sides over high heat, seasoning each side with salt and pepper after it has browned. Reduce the heat and cook the chops — without turning them again — until done.

2 **Searing.** Set the broiler rack and pan on a shelf about 3 inches [8 cm.] from the heat source if the meat is no more than 1 inch [2½ cm.] thick. For 2-inch [5-cm.] steaks or chops, the shelf should be 4 inches [10 cm.] from the heat. Preheat the broiler at its highest setting for 15 minutes. Discard the sprigs of dill and place the steaks on the broiler rack. After the first side has browned, turn the meat with tongs (above) or a fork inserted into a fatty edge.

3 **Testing for doneness.** After the second side is seared, lower the rack about 2 inches [5 cm.] farther from the heat source. Continue broiling for about four minutes, turning the meat once as it cooks. Slide the rack partway out of the broiler and press the meat with your finger: When the lamb feels soft but springy, it is rare; when it feels firm and unyielding, it is well done.

4 **Carving and serving.** Remove the steaks from the broiler and season both sides with salt and pepper. Place the steaks on a cutting board and, with a sharp knife, carve around the leg bone. Remove the bone with the tines of a serving fork. Slice the boned steaks down the center to serve them.

The Uses of Skewers

Ground Lamb Shaped into a Sausage

Almost any cut of lamb can be grilled or broiled if it is cubed or ground up and impaled on skewers. Tender sirloin and loin are good candidates for cubes; tougher cuts such as shoulder or shank become tender with grinding.

Skewer-cooked meats, shown here in both their cubed and sausage-like variations, are generally known by their Turkish name, kebabs. They are traditionally cooked over wood or charcoal embers. However, oven broiling is as appropriate as grilling—and safer for kebab sausages, which tend to stick to grill racks or broiler pans and break apart.

In these demonstrations, both kinds of kebabs are oven broiled. The skewers are suspended over a shallow baking pan to prevent the meat from sticking or frying in the fat that collects in the pan.

Shaped into cubes or sausages about 1 to 1½ inches [2½ to 4 cm.] thick, kebabs will be ready to eat as soon as they are seared on all sides. Grill them 3 inches [8 cm.] from the embers, or broil them 1 inch from the flame or heating element. Cubes will be rare after about five minutes of grilling or broiling; sausages will need eight to 12 minutes.

So that the skewered meats can be turned easily, use skewers with square or flat blades: The kebabs would slip on round skewers. Smear the skewers with oil to make it easier to slide the meat off for serving, and smear the kebabs with oil to keep the meat surfaces moist.

All kebabs lend themselves to additional flavoring. The sausages may be enhanced by chopped onion, garlic, green pepper, and herbs such as parsley, coriander or oregano, as well as various spices: cumin, cinnamon, paprika, cayenne pepper, nutmeg or mace. The blend here is mixed with beef marrow, which not only contributes flavor but helps to keep the meat juicy (recipe, page 91).

Cubed meat can be marinated (page 14) or simply sprinkled with herbs and spices. And a whole range of vegetables or fruits can be cut into slices or chunks and threaded on the skewers between the meat cubes. Zucchini slices are shown opposite at bottom; the alternatives include whole mushrooms or cherry tomatoes, strips of red or green pepper, orange segments or chunks of tart apple.

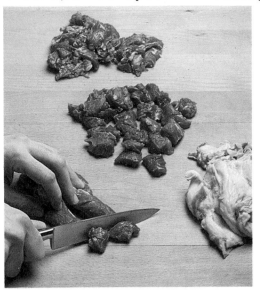

1 **Trimming meat.** Using a sharp knife, trim away every trace of fat and connective tissue from the meat — in this case, a boned lamb shoulder (pages 12-13). Then cut the meat into chunks.

2 **Grinding the meat.** Fit a food grinder with its medium disk. Put a few meat chunks into the mouth of the machine, and use a pestle to push them onto the revolving screw. Continue adding the cubes a few at a time until all of the meat has been ground once.

6 **Turning the kebabs.** Place the oiled kebabs 1 inch [2½ cm.] from the flame or heating element of a preheated broiler. Broil them for a total of about 10 minutes, turning them only once, halfway through the cooking time. If necessary, ease a spatula under each kebab to help lift it for turning.

7 **Serving the kebabs.** When they are done, remove the kebabs from the broiler and place them on a warmed serving platter. Garnish them, if you like, with parsley sprigs and lemon. Use a fork to slide the meat off the skewers onto individual serving plates.

3 **Flavoring the meat.** With a small knife, pry the marrow from short sections of beef shank bone. Then chop the marrow, an onion, parsley and coriander. Mix them with the meat. Season the mixture with cayenne pepper, salt, cumin, cinnamon and paprika, and pass it through the grinder two more times, using the fine disk.

4 **Molding sausages.** Knead the meat-and-flavoring mixture thoroughly. Refrigerate it for 30 minutes to make it firmer. With lightly wetted hands, lift up a handful of the mixture and mold it around an oiled skewer, shaping the mixture into a sausage that is 4 to 5 inches [10 to 13 cm.] long and 1½ inches [4 cm.] in diameter.

5 **Oiling the kebabs.** Rest the ends of the skewers on the sides of a baking pan to suspend the kebabs above the pan bottom. To keep the meat succulent and moist as it cooks, paint oil on the surfaces with a brush, or carefully rub oil onto the meat with your hand.

Cubed Meat Kebabs Interleaved with Zucchini

1 **Preparing the ingredients.** Pare any fat and connective tissue from the meat — in this case, sirloin — and cut the meat into neat cubes about 1 inch [2½ cm.] square. Cut small zucchini into slices about ¼ inch [6 mm.] thick.

2 **Threading the skewers.** Oil flat-bladed skewers and thread them with alternating lamb cubes and zucchini slices. Suspend the kebabs over a baking pan (above). Brush the meat and vegetables with oil and sprinkle on salt and chopped herbs — in this case, thyme, savory, marjoram and oregano.

3 **Broiling.** Position the kebabs 1 inch [2½ cm.] from the flame or heating element of a preheated broiler. Broil the kebabs for about five minutes, giving the skewers a quarter turn every minute or two. Serve the kebabs as soon as they are done — if you like, on a bed of rice. Use a fork to slide the meat and zucchini off the skewers.

Sautéing — and Creating a Sauce from the Pan Juices

Sautéing small, tender lamb cuts—that is, frying them rapidly in just enough butter or oil to keep them from sticking to the pan—preserves every bit of the meat's delicate texture and flavor. And the sautéing method wastes nothing: The juices from the meat coagulate on the bottom of the pan, and after cooking they can be loosened and recaptured with a splash of liquid *(Step 5)*—water, stock, lemon juice or wine. This process, called deglazing, provides a sauce for the meat.

Chops, steaks and boneless slices of lamb, such as the eye of loin and tenderloin in this demonstration, can all be sautéed. Their thickness may range from ½ inch [1 cm.] to 1½ inches [4 cm.]. Before sautéing, the meat should be trimmed of fat, then dusted with flour. The flour will form a hint of crust around the meat and ultimately help to thicken the sauce.

Use a skillet or sauté pan just large enough to accommodate the lamb pieces without crowding. If the pieces blanket the bottom of the pan, steam will be trapped and the meat will stew rather than fry; if there is too much space in the pan, the oil or butter not covered by the meat is likely to burn.

Thin chops or slices need only brief cooking; for rare meat, searing alone may be sufficient. If you prefer lamb well done, or if you are frying thicker cuts, cook the meat a few minutes longer after reducing the heat.

Once the meat has been seared, a garnish of raw or partly cooked vegetables may be added to the pan. The finely diced green peppers and chopped ripe olives used here *(recipe, page 93)* provide a contrast in flavor, texture and color. Sliced mushrooms or zucchini or peeled, seeded and chopped tomatoes would be equally effective complements.

1 Slicing lamb. Using a sharp knife, trim any fat from boneless lamb — in this case, eye of loin and tenderloin. Cutting across the grain, slice the eye into pieces ¾ inch [2 cm.] thick. Divide the tenderloin into three or four pieces.

2 Preparing a garnish. Broil a green pepper until its skin blisters all over. Cool it under a damp towel to loosen the skin. Peel the pepper, tear it open and remove the seeds; dice the flesh. Pit ripe olives and chop the flesh. Squeeze the juice from half a lemon. Set the garnish and lemon juice aside.

5 Deglazing the pan. Pour the lemon juice over the meat and garnish. Add a generous splash of water or, as here, white wine *(above, left)*. With a wooden spoon, stir the liquid as it comes to a boil and scrape the pan to loosen the meaty deposits *(right)*.

3 **Sautéing the meat.** Season the pieces of lamb with salt and pepper, and dust them with flour. Heat a little oil or butter in a heavy pan over high heat and put in the lamb pieces *(above, left)*. Sear them for about two minutes, then turn them over with a spatula or fork *(right)*. Sear the other side. Reduce the heat to medium.

4 **Garnishing the lamb.** Scatter the diced peppers and chopped olives over the meat. If you like, sprinkle thyme, oregano, marjoram or parsley on top.

6 **Serving the lamb.** When all of the pan deposits have been scraped free and blended into the liquid, remove the pan from the heat. With a spoon and fork, serve the lamb and the garnish. Spoon some sauce over each portion.

A Savory Coating to Hold In Succulence

Applying a coating of bread crumbs and egg to a piece of lamb before it is fried yields a crunchy envelope that seals in the meat's juices. Because the coating is fragile, the meat must be turned only once during cooking. For this reason, the layer of fat in which the pieces fry must be deep enough to cover them halfway. In the demonstration at right, a combination of butter—chosen for its flavor—and oil is used as the frying medium, but butter or oil alone could also be used.

Any small, tender chops or boneless slices cut ½ to 1 inch [1 to 2½ cm.] thick can be fried in a coating. Thicker cuts would burn before cooking through. To help the crumbs and eggs adhere, the meat can first be given a light dusting of flour; however, flour tends to turn into a pasty skin during frying. A better alternative is an undercoating of melted butter and grated Parmesan cheese (recipe, page 92). The butter keeps the cheese in place; the cheese provides a dry, textured surface to which the crumb coating can cling. And, while the chops are frying, the cheese melts to a succulent film.

1 **Preparing rib chops.** With a sharp knife, trim off the fat from around each of the chops, leaving a border only ¼ inch [6 mm.] wide. Then pare and scrape all of the fat and meat from the last 2 inches [5 cm.] of the rib bone to clean it completely. Save the meat trimmings for later use in stuffings and stews.

A Bright-hued Sauce of Puréed Tomatoes

In summer, the most delicious of tomato sauces can be prepared by simmering pieces of unpeeled fresh tomatoes with a few chopped onions, garlic cloves, some coarse salt, and fresh or dried herbs (recipe, page 165). In this demonstration, only thyme and a bay leaf are used, but you could add or substitute parsley, basil or oregano.

The tomatoes will quickly collapse to a pulp that can be forced through a sieve to rid the mixture of the skins and seeds. The resulting purée is then simmered until it has reduced to the consistency you want.

In other seasons, when local vine-ripened tomatoes are not available, the best sauce is made from canned tomatoes. Simply press them through a sieve, add flavorings and simmer the sauce to reduce it.

1 **Cooking the sauce.** Put cut-up tomatoes, whole garlic cloves, chopped onion, a bay leaf, thyme and coarse salt into a heavy pan. Bring the mixture to a boil, then reduce the heat to low. Stirring occasionally, cook until the tomatoes are reduced to a pulp.

2 **Sieving the sauce.** With a pestle, press the tomato pulp through a sieve into a clean pan. Discard the skin, seeds and herbs left in the sieve. Simmer the purée until it has reached the desired thickness. Taste the purée and correct the seasoning.

2 **Coating the chops.** Dip each chop in melted butter and dredge both sides with grated Parmesan cheese. Dip the chop in beaten egg, then lay it in a bed of bread crumbs. Sprinkle more bread crumbs over the top *(above)*. Gently shake off any excess crumbs. If you have time, set the chops aside for about an hour in order to dry them and firm their coating.

3 **Frying the chops.** In a skillet, heat a deep layer of butter and oil, including any melted butter that is left over from coating the chops. Arrange the chops in a single layer in the pan and fry them over high heat for about four minutes, or until the undersides are crisp and brown. Taking care not to pierce their crusts, gently lift the chops with a fork or spatula and turn them over.

4 **Serving the chops.** For rare lamb, remove the chops from the pan as soon as their second sides are browned; if you prefer lamb well done, turn down the heat and fry the chops a little longer. Drain the chops briefly on paper towels, arrange them on a warmed plate, and serve them alone or, as here, with a tomato sauce *(box, left)*.

2

Roasting
A Range of Effects
from Elemental to Opulent

A choice of vegetable garnishes

Approaches to carving

Cuts that accommodate stuffing

Deglazing the roasting pan

Roasting a whole baby lamb

In roasting, every surface of the meat is simultaneously exposed to dry heat. This cooking method is ideal for large cuts of tender meat, crisping and browning the exterior evenly while bringing the interior to succulent perfection. Because lamb and mutton are naturally so tender, most cuts can be roasted. Only the neck and shanks of lamb and the neck, shanks, breast and shoulder of mutton require the moist, gentle heat of braising and poaching.

As for roasting temperatures, approaches vary. Some cooks roast lamb at a constant 325° F. [160° C.] to minimize its loss of juices and thereby prevent shrinkage; others keep the oven at 400° F. [200° C.] to speed the roasting process and ensure a richly colored crust. However, a two-stage strategy—searing the meat first at 450° F. [230° C.], then cooking it through at 350° F. [180° C.]—combines the advantages of both approaches, yielding well-browned roasts with relatively little shrinkage. The only lamb roast that cannot be seared is baby lamb. Its thin, delicate flesh must be cooked at a constant, moderate heat; otherwise, the flesh would dry out.

To promote rapid formation of the crust, the oven should be preheated for a minimum of 15 minutes. And the surfaces of the lamb, especially those that are not protected by fat, should be smeared with oil unless the roast has been marinated beforehand *(page 14)*. After the initial searing period, baste the lamb at 10- to 15-minute intervals with its juices—supplemented, if necessary, by a little water, wine or stock; basting keeps the roast moist and produces an appealing amber glaze. At the end of roasting, the juices can be skimmed to degrease them, then used as a simple sauce for the lamb; or you can use the juices to form the base for a more generous sauce by deglazing the pan with liquid *(page 24)*.

A sharp knife divides the shoulders of a lordly lamb foresaddle *(pages 42-43)*. Surrounding the roast are thick slices already taken from the rib end of the meat. Before the cut was roasted, the breast and rib bones were removed, and the capacious inner cavity was stuffed with a savory mixture of chopped spinach and ground pork.

Roasted lamb should always be left to rest for at least 10 minutes before it is carved, and large cuts can safely wait for up to 20 minutes without cooling appreciably. Several changes will take place during the resting period: The lean parts of the meat will continue to cook slowly as they absorb heat from hotter pockets of fat; as the cut begins to cool, the fat will stabilize and the juices will settle. Rested meat thus will be firmer and easier to carve, and it will better retain its flavorful juices.

Vegetable Accompaniments to Roasts

The flavors of certain vegetables marry so well with roast lamb that they have become classic accompaniments. Foremost among these are beans and such members of the onion family as garlic, shallots, and Spanish or yellow onions.

Both fresh and dried beans are delicious complements of lamb. A mixture of the two gives an interesting juxtaposition of flavors, textures and colors. At right, top, fresh green beans are combined with *flageolets*—pale-green dried beans imported from France *(recipe, page 167)*. Fresh wax beans and dried navy or pea beans could be substituted. The dried beans are soaked overnight, simmered in fresh water until they are tender—about one and one half hours—and added to the parboiled fresh beans. Then all of the beans are tossed together in butter. A little chopped parsley may be added.

When a roasting pan or dish is deglazed *(page 36, Step 5)*, the resulting liquor can be used to cook garlic cloves or shallots. In the center demonstration, parboiled garlic cloves simmer in deglazed juices until they are soft but still intact. The cooking gives the cloves a mild, delicately sweet flavor, and the garlic lends its flavor to the sauce.

Another traditional accompaniment to lamb is the onion purée known as soubise *(recipe, page 166)*. Large onions are baked for one and one half hours, or until they are soft. They are then chopped and heated gently with cooked rice, which gives body to the purée.

Fresh and Dried Beans with Butter

1 **Combining beans.** Soak, cook and drain *flageolets*. Put them in a heavy pan. Parboil and drain fresh green beans, then add them to the pan.

2 **Adding butter.** Over low heat, toss the beans together. Turn off the heat. Add butter, parsley, salt and pepper, and toss until the beans are coated.

Garlic Cloves Simmered in Pan Juices

1 **Parboiling garlic.** Peel the skins from garlic cloves. Parboil the cloves in water for 10 minutes, or until tender but still slightly firm, then drain them.

2 **Degreasing.** Pour deglazed roasting juices into a pan *(page 36, Step 5)*. Add the garlic and simmer for five to 10 minutes. Skim off fat as it rises.

Soubise: A Purée of Onions Thickened with Rice

1 **Baking onions.** Individually wrap peeled onions in foil and bake at 350° F. [180° C.] until tender. Unwrap the onions and chop them coarse.

2 **Simmering.** Put the chopped onions in a pan. Add boiled rice. Stirring occasionally, simmer until the rice has absorbed all of the onions' liquid.

3 **Puréeing.** Purée the mixture in a food processor or pass it through a food mill. Sieve the purée into a pan. Heat it gently, then stir in butter and salt.

Cooking and Carving a Leg

For most people, roast lamb means leg of lamb—and with good reason. The leg has a high ratio of lean, succulent meat to fat and bone, making it a delectable cut for roasting. Furthermore, its compact shape ensures even cooking in the all-around heat of an oven, resulting in meat that is done to the precise degree desired.

Before roasting a leg of lamb, trim off as much excess fat as possible. Many people find lamb fat unpalatable, and any moisture the fat might have yielded can be provided by rubbing the surface of the leg with oil.

Additional flavor can be imparted by marinating the lamb in an oil-rich blend or by stuffing surface slits with garlic, bits of lemon peel, fresh herbs, or the paste made of pounded garlic and dried herbs that is shown here.

To sear the meat, start the roasting in a hot oven, then reduce the heat and baste the meat occasionally with pan juices to keep the surface moist. When the juices begin to solidify on the bottom of the baking dish or pan, they can be dissolved with liquid—water, wine or the liquid from a marinade.

The total roasting time for a leg of lamb will vary with the idiosyncracies of your oven, the size of the cut and how pink you want the interior to be. The box on page 34 explains the methods of calculating the required minutes per pound and of testing the meat's doneness.

A roast leg of lamb presents special challenges to the carver: Because of its rounded shape, the leg tends to slip on the platter. If you or the butcher cuts the shank bone off above the joint, you can screw on a *manche à gigot*—a special carving handle obtainable at fine kitchenware stores or from dealers in antique silver *(overleaf)*—to steady the leg. Another strategy is to use the bone itself as a handle, wrapping your hand in a napkin to ensure a good grip. If the butcher has broken the shank bone, steady the leg with a fork *(box, page 33)*. In any case, partially boning the sirloin end before cooking *(pages 10-11)* simplifies slicing.

The lamb contains different kinds of meat on the shank end, the rounded side of the sirloin end and the flatter inner side of the sirloin; every diner should receive a portion of each kind.

1 **Preparing leg of lamb.** Prepare the shank bone according to the carving method you plan to use, and remove the pelvic bone *(pages 10-11)*. Here, the shank has been sawed to accommodate a *manche à gigot*. Cut away all excess fat. In a mortar, pound together a garlic clove, dried herbs — in this case, thyme, savory, marjoram and oregano — salt and pepper. Add enough white wine to form a thin paste. Make several slits on both sides of the leg *(above, left)*, and spoon some paste into each slit *(right)*. Push the paste deep into the slits with your finger.

2 **Marinating the meat.** Smear any remaining paste over the meat. Coat the entire surface of the leg with oil; the oil will flavor the lamb and moisten it as it cooks. Pour a generous splash of white wine onto the meat *(above, left)*, and rub the wine over the surface, turning the meat to coat all sides *(right)*. Cover the meat with foil and, turning it from time to time, let it marinate for three hours at room temperature or at least nine hours in the refrigerator. ▶

3 **Tying the meat.** Transfer the leg of lamb to a work surface; reserve the marinade liquid. To form a compact shape for roasting, pull the loose folds of meat at the sirloin end together and tie them securely with two loops of string. Place the meat, rounded side up, in an ovenproof dish or a roasting pan and pour a little oil over it.

4 **Roasting.** Put the meat in a preheated 450° F. [230° C.] oven. After 10 minutes, reduce the heat to 350° F. [180° C.]. Baste the meat with its roasting juices after 30 minutes; 10 minutes later, pour the reserved marinade over the meat *(above)*. Continue to roast the meat, basting periodically, until it is done to your taste *(box, page 34)*.

5 **Preparing to carve.** Transfer the leg to a cutting board or warmed platter, and let the meat rest for 10 minutes. Meanwhile, strain the roasting juices into a small saucepan. Add any flavorings — in this case parboiled garlic *(page 30)*. Bring the juices to a boil and skim off the fat to make a sauce. Screw a *manche à gigot* to the shank bone.

6 **Carving the rounded side of the leg.** Snip off the strings and discard them. Gripping the *manche à gigot,* lift the shank end slightly to tilt the meat. Start carving from the rounded side of the leg *(above, left)*. Slice the meat thin — always cutting away from yourself and keeping the knife blade almost parallel to the bone.

7 **Carving the inner side.** When you have carved one slice of meat for each diner, turn the leg around and carve the same number of slices from the flatter muscle on the opposite side of the bone. The slices from the inner side of the leg will be somewhat more tender.

Bracing a Short-shanked Leg

Unless you make a specific request to the contrary, many butchers break the joint between the shank and leg bones and bend the end of the shank back so that the leg can be fitted easily into a small roasting pan or dish. Unfortunately, once the joint—or the bone near it—is severed, there is no handle to grasp when you carve. As a result, the meat tends to slip. To minimize slipping, carve the meat on a cutting board, and hold the leg securely in place with a carving fork as you work.

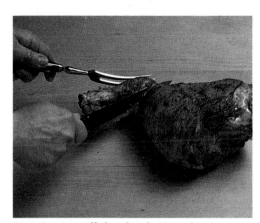

1 **Cutting off the shank.** Transfer the roasted leg from the pan to a cutting board and let it rest for 10 minutes. Steady the end of the shank bone with the back of a carving fork. Cut through the flesh where the bone was broken.

2 **Carving the rounded side.** Set aside the cut-off shank. Hold the roast firmly with the back of the fork. Keeping the knife almost parallel to the leg bone, slice through the rounded section of the leg. Carve one slice for each diner.

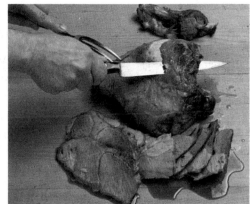

3 **Carving the inner side.** Turn the leg onto its flat, carved side. Steadying the meat with the fork, cut one slice for each diner from the inner side of the leg. Finally, carve the same number of slices from the shank.

8 **Carving the shank.** Starting near the shank end, and keeping the knife blade almost parallel to the bone, carve thin slices of meat from the shank. Because it is so small, the shank end is always well done. However, this meat is rich in gelatinous connective tissues, so it will have acquired a melting succulence as it cooked.

9 **Serving the meat.** Put the degreased, roasting-juice sauce in a heated sauceboat; add the juices exuded during carving. Serve each diner meat from each of the sections you have carved. Offer the sauce — and any other accompaniments — with the meat. Place any uncarved meat in a slow oven to keep it warm.

The Tenderest Cut of All

A double-loin roast—often called a saddle—has a large proportion of bone, and even a 5-pound [2½-kg.] saddle such as the one shown here will serve only six people. But the limited quantity is more than offset by the quality: This cut is the tenderest of all lamb. Moreover, the configuration of the roast—the meat lies in four discrete lengthwise strips along the backbone—makes for neat carving and an elegant presentation.

When buying a saddle, ask the butcher to leave the long flaps of tough flank attached to the sides of the roast. These flaps, called the aprons, can be folded underneath the meat during roasting *(box, below);* there they will protect the small tenderloins from overcooking before the larger eyes of the loin are done.

After roasting, the aprons are generally cut off and set aside for later use in making stock. Then the eyes are cut into neat, regular slices and the tenderloins sliced crosswise into round pieces, called medallions because of their shape. Each diner should receive at least one slice of eye and one medallion of tenderloin.

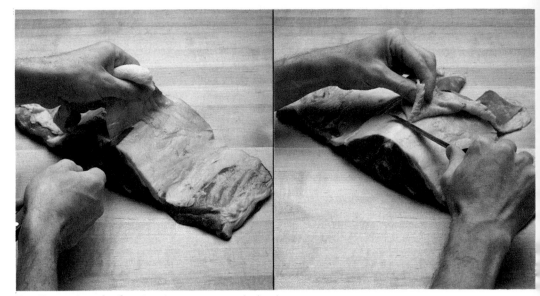

1 **Removing the fat.** Set the roast, rounded side up, on a cutting board. Starting at the bottom edge of one apron, peel the paper-like outer membrane, or fell, and the underlying layer of attached fat away from the meat. Use a knife to loosen the fat where it resists *(above, left).* Leave the flap attached to the backbone while you peel the other side of the roast, then slice through the fat and cartilage covering the backbone to free the sheet in one piece *(right).* Turn the meat over and trim away any excess fat from the underside.

Roasting Temperatures and Times

The amount of heat and length of time needed to roast lamb or mutton depends on the kind and size of the cut and the degree of doneness you prefer.

Most lamb and mutton roasts are seared for 10 minutes at 450° F. [230° C.], then finished at 350° F. [180° C.]. If you like rare meat—bright pink inside—roast it for 10 minutes per pound [½ kg.], including searing. For medium meat—pale pink inside—allow 12 to 15 minutes per pound. Allow 20 minutes per pound for well-done meat.

Roasts larger than 8 pounds [4 kg.] will lower the oven temperature when they are first put in; to compensate, increase the searing time to 15 minutes. Because these roasts have a high proportion of heat-absorbing surface area, however, you must decrease the total time by two or three minutes per pound. Dense boneless roasts need three to five minutes more per pound. Weigh stuffed roasts after you stuff

them; a stuffed foresaddle *(pages 42-43)*—an exceptionally dense roast—should finish cooking, after searing, at 325° F. [160° C.] instead of 350° F.

Baby lamb, whether whole or cut up, is too delicate to be seared and tastes best well done. Roast it for 15 minutes per pound at a constant heat of 350° F.

Because roasting times provide only an estimate of the meat's doneness, test the internal temperature with a thermometer. Lamb is rare at 140° F. [60° C.], medium at 150° F. [65° C.] and well done at 160° F. [70° C.].

You may test with a standard meat thermometer, inserting it when the meat is about three quarters done, but the tip will form a hole. Or you can use a rapid-response thermometer; it is pushed in and pulled out so fast that the hole it forms closes. Insert either kind in the fleshiest part of the roast, avoiding stuffing, fat or bone, which heat at different rates from flesh.

5 **Carving the eyes.** Starting ¾ inch [2 cm.] from the top of the backbone and cutting to the bone, slice diagonally into the eye to remove a wedge. Set it aside. Then carve the eye into slices ¼ inch [6 mm.] thick, making the angle of the knife increasingly horizontal as you proceed. Carve the meat on the other side of the roast similarly.

2 **Marinating.** Rub oil onto the meat and set it with the aprons extended in a baking dish or roasting pan. Pat fresh chopped herbs — here, sage, oregano and thyme — over the meat. Turn it rounded side up, and let it marinate for about three hours at room temperature or nine hours in the refrigerator. Season with salt and pepper, and fold the aprons under the meat, overlapped slightly.

3 **Roasting.** Sear the meat in a preheated 450° F. [230° C.] oven for 10 minutes; reduce the heat to 350° F. [180° C.]. After about three quarters of the estimated roasting time has elapsed (box, below), test the internal temperature of the meat with a thermometer. When the meat is done, remove the roast from the oven and let it rest for 10 minutes before carving.

4 **Removing the aprons.** Transfer the meat, rounded side up, to a carving board. Use the back of a carving fork to steady the roast. With a sharp knife, slice off the aprons (above) and set them aside. Then free the eye meat from one side of the vertical blade of the backbone by cutting straight down alongside it to the point where the vertical blade meets the horizontal blade.

6 **Carving the tenderloins.** Invert the roast. Following the bones' contours, cut the tenderloin from each side in one piece (inset). Carve each tenderloin across the grain into medallions ⅓ inch [1 cm.] thick. Serve each diner slices of eye and tenderloin (right), accompanying them, if desired, with soubise (page 30).

A Rolled Roast Flavored from Within

Rolling a boned lamb shoulder *(pages 12-13)* before roasting it not only simplifies its carving, but also allows the meat to be flavored from inside. In this demonstration, the inner surface of a boned shoulder is spread with a blend of butter and *persillade (page 14)*. The meat is then rolled up and tied to hold the mixture. As the roast cooks, the butter bastes the interior and the *persillade* imbues the lamb with the robust flavor of parsley and garlic. Olive oil could be substituted for the butter, and—for a subtler effect—the *persillade* could be replaced by chopped fresh dill, rosemary or fennel.

During roasting, the juices rendered by the lamb and the *persillade* mixture are spooned over the shoulder to glaze its exterior. The juices also can be used as an aromatic medium in which to cook a garnish vegetable such as boiling onions, small carrots or, in this case, unpeeled shallots. Afterward the juices can be degreased and the meaty pan deposits dissolved with water, stock or wine to produce a simple but richly flavored sauce.

1 **Spreading the flavoring.** Bone and remove the interior fat from a lamb shoulder *(pages 12-13)*. Soften butter and blend it with *persillade*. With a spatula, spread the mixture first into the channels left by the removal of the bones and then over the entire inner surface of the meat.

2 **Rolling the shoulder.** Starting at the thin side of the meat, roll the shoulder lengthwise to form as neat and tight a cylinder as possible. Turn the roast over so that the open edge lies underneath.

4 **Roasting.** Rub the tied meat with oil and set it in a baking dish or roasting pan. Roast in a preheated 450° F. [230° C.] oven for 10 minutes. Then reduce the heat to 350° F. [180° C.]. Baste the meat with its juices every 15 minutes. About 30 minutes before the roast is done *(box, page 34)*, surround it with unpeeled shallots. When the lamb is done, rest it on a cutting board for 10 minutes.

5 **Deglazing.** Transfer the shallots to a small bowl. Carefully tilt the roasting pan at a slight angle and skim the surface fat from the juices. Add liquid—in this case, water—then set the pan over high heat. Stir the liquid as it comes to a boil, scraping up the pan deposits with a wooden spatula to disperse them through the liquid. Pour this sauce into a warmed sauceboat. Peel the shallots.

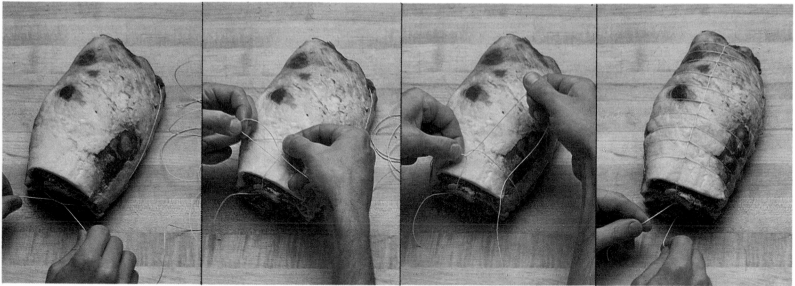

3 **Tying the shoulder.** Loop a piece of kitchen string about 2 feet [60 cm.] long lengthwise around the roast, halfway up its sides; tie a knot at one end *(above, left)*, leaving a 3-inch [8-cm.] tail of string. Draw the long end of the string up over the edge of the roast and hold a short, 2-inch [5-cm.] section taut *(center, left)*. Pass the string crosswise around the meat and loop it under the string you are holding taut *(center, right)*. Repeat this process at ¾-inch [2-cm.] intervals along the length of the roast. Then draw the string lengthwise under the meat and tie it to the first knot *(right)*.

6 **Carving and serving.** Using kitchen scissors or a knife, snip the string tied around the meat and remove it. Carve the roast into slices ½ to ¾ inch [1 to 2 cm.] thick. Arrange the slices on a warmed platter *(inset)*, and garnish the platter with the peeled shallots. Spoon some of the sauce over the slices *(right)*, and serve the rest in the sauceboat.

Racks Interlaced for a Striking Display

Depending on how it is trimmed and arranged, the rib roast—or rack—of lamb will provide a simple or a spectacular presentation. A single rack forms a neat, easily manageable roast that affords four generous two-rib portions. For a festive meal, you can serve a pair of racks, transformed into a guard of honor—demonstrated here—or a crown roast.

For the single-rack roast, ask your butcher to saw through the chine—the chunky part of the backbone—but not to remove it. Trim the rack and strip the rib ends as in Steps 1 to 3. Position the rack in a small baking dish or pan with the rounded side of the meat upward and the rack resting on the rib tips and severed bone. The bones will hold the meat out of the drippings as it cooks. And the chine will be easy to remove before the rack is set on a carving board.

To make a guard of honor, ask your butcher for two matching racks from the same animal—mismatched racks would mar the final symmetry of the dish. Have the chine removed by the butcher; you can trim the meat and strip the rib tips at home. Shape the rib tips neatly *(Steps 4 and 5)*. Then, to turn the racks into a guard of honor—so called because it resembles the crossed swords of a military honor guard—stand the racks on end, press them together and interlace the ribs *(recipe, page 108)*.

If you want to make a crown roast *(recipe, page 107)*, prepare two chined racks as you would for a guard of honor *(Steps 1 to 5)*. Lay the racks end to end and stitch the adjacent ends together. Then gently curve the racks into a circle and join the other ends with stitches. The central cavity logically demands to be filled. But a raw stuffing will take longer to cook than will lamb that is roasted to rare or medium rare: Unless you like lamb well done, cook the roast empty and fill the cavity afterward with a vegetable that has been cooked separately—sautéed mushrooms, for example, or a purée of peas.

1 **Preparing racks.** Position each chined rack, rounded side up, on a cutting board. Slit open the end near the longest ribs and pry out any remnants of the shoulder-blade bone *(above)*. Turn the rack over and, with the point of a knife, free the yellow strip of connective tissue running underneath the backbone. Grasp the tissue and pull it out.

2 **Exposing the rib ends.** Turn the rounded side of the racks upward. Score a straight line across each rack, about 4 inches [10 cm.] from the tips of the ribs. Cut off the layer of fat and meat between the line and the rib tips, pulling it away as you slice, to expose the bones.

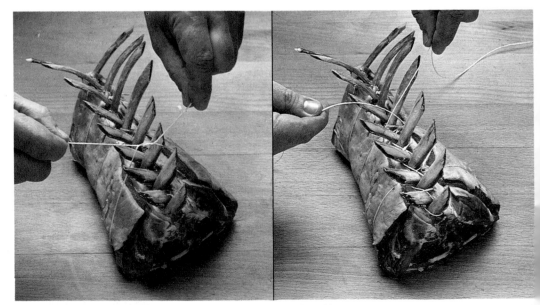

6 **Joining the racks.** Stand the two racks on their backbone edges, concave sides facing each other, and press the racks together. Interlace the bone ends. Cut three lengths of string—each about 18 inches [46 cm.] long—and tie each length vertically around the racks *(above, left)*. Cut another length of string—about 30 inches [75 cm.] long—and weave it in and out of the crossed ribs *(right)* from one end to the other. Bring the ends of the string back along the outside of the crossed ribs and tie them. Place the meat in a baking dish and smear it with oil, herbs and salt.

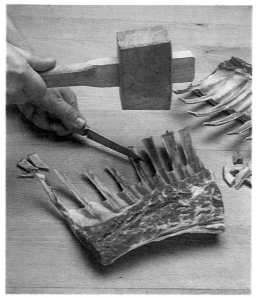

3 **Slitting between ribs.** With a knife, cut out the meat and fat from between the bared rib ends. Save these strips of meat to use in stuffings or stews. Cut off the outer covering of parchment-like fell from the remainder of the meat. Then trim the fat, if necessary, to form a layer about only ¼ inch [6 mm.] thick over the meat.

4 **Shaping the rib tips.** Turn the racks concave side up. Hold a sharp knife diagonally over each tip, making sure that the rib is flat against the board. Tap the knife sharply with a wooden mallet. If you like, graduate the length of the ribs so that when the racks are joined together, the ribs decrease in height toward the broader ends of the meat.

5 **Scraping the ribs.** Holding each rack firmly, scrape the exposed rib bones with a knife to remove any remaining bits of meat and fat. Be careful not to split the fragile bones.

7 **Roasting the meat.** Wrap foil over the rib ends to prevent charring. Sear the meat in a preheated 450° F. [230° C.] oven. After 10 minutes, reduce the heat to 350° F. [180° C.]. Continue roasting, basting the meat occasionally, until it is done (box, page 34). Take the roast from the oven and lift off the foil.

8 **Carving and serving the roast.** Let the meat rest in a warm place for 10 minutes. Place it on a cutting board and snip off the strings with scissors or a knife. Carve the roast by slicing down between the crossed ribs (above). In this case, the resulting rib chops are served with *flageolets* and green beans (page 30).

A Glazed Package for a Robust Stuffing

Although lamb breast is usually cooked by poaching or braising, it can make a compact roast if it is first boned *(pages 10-11)* and wrapped around a stuffing. Because the firm, gelatinous meat requires somewhat longer cooking than more tender cuts, the breast should be roasted until well done—ample time for an enclosed stuffing to cook through.

Remove superficial fat from the meat's boned surface before stuffing the breast. However, leave the fat and the fell on the outer surface in place; the fat will melt during roasting to lubricate the meat, and the membrane will help keep the stuffed parcel intact.

Any hearty stuffing is suitable *(page 15)*. In this demonstration, the parcel is filled with a mixture of ricotta cheese, ham and finely chopped cooked spinach. During roasting, the meat will shrink and the stuffing swell: By the end of cooking, the flat parcel becomes a plump pillow. To keep the parcel from bursting its seams, do not overstuff the breast. The 2-pound [1-kg.] breast shown holds about 2 cups [½ liter] of stuffing.

After the initial searing, the stuffed breast should be moistened so that the meat does not dry up during the long roasting. The options for moistening the meat are many: You can use white or red wine, beer, stock, even tomato juice. Frequent basting with the resulting pan juices will build up a dark golden glaze on the surface of the roast. At the end of cooking, the pan juices can be skimmed of fat to provide a richly flavored sauce to accompany the stuffed breast.

1 **Stuffing a breast.** Bone a lamb breast and trim the fat from the boned surface. Spoon stuffing into the pocket that was opened up at one corner when the breast was boned *(above)*. Spread a thick layer of stuffing over about two thirds of the surface of the exposed meat, leaving a margin about 1 inch [2½ cm.] wide around the edges.

2 **Enclosing the stuffing.** Fold the uncovered flap of meat over the stuffed surface and the mouth of the pocket. If you have any difficulty enclosing the stuffing, remove some of it: An overstuffed roast may burst in the oven while it is cooking.

4 **Preparing for roasting.** Place the parcel, rounded side up, in a small, shallow baking dish or roasting pan. Rub oil, salt, pepper and dried herbs — here, thyme, savory, marjoram and oregano — onto the surface of the meat. Place the roast in a preheated 450° F. [230° C.] oven; after 10 minutes, reduce the heat to 350° F. [180° C.].

5 **Pouring on wine.** After about 30 minutes of roasting, take the lamb out of the oven. Baste the breast with its rendered fat, then spoon as much fat as possible out of the dish or pan. Put the breast back into the oven. About 15 minutes later, take out the lamb again and pour over it a cup [¼ liter] or so of white wine or other liquid.

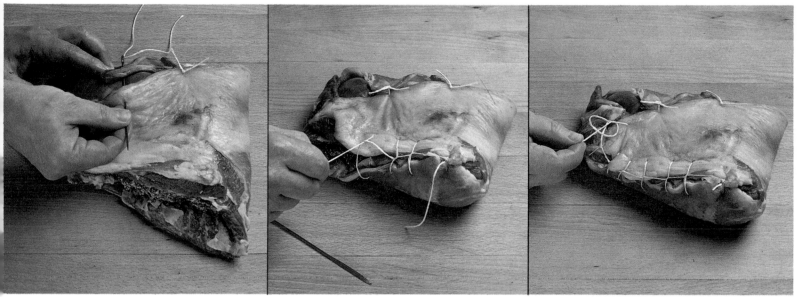

3 **Sewing up the meat.** Thread a trussing needle with a short length of kitchen string. Make two separate stitches, about 1½ inches [4 cm.] apart, to attach the edge of the flap to the far edge of the pocket*(above, left)*. Knot the string. Rethread the needle with an 18-inch [46-cm.] length of string, and make a line of looped stitches to close the opposite, open side of the parcel*(center)*. Finish off by stitching the short side of the flap to the pocket *(right)*. Do not pull the stitches too tight, lest the parcel burst.

6 **Basting.** Replace the breast in the oven and baste it frequently — every 10 minutes or so — until it is well done *(box, page 34)*. Add more wine as the liquid evaporates.

7 **Serving.** Move the breast to a cutting board or a platter and let it rest for 10 minutes. Meanwhile, skim the fat from the pan juices. Cut the strings from the roast and carve the breast crosswise so that each slice contains stuffing. Spoon juices over the slices.

The Foresaddle: A Cut Proportioned for Feasting

The foresaddle of lamb comprises the two shoulders, both racks of ribs, the whole breast and the foreshanks, and produces a regal feast if roasted as one piece. Because of its size and bone structure, the cut is naturally unwieldy. However, removing the ribs and breast bones will make the rigid form of the foresaddle more flexible and create a capacious cavity for stuffing. The meat is then sewed and trussed to secure the stuffing, giving the foresaddle a more compact shape.

The foresaddle must be ordered in advance from the butcher, and should come from a small lamb. The roast shown here weighs about 18 pounds [9 kg.] and holds a lavish 5 to 7 cups [1¼ to 1¾ liters] of stuffing: It provides enough meat and stuffing for at least 20 servings.

So that the heat penetrates the dense meat and stuffing without overcooking the surface—or drying out some parts of the meat before others are cooked—the foresaddle should be roasted at 325° F. [160° C.], a slightly lower temperature than that used for other lamb cuts.

1 Removing bones. Cut into the flap on the inner surface of each breast to open up a pocket. Slice through the cartilage that connects the breast bones to the ribs; remove the breast bones *(pages 10-11)*. Use a small knife to free each rib bone from the flesh *(above)*. Cut and twist the ribs from the backbone; reserve the bones. Remove excess fat.

2 Stuffing the meat. Make a stuffing—ground pork with chopped cooked spinach is used here *(recipe, page 121)*. Stuff the pockets that were opened when the breasts were boned, and fill any cavities left when the excess fat was stripped away. Distribute the remaining stuffing over the backbone and to either side of it.

6 Roasting. Place the foresaddle in a preheated 450° F. [230° C.] oven. After 15 minutes, reduce the heat to 325° F. [160° C.]; continue to cook the meat, basting it with the pan juices at half-hour intervals. After two hours, pour off any fat and add some white wine. Basting it regularly, cook the meat until it is done to your taste *(box, page 34)*.

7 Preparing to carve. Put the meat on a large, warmed platter and let it rest 10 minutes in a warm place. Meanwhile, deglaze the roasting pan with white wine *(page 36, Step 5)* to make a sauce. Strain the sauce into a saucepan and skim off the fat. Cut away the strings, then cut along each side of the backbone and lift the bone away *(above)*.

8 Carving the rib end. Slice off the meat attached to the backbone. Steady the foresaddle with the back of a fork and slice across the rib end of the meat, carving the slices thick so that the stuffing does not fall away from the meat. At the shoulder end, cut the roast in half to separate the shoulders.

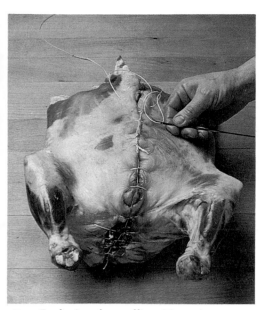

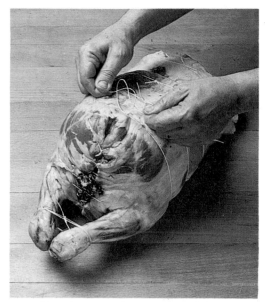

3 **Enclosing the stuffing.** Thread a trussing needle with 24 inches [60 cm.] of kitchen string. Bring the edges of the shoulders and breast together around the stuffing. Join the neck ends of the shoulders with a few long stitches, passing the string through the loop of each preceding stitch as you sew. Then stitch from the neck end to the rib end.

4 **Sewing the rib end.** Turn the meat around and, without cutting the string, sew up one half of the rib opening, working from the center outward. Cut and knot the string. Working from the opposite end, toward the center, sew up the other side of the opening.

5 **Trussing.** Wind string around the knuckle ends of the shank bones and tie it. Turn the roast over (above) and tie separate lengths of string around it. Set the meat — with the reserved bones — backbone up in a pan. Rub the meat with oil and dried herbs; if available, push rosemary twigs under the string. Let the meat marinate for three hours.

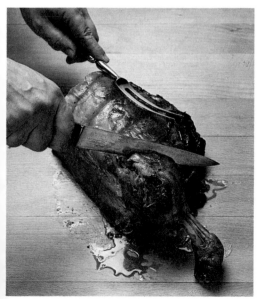
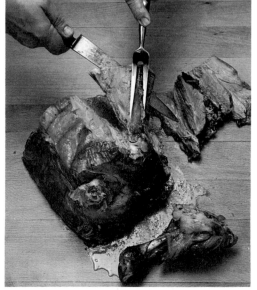

9 **Cutting off the shank.** Transfer one shoulder — rounded side up — to a cutting board. Steady the meat with the fork and, holding your knife at a slant, cut through the joint connecting the shank to the shoulder. With your hands, twist away the shank.

10 **Boning the shoulder.** At the end of the shoulder opposite the shank, carve the meat horizontally off the top of the blade bone. When the blade bone is bare, cut around and underneath it, then lift it out (above); the knobby end of the arm bone will be exposed. Slit the meat over the arm bone and cut the bone free.

11 **Slicing the shoulder.** Carve the boned shoulder crosswise into thick slices; cut the meat from the shank. Bone and carve the second shoulder in the same way as the first. Transfer all of the shoulder and shank slices to the platter. Serve the meat with the sauce made from the pan juices.

A Special Technique for Stuffing a Leg

Lamb's fell, or outer membrane, permits stuffing to be added to cuts that lack an ample cavity. This stuffing strategy seems made-to-order for a leg of lamb: The fell covers the leg like a glove. After the fell is peeled off *(right)*, the stuffing is smeared over the exposed surface of the meat and the fell is eased back over the leg. A few stitches at the sirloin end ensure that the fell will stay in place during roasting.

Because the amount of stuffing that can be accommodated is small, a highly flavored one is best. The stuffing used in this demonstration includes salt pork, mushrooms, scallions and herbs bound with soft butter *(recipe, page 98)*.

The stuffed leg can be roasted in exactly the same way as an unstuffed leg *(pages 31-33)*. But if you want to give a crisp surface to the layer of stuffing, sprinkle the leg with bread crumbs for the last few minutes of roasting. The deglazed juices from the pan—sharpened, if you like, with lemon juice or a mixture of orange juice and lemon juice—provide a sauce.

1 Peeling back the fell. Remove the section of pelvic bone from the leg and prepare the shank bone according to your carving method *(pages 32-33)*. Starting at the sirloin end, carefully peel the fell — and the layer of fat that clings to its underside — away from the meat *(left)*. Gently force the fell free with your finger tips, using a knife tip to loosen it where necessary. Try not to pierce the fell — although if you do, a hole or slight tear will not be a disaster. Leave the fell attached at the shank end of the leg *(right)*.

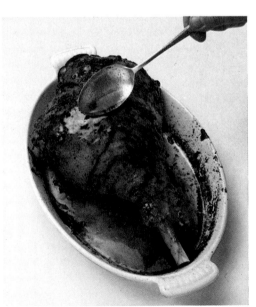

5 Roasting. Sear the leg in a preheated 450° F. [230° C.] oven. After 10 minutes, reduce the heat to 350° F. [180° C.]. Twenty minutes later, begin basting the meat with its juices at 10-minute intervals. About 10 minutes before the estimated roasting time has elapsed *(box, page 34)*, transfer the leg to a heated platter to keep it warm.

6 Deglazing. Turn up the oven to 400° F. [200° C.]. Remove the excess fat from the baking dish, then put the dish over high heat and add a splash of white wine. With a wooden spoon, stir the liquid as it comes to a boil; scrape the deposits on the dish to dislodge them and blend them into the liquid.

7 Browning the leg. Pour the deglazed juices into a small saucepan. Replace the leg in the baking dish and sprinkle the surface of the meat with fine bread crumbs. Put the leg into the hot oven and cook it for about 10 minutes, until the surface is golden and crisp.

2 **Stuffing the leg.** Smear a ¼-inch [6-mm.] layer of stuffing over the exposed surface of the leg. Pat the stuffing down firmly so that it sticks to the meat in a uniform layer.

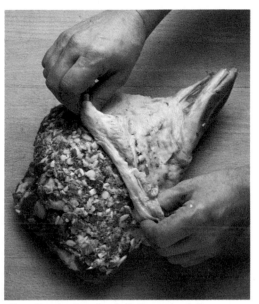

3 **Replacing the fell.** Ease the fell back over the stuffing, molding it into place with your hands. Take care not to stretch and break the fell as you pull it back toward the sirloin end.

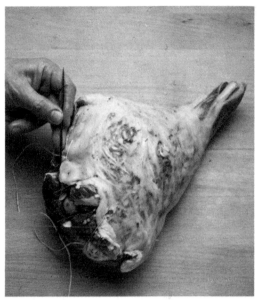

4 **Stitching the fell.** Thread a trussing needle with a 16-inch [40-cm.] length of kitchen string. Stitch the edges of the fell to one another across the sirloin end. Put the leg, rounded side up, in a roasting pan or heavy baking dish — here, an enameled iron dish is used. Pat a little oil over the surface of the meat.

3 **Preparing sauce.** Bring the deglazed juices to a boil over medium heat. Reduce the heat to low and set the pan half off the heat. Skim off the fat on the cooler side of the sauce until no more fat rises. Add chopped shallots and cook gently for about 10 minutes, until soft. Add the lemon juice or orange juice sharpened with lemon juice.

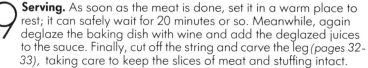

9 **Serving.** As soon as the meat is done, set it in a warm place to rest; it can safely wait for 20 minutes or so. Meanwhile, again deglaze the baking dish with wine and add the deglazed juices to the sauce. Finally, cut off the string and carve the leg (pages 32-33), taking care to keep the slices of meat and stuffing intact.

The Redoubtable Baron

A baron of lamb consists of the entire rear half of the animal, including both loins and the two legs, making it an impressive roast for a large party. Available by request from butchers, a baron must be ordered carefully: To fit into most home ovens, it must be less than 20 inches [50 cm.] long; a baron this size will be under 20 pounds [10 kg.] in weight.

Before roasting, strip off the fell and trim away the excess fat so that the surface will turn a deep brown in the oven. To permit neat trussing of the roast, remove the two easily accessible rib bones at the loin end; if left in place, they would make it impossible to tuck the flaps of the flanks under the loins. Unlike the foresaddle *(pages 42-43)*, the baron does not have a cavity ample enough to fill with sufficient stuffing to accompany such a large amount of meat.

During the roasting, this big cut will exude a wealth of juices. Add water or wine from time to time to dissolve the juices as they coagulate in the pan. The deglazing liquid can be used for basting and as a rich sauce to go with the meat.

1 Removing the fell. Set the baron on its belly. Starting at the loin end, pull away the fell and the layer of fat that clings to it. Where the fell sticks to the loin and flanks, cut it free. The fell covering the sirloin and legs is thin and in places tightly attached: Leave it intact, but cut away any large lumps of fat.

2 Preparing the meat. Trim all but a ¼-inch [6-mm.] layer of fat from the back, the flanks and the area between the legs. Cut away the rib bones from the front of the loin. Sprinkle salt, pepper and herbs inside the meat. To close the belly, fold in the flank flaps, one over the other *(above)*; tie the loin and sirloin with string to secure the flaps. Rub oil, herbs, salt and pepper onto the meat.

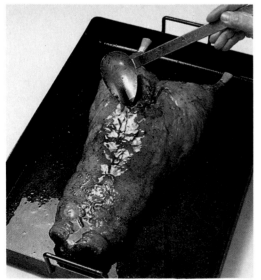

3 Roasting. Sear the baron in a preheated 450° F. [230° C.] oven for 15 minutes. Reduce the heat to 350° F. [180° C.]. After one hour, spoon excess fat from the pan, deglaze the pan and baste the meat. Deglaze and baste regularly for the rest of the roasting time *(box, page 34)*.

4 Removing the loins. Transfer the baron to a large platter and let the meat rest for about 10 minutes; skim the fat from the pan juices. To carve the meat, remove the strings and cut all the way down one side of the backbone. Make a second cut, at right angles to the first, between the sirloin and loin *(above)* to dislodge one loin; repeat these cuts to free the other loin.

5 Carving the legs. Transfer both loins to a cutting board, slice them and arrange the slices around the platter. Carve the legs one at a time, taking slices first from the sirloin and then from the side of each leg. Distribute the slices around the roast. Serve the sliced meat with the pan juices.

A Young Animal Cosseted in Caul

Once available only in spring, baby lamb is now obtainable by special order in any month of the year. To the age of about eight weeks, the lamb will weigh no more than 18 pounds [9 kg.] and can be roasted whole in a home oven.

The meat of a baby lamb that has fed on nothing but milk differs from that of an older lamb that has eaten grass: Baby lamb is markedly leaner, paler in color and more delicate in texture. And, while the meat of older lambs is usually served rare or medium rare, baby lamb is best well done. Milk-fed kid is similar to baby lamb; the same rule applies.

Keeping the lean meat of baby lamb or kid moist during roasting calls for protective tactics. Some recipes suggest that the meat be smeared with softened lard; in others, the meat is barded, or wrapped with thin sheets of fresh pork fat. A more delicate wrapping is pork caul *(right)* — a fatty stomach-and-intestinal membrane available fresh or salted from butchers. Before use, fresh caul must be rinsed well. If salted, it should be soaked for 30 minutes in warm water acidulated with a little lemon juice or vinegar. The caul swathes the lamb like a lacy shawl, melting slowly and basting the roasting meat.

As an added safeguard against drying, baby lamb should be roasted at a constant, gentle temperature—not seared. Because the meat is no more than 1½ inches [4 cm.] thick, the cooking time will be relatively brief *(Step 3)*.

The techniques of carving a baby lamb vary with the animal's size. For a tiny lamb, simply cut the roast in half lengthwise and slice through the joints to divide each half into four or six pieces.

Carving a larger baby lamb, such as the 14-pound [7-kg.] animal shown here, is a little more intricate. First, cut the shoulders free from the body, then cut through the joint of each shoulder to separate the blade section from the foreshank. Next, remove the hind legs; slice the sirloin end of each leg parallel to the bone to yield two or three thick slices, and cut through the joint in order to free the hind shank. Slice straight across the loin to produce three or four double-width chops. Finally, remove the flesh from each side of the rib cage and slice each length of meat in two crosswise.

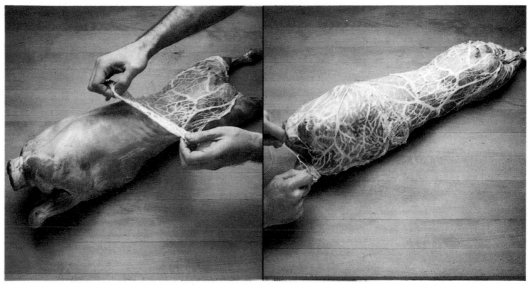

1 **Wrapping a baby lamb in caul.** Set the lamb on its belly on a cutting board. Wrap enough pieces of caul around the lamb to cover it completely *(above, left)*. Cross one hind leg over the other and wind a length of kitchen string around them several times to keep them together. With another length of kitchen string, tie the foreshanks together *(right)*.

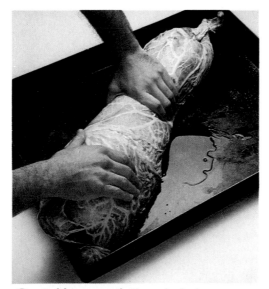

2 **Rubbing on oil.** Place the baby lamb in a large roasting pan. Pour a little oil onto the lamb and rub it over the entire surface with your hands. Rub salt, pepper and dried herbs onto the surface of the meat. Place the lamb in a preheated 350° F. [180° C.] oven.

3 **Roasting.** After the first 40 minutes of cooking, baste the lamb every 15 minutes with pan juices. Baste more frequently toward the end of the estimated cooking time — about 15 minutes per pound. When the skin is golden, pierce one thigh with a skewer; if the juices flow clear without a tinge of pink, the lamb is done. Let it rest for 10 minutes before carving.

3
Poaching and Braising
Tenderizing with Moist Heat

Unlikely candidates for poaching
Blueprint for a basic stew
Browning to bolster a braise
A choice of cooking liquids
Thickening and enriching sauces

A ladleful of fragrant daube is lifted from a cooking pot. The lamb was marinated in wine and olive oil to heighten its flavor, and larded with pork fat to keep it moist during the long cooking period. It was then simmered for many hours in the liquid from the marinade. Chopped aromatic vegetables, salt pork and pork rind were cooked with the meat until all of the flavors blended.

The combined application of moisture and gentle heat will make even the firmest cuts of lamb or mutton tender and juicy. Two cooking techniques that employ this principle are poaching and braising. Both methods use liquid held at a bare simmer; they differ chiefly in that poaching requires enough liquid to cover the meat, whereas braising uses only enough to keep the meat moist. Stewing is a form of braising; the term simply means that the meat is first cut into small pieces.

The cuts of lamb or mutton that benefit from moist heat are the shoulder, breast, shank and neck, all of which contain hard-worked muscles rich in connective tissue. When such cuts are poached or braised, much of the connective tissue is broken down into gelatin, which makes the meat tender; at the same time, fat melts to baste the meat from within. The process is a slow one: In most cases, at least one and one half hours of cooking are needed to achieve full tenderness.

Naturally tender cuts, on the other hand, produce little if any gelatin. But the lean meat of a leg or loin has enough streaks of internal fat, or marbling, to keep it juicy when poached to the rare stage *(pages 50-51)*.

The liquid for poaching lamb is most often water. By the end of the cooking, water becomes a savory broth, redolent of the meat. Lightly thickened with egg yolks or flour or both, the broth can yield an aromatic sauce *(page 51)*. Water is also commonly used for braising lamb. However, the liquid from a marinade *(page 14)*, the pulp of tomatoes, wine, stock, or a mixture of these may be substituted to enhance the dish. In many braises and stews, the liquid gains added flavor from a preliminary searing of the lamb: The crusty brown fragments deposited on the bottom of the pan dissolve when liquid is stirred into them. At the end of the braising, the liquid—now a complex essence of all the elements in the braise—is reduced and cleansed of fatty particles to form a rich sauce *(page 60)* or to burnish the meat with a mahogany glaze *(pages 66-67)*.

When lamb is poached or braised, it is usually accompanied by aromatic vegetables such as onions and carrots, which add their own flavors to the liquid and are then generally discarded and replaced with fresh vegetables *(pages 61-62)*. However, in some dishes—especially in a daube *(opposite)*—the original aromatic vegetables are left to merge into the liquid and become an integral part of the finished braise.

Brief Poaching for a Premium Cut

Poaching brings lamb to succulent tenderness while leaving its natural flavor largely intact. The lamb is immersed in liquid—usually water—and simmered gently to the desired degree of doneness. Tender cuts of lamb such as leg, loin and ribs have enough interior fat to remain moist during poaching, providing the cooking time is relatively brief: The meat must be kept rare to prevent too much of its juice from seeping out. For tougher cuts such as shank, shoulder or breast, the cooking time is prolonged in order to soften the gelatinous connective tissue and make the meat tender. Such cuts are poached until well done.

In this demonstration, a leg of lamb is poached in water flavored with aromatic herbs and vegetables. The aromatics are cooked in the water for a preliminary half hour. Then the leg—wrapped in cloth to preserve its compact form—is immersed in the flavored liquid.

Throughout the poaching, the water is maintained at a bare simmer; if it were to boil, the meat would become dry and stringy. The leg will be rare when its internal temperature registers 140° F. [60° C.] on a meat thermometer (box, page 34)—after poaching for about 15 minutes per pound [½ kg.]. Tougher cuts should be poached to 170° F. [75° C.]—about 30 minutes per pound.

When the lamb is ready, the vegetables cooked with it will have lost most of their flavor. You may serve them with the lamb, but fresh vegetables, cooked separately in some of the poaching liquid, will have better taste and texture.

The poaching liquid can also be served as a broth or used as a base for a sauce to accompany the meat. In the caper sauce demonstrated opposite (recipe, page 112), some of the poaching liquid is thickened with a flour-and-butter roux, then enriched with egg yolks that have been lightened by lemon juice; for an even more luxurious result, cream could replace the lemon juice. Capers give the sauce a piquancy that marries well with the hearty flavor of the poached leg.

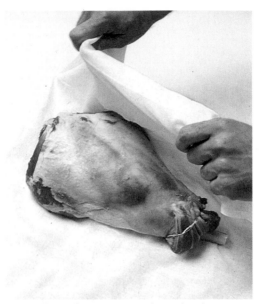

1 **Wrapping.** Remove the pelvic bone from a leg of lamb (pages 10-11). Trim off excess fat. If, as here, the shank bone has been sawed short, tie the flap of meat at the shank end with string. Fold a large piece of muslin or cheesecloth in half; put it on a work surface. Place the leg in the center of the cloth and wrap it into a tube around the meat.

2 **Tying the leg.** At each end of the tube, gather the cloth, twist it, and tie it with kitchen string; with scissors, cut the ends of the cloth off short. Tie separate lengths of string around the leg at about 3-inch [8-cm.] intervals.

6 **Serving the lamb.** Carve the poached leg of lamb just as you would a roasted one (pages 32-33). Drain the vegetables. Arrange them on the serving plate with the meat. Serve caper sauce separately in a warmed sauceboat.

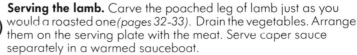

3 **Poaching.** Put an unpeeled garlic bulb, a bouquet garni, peeled carrots, and peeled onions stuck with whole cloves into a pot of cold water. Cover and simmer for 30 minutes. Lower the leg into the liquid. Set the lid ajar and increase the heat. When the liquid returns just to the simmering point, adjust the heat to maintain a bare simmer.

4 **Preparing vegetables.** Peel turnips and carrots, and cut the carrots into large pieces; scrub new potatoes. Put all of the vegetables into a pan and cover with some of the poaching liquid *(above)*; add warm water to the pot containing the lamb to keep it submerged. Cook the vegetables at a light boil until they are tender — about 20 minutes.

5 **Removing the lamb.** When the lamb is done, lift it with a large skimmer or two perforated spatulas. Hold the meat over the pot until most of the liquid has drained from the cloth. Then put the lamb on a work surface, cut the strings and unwrap the meat. Transfer the leg to a large, warmed platter.

A Piquant Partner

1 **Preparing a roux.** About an hour before the leg is done, melt butter in a pan over medium heat. Using a whisk, stir in flour to make a smooth roux. Draw the pan off the heat and whisk in a large ladleful of the hot poaching liquid from the lamb. Whisk until the roux and poaching liquid blend, then whisk in two or three more ladlefuls.

2 **Flavoring the sauce.** Return the pan to the heat and bring the sauce to a boil. It should be thin and creamy; if it is too thick, add more poaching liquid. To rid the sauce of any floury taste, reduce the heat to low, place the pan half off the heat and simmer the sauce for about 40 minutes, skimming it several times. Beat egg yolks lightly with strained lemon juice. Blend a little sauce into the yolks to warm them. Then, off the heat, whisk the yolks into the sauce *(above, left)*. Put the pan back on low heat and stir the sauce until it thickens, but do not let it boil. Finally, rinse and drain capers, and stir them into the sauce *(right)*.

Concentrating Flavors for a Perfect Stew

When meat is cut up small for a stew, it can be packed tightly into a cooking pot so that relatively little liquid is needed to cover it. The stew may be moistened with water or, for more flavor, wine, puréed tomatoes or meat stock. In the stew demonstrated at right and on the next page, stock serves as the cooking liquid for pieces of lamb breast.

A meat stock is produced by simmering meaty bones and aromatic vegetables in water (box, below). When the meat and vegetables have surrendered their flavors to the liquid, they are strained out. In this case, the stock is made with lamb bones and a veal shank, included for its gelatin content. The aromatics are carrots, garlic, a bouquet garni and onions studded with whole cloves (recipe, page 164). A beef or veal stock could be used instead, but the distinctive flavor of lamb stock makes it an ideal complement to lamb stews and braises.

Stews always include additional aromatic vegetables for extra flavor; here, carrots and onions are cooked with the lamb pieces. Cooking may proceed in either of two ways. For simplicity, you can simmer the stew in a tightly covered pan until the meat is tender—about two hours. For an especially rich taste, you can cook the stew uncovered for about 40 minutes to reduce the stock and concentrate its flavor, then simmer it covered for about two hours more.

In either case, when the lamb is ready to eat, the vegetables should be discarded: They will have lost most of their flavor during the long cooking; and if a fatty cut of meat is used, as here, they will have absorbed a good deal of fat from the meat. The lamb and the cleansed cooking liquid, reduced to a fragrant sauce, then may be combined with one or more garnishing vegetables to produce a variety of different dishes.

In this instance, quartered turnips, sautéed in butter until they are golden brown, are served with the lamb. You could substitute carrots, cut into 1½-inch [4-cm.] lengths and sautéed; tiny onions, sautéed whole; parboiled new potatoes; or chunks of cucumber, parboiled and then sautéed.

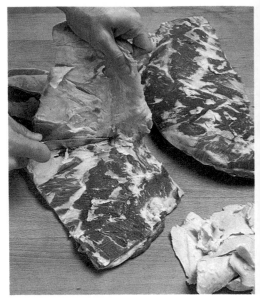

1 **Removing fat.** Place lamb breast meaty side up, and insert the tip of a small, sharp knife between the surface fat and the meat. Grasp the edge of the fat layer and peel it back, using the knife to cut the fat free where it clings to the meat underneath.

Making Stock from Lamb Bones

1 **Removing scum.** Place lamb bones and trimmings and a cut-up veal shank on a rack in a pan. Cover with cold water; bring slowly to a boil, skimming off rising scum. Add water and skim as the liquid returns to a boil.

2 **Straining the stock.** Continue to skim the liquid until no more scum rises. Add aromatics and reduce the heat to very low. Simmer the stock, partly covered with a lid, for five hours. Strain the stock through a cloth-lined colander.

3 **Degreasing.** Refrigerate the strained stock overnight to set it into a firm jelly. Its fat will rise to form a white, solid mass on the surface. Scrape the fat off with a spoon; pick up any remaining particles of fat with a warm, damp paper towel.

2 **Cutting up the meat.** Turn over the breast. Cut through the breastbone and between the ribs to divide the meat into sections of two or three ribs each.

3 **Assembling the stew.** Slice enough onions and carrots to cover the bottom of a large sauté pan. Arrange the pieces of lamb on top. Place a bouquet garni — in this case, celery, leek, thyme, a bay leaf and parsley — in the center of the pan. Season with salt.

4 **Cooking the stew.** Bring lamb stock to a boil and ladle some of the hot stock into the pan. Simmer uncovered until most of the stock has evaporated, about 40 minutes. Then add enough stock to submerge the meat. Cover the pan and let the stew simmer gently over low heat for about two hours, until the meat is tender.

5 **Preparing a garnish.** Peel about a dozen small, round turnips. If you prepare them in advance, place them in a bowl of cold water to prevent them from discoloring. When the meat is almost cooked, quarter the turnips and dry them on paper towels.

6 **Sautéing the turnips.** Melt butter in a skillet. Toss in the turnip quarters, and gently sauté them until golden brown and tender — 20 to 30 minutes. To brown the quarters evenly, turn them carefully with a wooden spoon or shake the skillet from time to time.

7 **Removing bones.** Take the stew off the heat and, with a slotted spoon, lift out the meat. Remove the large bones, cutting around them if necessary to free them from the meat. Leave any small bones in place. Place the meat in a clean sauté pan, cover it, and keep it warm while the sauce is prepared *(overleaf).* ▶

8 **Straining the sauce.** Tip the liquid and vegetables from the sauté pan into a strainer held over a skillet. With a wooden spoon, press the vegetables against the mesh of the strainer to extract as much juice as possible. Discard the pulp remaining in the strainer.

9 **Cleansing the sauce.** Bring the liquid in the skillet to a boil; set the skillet half off the burner, and adjust the heat to maintain a light boil on only one side of the surface. When a skin of fat forms on the cooler side of the liquid, skim it off.

10 **Assembling the stew.** Continue cooking and skimming the liquid for about 30 minutes, or until no more fat rises and the liquid has been reduced to a syrupy sauce. Distribute the sautéed turnips over the meat chunks in the sauté pan, and pour the sauce over them.

11 **Serving the stew.** Simmer the stew over low heat for a few minutes to blend the flavors of the meat, the sauce and the turnips. Serve the meat on warmed plates, and spoon some turnips and sauce over each portion.

Potatoes to Thicken the Cooking Liquid

A stew's cooking liquid may be thickened by reduction *(opposite, Steps 9 and 10)* or, for a heartier sauce, by the addition of a thickening agent such as flour or egg yolks. Starchy russet potatoes are another possibility: As the stew cooks, they disintegrate to give the liquid body.

The stew demonstrated on this page *(recipe, page 125)* incorporates two kinds of potatoes: large russets for thickening, and small, waxy new potatoes, which remain whole and provide a garnish for the meat. The new potatoes can be prepared in advance and kept in water so they do not discolor. However, the large potatoes should be peeled and sliced at the last minute; putting them in water would wash off their superficial starch.

In this stew, neck slices and shoulder chops are sandwiched between layers of sliced onions and the russet potatoes. The new potatoes are arranged on top and water is added. Tightly sealed, the stew is left to cook undisturbed in the oven until the meat is tender and the sliced potatoes have collapsed almost to a purée.

1 Preparing ingredients. Peel or scrub small new potatoes. Place them in a bowl of cold water to prevent discoloration. Peel and slice large russet potatoes and arrange them in a fairly thick layer on the bottom of a casserole; cover the potatoes with a layer of sliced onions. Arrange pieces of lamb on top of the sliced onions.

2 Adding more layers. Season the meat with coarse salt and herbs — here, dried thyme. Cover the meat with a second layer of potato slices, then a second layer of sliced onions. Season again with salt and herbs.

3 Adding water. Cover the final layer of onions with a close-packed layer of the new potatoes. Pour in enough water to come just above the last layer of onions.

4 Cooking the stew. Cover the casserole with aluminum foil to minimize the loss of liquid. Place a tightly fitting lid on top and put the casserole in a preheated 350° F. [180° C.] oven. Let the stew cook undisturbed for about two and one half hours.

5 Serving the stew. Remove the casserole from the oven and take off the lid and foil. Ladle stew onto warmed plates. Each portion should include some meat, some of the potato-thickened liquid and some intact new potatoes.

55

Exotic Components of a North African Classic

Olive oil will lend a distinctive flavor to a stew. In this demonstration, water and a generous splash of olive oil provide the cooking liquid for a *tajine*, the Moroccan term for a stew. As the stew simmers, the oil suffuses the meat—in this case, shoulder—with its fragrance and combines with the water to form a rich braising medium that yields a silken sauce.

Much of the character of this particular *tajine (recipe, page 130)* derives from the saffron, ginger and garlic used to season the meat, and the olives and preserved lemon peel added before the final cooking. Partially ripened olives, which have a violet tint, are shown, but they could be replaced by fully ripened black olives. The preserved lemon *(box, opposite; recipe, page 166)* contributes a spicy, slightly bitter taste; if not available, omit lemon altogether—fresh peel cannot be substituted. Vegetables to serve with the meat—here, broad beans and artichoke bottoms—are cooked separately in the braising liquid to preserve their textures and unique tastes.

1 Stewing lamb. Cut lamb shoulder into large pieces and trim off fat. Place the meat in a pot, and add ground saffron and ginger, lightly crushed garlic cloves and coarse salt. Pour in olive oil. Cover the meat with cold water and bring it to a boil. Reduce the heat, cover the pot and simmer gently for about two hours, until tender.

2 Preparing beans. Pinch each bean pod near the stem end to split it, then run your thumbnail down its seam. Run the tip of your thumb down the inside of the pod to free the beans, then—again using your thumbnail— split the skin on each bean lengthwise and peel the skin *(above).* Put the beans in a pan; discard the pods and skins.

4 Rinsing olives and lemons. To rid the olives of excess saltiness, rinse them and then soak them in cold water for about 30 minutes. Meanwhile, rinse a preserved lemon, separate it into quarters and, with a teaspoon, scoop out all of the pulp. Discard the pulp and cut each lemon quarter into four pieces.

5 Adding liquid. When the meat is tender, remove it from the pot. Strain the liquid to extract the garlic. Place the beans and the drained artichokes in separate pans. Divide all but one ladleful of the strained liquid between them. Return the meat to the stewpot and add the last ladleful of liquid. Keep the meat warm over very low heat.

6 Cooking the vegetables. Bring the beans and artichokes to a boil, then simmer them until tender: two to five minutes for the beans and 10 to 15 minutes for the artichokes. Strain the cooking liquid into a saucepan and add the vegetables to the meat. Put the olives and the preserved lemon peel into the stew, cover it, and keep it warm.

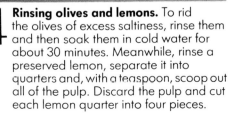

Spiced Lemons Preserved with Salt

3 **Preparing artichoke bottoms.** Break off the artichoke stems. Bend each outer leaf back from the fleshy base and snap it off. When you reach the tender, yellow-green inner leaves, use a sharp, stainless-steel knife to cut off the top two thirds of the artichoke. Starting at the stem end and cutting in a spiral, peel away the bases of the outer leaves from the artichoke bottom *(above, left)*. Quarter the bottom and cut out the hairy choke *(right)*. To prevent discoloring, immerse the quarters in a solution of 1 teaspoon [5 ml.] of lemon juice to 1 quart [1 liter] of water.

Preserving lemons. Make two crosswise slits from the top to within ½ inch [1 cm.] of the bottom of each lemon. Pack the slits with coarse salt *(above, left)*. Place a layer of salt in a clamp-top jar. Add lemons, pressing them to release their juice. Add a bay leaf and spices — here, coriander, cinnamon, cloves and black peppercorns. Layer in more salt, lemons and spices, ending with salt. Pour in lemon juice to cover the lemons *(right)*. Close the jar; store in a warm place for at least a month.

7 **Reducing the sauce.** Place the saucepan containing the braising liquid over high heat and boil until the liquid is reduced to a slightly syrupy sauce. As it thickens, stir it from time to time with a wooden spoon to prevent it from sticking *(inset)*. When the sauce is thick, pour it over the meat and vegetables *(above)*. Simmer the stew over low heat for about 15 minutes, to let the flavors mingle.

8 **Serving the stew.** Using a slotted spoon, remove the meat and vegetables to a large, warmed serving dish. To add a hint of sharpness, sprinkle the juice of a fresh lemon over the stew. Ladle the sauce remaining in the stewpot evenly over the meat and vegetables. Serve the stew on warmed plates.

A Rich Amalgam Nurtured by Low Heat

When pieces of meat and chopped vegetables are stewed together gently for seven or eight hours, the flavors merge into a rich blend while the vegetables soften almost to a purée. In France, an unhurried braise of this type is known as a daube; the one demonstrated here *(recipe, page 130)* is native to Provence.

The meat for a lamb daube is often the leg. However, the shoulder, chosen here, possesses certain advantages: It has a stronger flavor to contribute to the stew and, while only the shank of the leg yields sufficient gelatin to remain moist with long cooking, the entire shoulder is highly gelatinous. Succulence can be further ensured by lacing the meat with strips of pork fat, called lardons *(Steps 1-3)*. As the stew cooks, the lardons slowly melt, basting the meat from within. For additional flavor, the lardons can be seasoned and the meat marinated.

The other ingredients of a daube are largely a matter of personal choice. Such gelatinous cuts as pork rind and pig's or calf's feet will add body to the stew. The aromatic vegetables in this demonstration are carrots, onions, garlic and dried cepes, but these could be replaced or augmented by celery, turnips, ripe olives, parsnips, tomatoes or fresh mushrooms. A wide range of suitable herbs includes thyme, savory, marjoram, oregano, chervil, bay leaf, rosemary and parsley.

Traditionally, a daube is cooked in a special vessel that gives the stew its name—the *daubière,* which has a narrow neck to minimize evaporation. Any deep, heavy ovenproof vessel, such as the earthenware pot at right, will serve as well. To hold in moisture, place a layer of foil on top of the vessel before lidding it.

After cooking, a daube can be skimmed of surface fat and served at once. But if refrigerated for one to four days before serving, the flavors of the daube will blend further, and it will taste even better. Chilling the stew has another advantage. As the liquid gets cold, additional fat rising to the top solidifies; it can be easily removed with a spoon *(Step 9)* before the daube is reheated.

Present the daube along with a simple accompaniment—pasta moistened with the daube's cooking liquid, perhaps, or boiled dried white beans or *flageolets.*

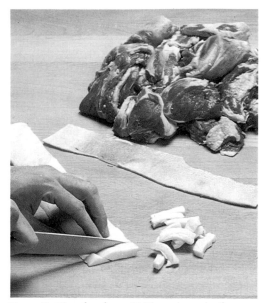

1 Cutting lardons. With a sharp knife, cut meat — in this case, boned lamb shoulder *(pages 12-13)* — into large chunks of roughly equal size. Trim the rind from a piece of pork fat, and cut the fat into lardons approximately 1½ inches [4 cm.] long and ¼ inch [6 mm.] wide. Reserve the rind to add to the daube.

2 Seasoning the lardons. In a mortar, pound garlic cloves, coarse salt, pepper and dried herbs — here, thyme, savory, marjoram and oregano — to a paste. Add finely chopped parsley and a splash of brandy. Toss the lardons in the paste to coat each one evenly.

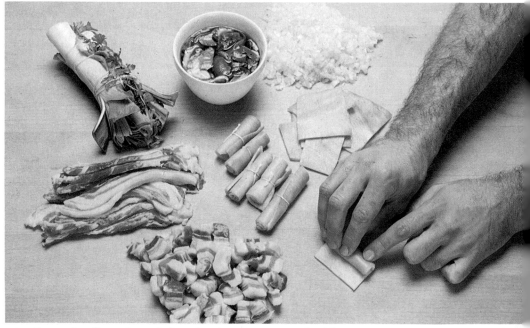

6 Preparing flavorings. Soften dried cepes in water for 30 minutes. Chop onions and assemble a bouquet garni. Slice salt pork, then dice half the slices. Chop the reserved pork rind or, as here, cut it in squares, then roll each square into a cylinder and tie it. Blanch the salt pork in boiling water for five minutes and the pork rinds for 15 minutes. Drain the cepes, reserving the liquid, then chop them and mix with the onions and diced salt pork.

3 **Larding the meat.** With the point of a small, sharp knife, pierce each piece of meat in one or two places. Push one of the seasoned lardons into each slit with your fingers.

4 **Preparing marinade.** Assemble the marinade ingredients — carrots, onions, garlic, thyme, a bay leaf, parsley sprigs, red wine and olive oil are shown. Chop the onions and carrots fine *(above)*. Crush the garlic to a paste. Place the meat in a large bowl; scatter the herbs and vegetables over and around the pieces of meat.

5 **Adding wine.** Pour olive oil over the meat and vegetables, then add enough red wine to cover all of the ingredients. Cover the bowl, and marinate the meat for several hours at room temperature or overnight in the refrigerator.

7 **Layering.** Line the bottom of a deep, heavy pot with half of the slices of salt pork and a few pork rinds. Fill the pot with alternate layers of the lamb, cepe mixture, vegetables from the marinade and pork rinds. Salt each lamb layer. Put the bouquet garni in the center, and finish with vegetables and the remaining salt pork.

8 **Moistening.** Pour the reserved cepe liquid and the marinade liquid into the pot. Add just enough stock *(box, page 52)* to cover the dry ingredients. Cover the pot with foil and the lid. Put it in a 250° F. [120° C.] oven or over very low heat, and cook for seven hours.

9 **Serving.** Skim the fat off the surface of the daube, discard the bouquet garni and serve. Alternatively, refrigerate the daube overnight — or for up to four days — then lift off the solid fat from the top with a spoon *(above)*. Reheat the daube very slowly for about two hours. Skim off any fat that rises to the surface, then serve.

Garlic-scented Lamb Braised in Its Own Juices

When they are cooked over gentle heat, gelatinous pieces of lamb—neck slices, chunks of shoulder or the shanks shown here—release enough liquid so that they can braise in their own juices *(recipe, page 121)*. Maintaining low, even heat is critical to success. The pan must be a heavy one that diffuses heat uniformly, and its lid must fit tightly to prevent evaporation.

To keep the lamb from sticking at the start of the braising, add a film of oil to the pan. Brown the lamb lightly to begin melting the surface fat, then add seasonings—herbs and garlic in this case—and cover the pan. Check the meat periodically. The amount of liquid exuded varies with the cut; neck and shank contain more fat and gelatin-yielding connective tissue than shoulder does. If the juices dry up, add spoonfuls of water or stock.

Because the volume of liquid is small, the flavors of the meat and seasonings concentrate in the brown deposits left in the pan during braising. These can be captured by deglazing with water, stock or wine to produce a sauce.

1 **Heating lamb.** Pour a thin layer of olive oil into a heavy pot or sauté pan, and heat it over medium heat. Put lamb pieces — in this case, shanks — into the pan and brown them lightly on all sides. Sprinkle in salt and mixed dried herbs, and scatter unpeeled garlic cloves over the lamb. Then reduce the heat to very low and cover the pan.

2 **Braising the meat.** As the pieces of meat cook, turn them from time to time with a wooden spoon. If the meat juices evaporate and the lamb begins to sizzle in fat, add a few spoonfuls of water.

3 **Deglazing with wine.** When the meat begins to fall from the bones — after one and one half to two hours — spoon out of the pan as much fat as possible. Add a splash of dry white wine; stir and scrape with a wooden spoon to loosen the deposits adhering to the bottom. With a slotted spoon, transfer the meat to a plate.

4 **Straining the sauce.** Pour the pan juices through a strainer into a small saucepan. Push the garlic pulp through the strainer with a wooden spoon or pestle; discard the peels. Skim off the surface fat, and reduce the sauce until it reaches the consistency of thick cream.

5 **Coating the meat.** Return the shanks to the braising pan. Grind black pepper over the meat. If you like, stir a little lemon or bitter-orange juice into the reduced sauce. Pour it into the pan, coating each piece of meat. Reheat the shanks gently before serving.

Searing for a Wealth of Flavor and Color

Browning the lamb for a stew before covering it with liquid produces a wealth of savory pan deposits. If the pan is deglazed before the liquid is added, the fragments can be blended with the liquid from the start, ensuring a hearty sauce.

A classic French stew that employs this stratagem is *navarin printanier*, or lamb stew with spring vegetables—demonstrated at right and overleaf *(recipe, page 134)*. Sugar is added to the browning meat to caramelize in the juices and deepen the color of the pan deposits. A sprinkling of flour is stirred in to thicken the braising liquid.

To ensure that all of the pan deposits are retrieved, the braising liquid is added in two stages: A small measure serves for deglazing; the remainder is poured in afterward *(overleaf)* to submerge the meat. In this case, white wine and water form the braising liquid. Water alone would suffice, or you could use stock, either by itself or combined with wine.

Aromatic vegetables for the braise can be browned with the meat or, as here, sautéed separately. Either way, the aromatics will have yielded up their flavors by the time the meat is tender, and they should be replaced at the end of the cooking with fresh vegetables.

The final complement of vegetables for *navarin printanier* should be young and fresh: Parboiled carrots and broad beans and sautéed boiling onions and turnip quarters are the choice here, but you could add, or substitute, sautéed artichoke bottoms or parboiled peas, cauliflower florets or celeriac cubes. Such vegetables are simmered only briefly in the stew to intermingle their flavors without loss of their individuality.

A similar stew, made with dried beans instead of fresh vegetables, provides a heartier alternative. The demonstration on page 63 features white beans, but *flageolets*, pinto beans or lentils offer other possibilities. While the fresh flavors of young vegetables in the spring stew are kept distinct, the mild flavor of dried beans should be thoroughly integrated. Two procedures achieve this: The stew is moistened with some of the liquid used to cook the beans; and in braising, the meat is simmered with the beans long enough to merge all of the flavors.

1 **Sautéeing vegetables.** Peel carrots and onions, and cut them into chunks. Heat oil in a sauté pan; add the vegetables and soften them over low heat. After about 15 minutes, increase the heat slightly to brown the vegetables. Cook for another 15 minutes, stirring frequently to prevent sticking.

2 **Browning lamb.** Place the vegetables in a strainer to drain off excess oil. Remove all bits of onion from the pan — they would burn when the meat was seared. Cut lamb — here, shoulder — into large pieces; trim off fat. Salt the meat. Return the drained oil to the pan and, over high heat, brown the lamb on all sides — adding more oil if necessary.

3 **Deglazing the pan.** Sprinkle sugar over the lamb pieces; turn them gently with a wooden spoon until the sugar caramelizes. Sprinkle flour over the lamb *(above, left)*. Again, turn the meat pieces several times to brown all of the flour. Return the carrots and onions to the pan; mix them with the meat. Pour white wine over the meat and vegetables. Scrape the pan to loosen the caramelized deposits, and blend them into the cooking liquid *(right)*. ▶

4 **Adding water.** Cut tomatoes in quarters, as here, or chop them. Add the tomatoes to the pan with unpeeled garlic bulbs and a bouquet garni. Pour in just enough water to cover the ingredients. Bring to a boil over medium heat.

5 **Simmering the stew.** Reduce the heat to low and put a heat-diffusing pad under the pan. Place the lid on the pan. Or put the stew in a casserole, cover, and place it in a preheated 350° F. [180° C.] oven. Simmer the stew one hour, or until the meat is tender. With a disk skimmer or slotted spoon, remove the meat to a platter (above).

6 **Straining the sauce.** Lift the bouquet garni between two wooden spoons and squeeze its juices into the pan; discard the bouquet garni. Strain the sauce into a small pan. Discard the carrots; press the pulp of the other vegetables through the strainer with a spoon or pestle. Discard the skins and seeds left in the strainer.

7 **Preparing vegetables.** Sauté boiling onions gently in butter in a covered skillet for 20 minutes. Sauté quartered turnips in a separate pan for 15 minutes. Parboil cut-up carrots for 15 minutes, and shelled and peeled broad beans for two to three minutes. Return the meat to the sauté pan and scatter the drained vegetables over it.

8 **Simmering and serving.** Cleanse the sauce (page 54, Step 9) and, if necessary, boil the cleansed sauce to reduce it. Pour the sauce into the sauté pan, and stir so that all of the meat and vegetable pieces are coated (above). Put the pan over medium heat and bring the stew to a boil. Reduce the heat, cover and simmer the stew for 10 minutes. Serve the meat and vegetables on heated plates; ladle sauce over each portion (inset).

Dried Beans to Buttress a Winter Stew

1 **Softening beans.** Pick over dried white beans, removing the imperfect ones. Rinse the beans. Soak them in cold water overnight, or bring them to a boil in water and soak them for one hour in the same water. Drain the soaked beans; pour them into a saucepan. Add enough fresh water to cover them by about 1 inch [2½ cm.].

2 **Cooking the beans.** Bring the beans to a boil, skimming off scum from the surface. Add a carrot, a clove-studded onion and a bouquet garni. Cover and cook over low heat for one and one half hours, until the beans can be crushed easily between your fingers. Prepare and sauté the meat and aromatic vegetables *(page 61, Steps 1 and 2)*.

3 **Moistening the stew.** Add quartered tomatoes, garlic and a fresh bouquet garni to the stew. Ladle a small amount of cooking liquid from the beans into the stew, but leave enough liquid to keep the beans submerged. If more braising liquid is needed, add water.

4 **Adding the beans.** Cover and simmer the stew for about one hour over low heat or in a preheated 350° F. [180° C.] oven. Strain and cleanse the braising liquid *(page 54, Step 9)*. Drain the beans, reserving the cooking liquid, and add them to the meat.

5 **Melding the flavors.** Pour the cleansed sauce over the meat and beans. If necessary, add some of the reserved cooking liquid from the beans. Cook the stew over gentle heat for about 30 minutes to mingle the flavors of all the ingredients. Lift the meat onto warmed serving plates; cover each portion with a generous helping of the beans and sauce.

A Unique Presentation of Rib Chops

Rib chops—although a tender cut not usually considered a candidate for braising—are featured in an English stew called Lancashire hot pot. The reason is their structure: The chops are positioned upright on their meaty ends in a round casserole so that their curved bones arch up in a spiky, circular fence, enclosing aromatic vegetables and sliced potatoes.

Before the chops are arranged in the casserole, they are lightly coated with flour and seared in hot lard until their surfaces are crisp and brown. The fat used to sear them also serves to sauté the aromatic vegetables and, finally, when flour is added, to make a roux that will thicken the liquid for the stew. The searing of the chops and the thickness of the braising liquid minimize any juice loss, thus keeping this tender cut succulent.

In the demonstration here, the meat is flavored not only with the familiar carrots and onions, but also with oysters *(recipe, page 124)*. When oysters were inexpensive, they were often used to eke out meager supplies of meat. Nowadays, they are added not for economy but for the subtle, salty taste they bring to the hot pot. Oysters are obtainable already shucked, but—for the tangiest effect—should be bought in their shells. Before shucking them, sharply tap any specimens whose shells gape; if the shells do not close immediately, the oysters are dead and must be discarded.

For shucking, use an oyster knife, an implement with a short blade that has dull edges but a sharp tip. Wrap each oyster in a folded napkin with the flatter shell uppermost and the hinged end toward you. Hold the oyster firmly, and insert the tip of the knife into the gap in the hinge; twist the knife blade to snap the shells apart. Then slide the blade along the inside of the flat upper shell to sever the muscle that holds the two shells together. Discard the upper shell.

Without spilling the liquor contained in the curved lower shell, set the shell on a cutting board. Cutting toward yourself, run the blade under the oyster to sever the muscle attached to the shell. Remove bits of broken shell with the knife point, but save the oyster liquor for the stew.

1 Preparing oysters. Chop onions fine. Slice carrots and potatoes. Place the potatoes in cold water to prevent discoloration. Holding each oyster in a cloth to protect your hand, insert an oyster knife into the hinged end of the shell and twist it to open the shell. Cut the oyster free and transfer it, together with its liquor, to a plate.

2 Browning the chops. Trim rib chops and strip the rib ends *(page 39, Steps 4 and 5)*. Dust each chop with flour. Melt lard in a sauté pan and sear the chops on both sides over high heat. Remove the chops. Reduce the heat, and sauté the carrots and onions in the same fat— adding more lard if needed—until they are lightly colored.

5 Making a sauce. Put the sauté pan—still containing the fat and drippings—over medium heat. Sprinkle sugar into the fat. Sprinkle in flour, a little at a time, while using a whisk to stir it into the fat *(above, left)*. Stop adding flour when the roux has the consistency of a thin paste. Still whisking, pour boiling water into the pan all at once *(right)*; use the whisk to free deposits that cling to the pan bottom, and blend them into the liquid.

3 **Arranging the chops.** Place a layer of sautéed carrots and onions in a deep ovenproof casserole with curved sides. Stand the chops, upright on the meaty ends, on top of the vegetables.

4 **Adding vegetables and oysters.** Spoon the remaining carrots and onions into the casserole, packing them around the meat to hold the chops upright. Tuck in a bay leaf among the vegetables. Season with salt. Place the shucked oysters on top of the carrots and onions, and pour in the oyster liquor. Cover the oysters with a layer of overlapping potato slices.

6 **Adding the sauce.** Continue whisking until the sauce becomes smooth and begins to boil. Ladle the sauce into the stew—a little at a time to avoid disturbing the contents of the casserole—until the sauce reaches the level of the potatoes. Cover the casserole with a lid.

7 **Cooking and serving.** Cook the stew for two hours in a preheated 350° F. [180° C.] oven. Increase the heat to 375° F. [190° C.], remove the lid from the casserole and cook for 30 minutes more. If the potatoes have not browned, put the stew under a preheated broiler to give the potatoes a glossy, golden sheen (above). Spoon the stew onto warmed plates (inset).

Enclosing Stuffing in a Pair of Shoulders

For braising, as for roasting, whole lamb breast or shoulder forms a neat parcel when boned and tied or sewed into a compact shape *(pages 36-37 and 40-41)*. For an especially substantial meal, two shoulders may be sandwiched together to make the plump cushion shown here.

The cushion of lamb invites stuffing, and the requisite cooking time is sufficiently long so that raw mixtures can be used. Here, the stuffing is a savory pork blend *(recipe, page 166)* bound with egg and enlivened with blanched and peeled pistachios. Other possible options are a ham-and-cheese mixture flavored with *persillade (recipe, page 166)* or a mixture of rice, apricots and almonds *(recipe, page 106)*. Because the stuffing will swell during cooking, the cushion should not be packed too full: Two to three cups [½ to ¾ liter] of stuffing is sufficient.

For extra flavor, bones removed from the cut are browned ahead of time and their pan deglazed. The bones are then spread in the bottom of the braising vessel to enrich the liquid and to form a rack that will keep the meat from sticking.

1 **Browning the bones.** Bone two lamb shoulders *(pages 12-13)* and set the meat aside. Hack the bones into 1½-inch [4-cm.] pieces. Roast the pieces for two hours in a preheated 400° F. [200° C.] oven. Make a stuffing of ground pork and pork fat, egg, onion, bread crumbs, pistachios, parsley, garlic, herbs, salt and pepper.

2 **Spreading the stuffing.** Place the boned shoulders on a work surface, fell side down. Spread stuffing into the gullies left by the bones, leveling off the top of the stuffing even with the flesh. Turn over one shoulder and position it on top of the other, matching the thick end of one to the thin end of the other.

5 **Preparing the casserole.** Cut celery, onions and carrots into 1-inch [2½-cm.] pieces, and set them aside in a bowl. Place the roasted bones on the bottom of a large casserole. Sprinkle the vegetables over the bones and set the cushion on top.

6 **Braising.** Use 2 cups [½ liter] of water, wine or stock to deglaze the pan in which the bones were browned *(page 36, Step 5)*. Pour this liquid over the meat. Place the casserole over high heat and bring the liquid to a boil. Cover the casserole and put it in a preheated 300° F. [150° C.] oven. Cook for about three hours, or until the meat is tender.

7 **Finishing the sauce.** Transfer the meat to a clean roasting pan. Increase the oven temperature to 400° F. [200° C.]. Strain the braising liquid into a small pan, pressing down lightly on the vegetables. Discard the vegetables and bones. Boil the liquid until it is syrupy and is reduced to approximately one third of its original volume.

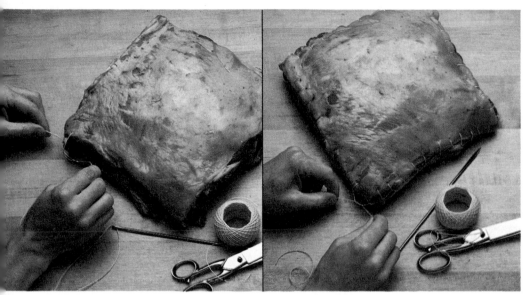

3 **Sewing the parcel.** Thread a butcher's needle with kitchen string. Starting about ½ inch [1 cm.] from the edge at a corner of the cushion, insert the needle into the bottom shoulder and push it upward through the fell, the two layers of flesh and the fell of the top shoulder. Make a loop and tie a knot (above, left), leaving a short tail of string. About ¾ inch [2 cm.] from the loop, push the needle up through the cushion again. Pass the string through the loop and pull the string tight. Repeat the stitch around the cushion; knot the end of the string (right) and cut off the excess.

4 **Browning the meat.** Pour oil into a heavy skillet to a depth of about ¾ inch [2 cm.]. Heat the oil over high heat. Place the meat in the skillet and brown the underside for eight to 10 minutes, moving the meat occasionally to ensure even cooking. Turn the cushion and cook until the second side has browned.

3 **Glazing the meat.** Set the roasting pan with the meat in the oven, pour the reduced liquid over the cushion, and cook the meat — basting occasionally — until the surface is glazed and a rich brown — about 15 minutes.

9 **Serving.** Let the meat rest for 10 minutes, then cut and remove the string. Carve the stuffed cushion into slices at least ½ inch [1 cm.] thick; thinner slices would fall apart along the lines between stuffing and meat.

4

Extensions and Encores

'echniques to keep leftovers tender
:ombinations of lamb and vegetables
\ classic moussaka and variations
'oached meat broiled to crispness
'inishes for ground lamb

The cook who ranges beyond the basic techniques for preparing lamb—broiling, frying, roasting, poaching and braising—will discover a territory full of variety and new delights. Lamb can be puréed, for example, and blended with cracked wheat to produce a Lebanese version of meat loaf *(pages 82-83)*. Or two cooking methods can be conjoined: Poaching followed by broiling ensures that lamb breast is juicy within and crisp on the outside *(pages 80-81)*. And some of the most rewarding dishes can be created from that humblest of starting points—leftovers.

Leftover lamb deserves—and indeed requires—at least as much attention as fresh meat; carelessly reheated meat can be tough. To understand why, consider the two structural components of lean meat and what happens to them during the first cooking. The two components are the muscle fibers and the tough connective tissue—largely composed of a substance called collagen—that holds the fibers together. Cooking meat to an internal temperature of 160° F. [70° C.] will shrink the muscle fibers and rob them of juices, thus toughening them. However, further cooking—particularly moist cooking—to 175° F. [80° C.] or higher will convert much of the collagen to semiliquid gelatin, compensating for the loss of juice from the muscle fibers and making the meat tender.

Leftover meat that was cooked initially by poaching or braising—both involving the slow application of heat in the presence of moisture—has become rich in gelatin and can be reheated with no danger of toughening. But meat cooked by the quicker methods of roasting or broiling, or by the brief poaching sometimes given to a prime cut *(pages 50-51)*, is ready to serve at an internal temperature of 140° F. [60° C.], before much gelatin has formed; if cooked further during reheating, the meat is likely to toughen and become dry.

One straightforward way to keep roasted or broiled meat tender is to warm it cautiously, as demonstrated on pages 50-51. The other approach is to cook the leftovers long enough to convert their collagen into tenderizing gelatin: Large chunks of meat will require a second cooking of about one and one half hours; finely chopped meat will need 20 to 30 minutes. With this technique, the dishes you can make with leftover roasted or broiled meat range from a rustic lamb-and-vegetable pie *(pages 74-75)* to the spectacular eggplant-sheathed mold shown opposite.

wedge is lifted from a molded ssembly of finely chopped leftover lamb nd vegetables enclosed in spiraling ggplant slices *(pages 78-79)*. To chieve this effect, the eggplant slices ere cut into shapes that would fit the ottom and sides of a charlotte mold, en sautéed long enough to make them alleable. After the mold was lined nd packed, the dish was cooked gently a water bath until the flavors of its mponents blended.

Gentle Reheating on a Bed of Leaves

Sliced thin and warmed briefly on a bed of a chopped-and-sauced leaf vegetable, roasted lamb will keep its original pinkness and tenderness when reheated for another meal. The slices must be arranged on the vegetable bed in a single layer so that the meat will heat through quickly and evenly, without cooking further and becoming tough. The vegetable, meanwhile, will insulate the slices from the heat of the pan bottom and will supply moisture—captured by covering the pan—to prevent the meat from drying out. This same technique can, of course, be applied to braised or poached lamb; although these leftovers will not toughen if reheated at higher temperatures or on their own, they will gain in flavor from being warmed with the vegetable.

Any leafy vegetable may be used to form the bed. The chicory shown in this demonstration *(recipe, page 157)* could be replaced by spinach, chard, cabbage or a lettuce such as romaine, escarole or butterhead. To soften the leaves and reduce their bulk, they are parboiled, drained well, squeezed dry and chopped into fine bits. Then the chopped leaves are moistened liberally so that they do not stick to the bottom of the pan. Velouté sauce sharpened with wine is the moistener used here; white sauce and heavy cream are two other possibilities.

After the lamb is placed on the leaves, the pan is covered and set on a fireproof pad, which keeps the heat low: The lamb should never reach a temperature higher than 140° F. [65° C.], and the sauced vegetable should never begin to simmer. Even so, 10 minutes will be ample time to warm the lamb through. If desired, cubes of bread can be sautéed into croutons during that time to provide a garnish.

1 **Parboiling leaves.** Remove any damaged leaves from several heads of chicory. Bring salted water to a boil in a large pot and drop in the heads. Parboil the chicory for five minutes.

2 **Chopping the chicory.** Drain the chicory in a colander. Run cold water over it to stop the cooking and to make it cool enough to handle. Set the colander over a bowl. With your hands, squeeze each head of chicory tightly to expel as much water as possible. Trim the main stem from each head, and chop the leaves fine.

5 **Adding the lamb.** Cut leftover lamb—in this case, the remains of a roasted leg—into thin slices. Arrange the slices of meat in one layer on top of the chicory. Cover the pan and set it on a fireproof pad placed over very low heat. Cook for 10 minutes, or until the slices of meat are just warmed through.

3 **Preparing velouté sauce.** Melt butter in a skillet set over low heat. Add flour and stir for a minute or two with a whisk to form a smooth roux. Increase the heat and pour meat stock into the roux *(left)*. Whisk continuously until the sauce boils. Then whisk in a little white or red wine, if you wish *(right)*. Reduce the heat and set the pan half off the burner. Simmer the sauce for about 40 minutes, skimming frequently to remove any impurities that rise to its surface on the cooler side of the skillet.

4 **Mixing chicory and sauce.** Pour the velouté sauce into a wide sauté pan. Put the chopped chicory into the sauté pan, and stir the mixture gently until the chicory is evenly moistened with sauce.

6 **Sautéing croutons.** Remove the crusts from thick slices of bread and cut the bread into cubes. Melt butter in a skillet over low heat. Toss the bread cubes in the butter for approximately 15 minutes, until they are crisp and golden brown *(inset)*. Spread the sauced chicory on a warmed platter, arrange the slices of lamb on top and garnish them with the croutons *(right)*.

Leftover Lamb Encased in Vegetables

A Wrapping of Parboiled Cabbage

Even a small amount of leftover lamb will yield a substantial meal when it is reheated inside a vegetable covering or case. Strips of meat, for example, can be wrapped in leaf vegetables—chard, spinach or cabbage *(top demonstration; recipe, page 153)*. Alternatively, tidy containers for diced or chopped lamb can be fashioned from tomatoes, eggplants, onions or zucchini *(bottom demonstration; recipe, page 154)*—or, even more easily, from such hollow vegetables as acorn squash or peppers.

How long the wrappers or cases must cook depends on the type of vegetable and perhaps on the type of leftover it holds as well. Previously roasted or broiled lamb must be cooked long enough to tenderize it: about one and one half hours if the lamb is cut into strips, about 30 minutes if it is diced or chopped. Previously poached or braised lamb needs no tenderizing, and cooking time is determined entirely by the vegetable that encloses it.

1 Preparing leaves. Separate cabbage leaves. Pare the thick central rib of each leaf. Layer the leaves in a pot and cover them with boiling water. Boil the leaves over high heat for a minute or so. Drain them, pour cold water over them to stop the cooking, drain them again and lay them on a towel to dry.

2 Cutting leftover meat. Carve slices ¾ inch [2 cm.] thick from a leftover lamb roast—in this case, a leg. Cut the meat slices into strips about 3 inches [8 cm.] long and ¾ inch wide.

Hollowed Halves of Zucchini

1 Scooping out shells. Chop onions and parsley fine. Make crumbs from slightly stale, crustless bread. Trim the ends from zucchini and halve them lengthwise. With a spoon, carefully scoop out most of the flesh from each half, leaving a shell ⅛ inch [3 mm.] thick. Chop the flesh into small pieces.

2 Preparing stuffing. Chop leftover lamb, place it in a pan and add enough stock to immerse the meat. Cover and simmer for 15 minutes. In a second pan, sauté the onions and chopped zucchini until they are just soft. Add the meat and stock to the vegetables *(above)*; cook for five minutes.

3 Mixing the stuffing. Transfer the meat-and-vegetable mixture to a bowl. Add the parsley and bread crumbs, and bind the stuffing with eggs. Season the mixture with salt and pepper, and stir to blend the ingredients thoroughly.

3 **Wrapping the lamb.** Place a strip of lamb near the base of each leaf. Sprinkle a little salt, pepper and herbs —finely chopped rosemary is used here —over the meat. Fold up the base (above), then fold in the sides of the leaf to enclose the meat. Roll up the leaf, from the base, to make a neat parcel. Place each parcel in a baking dish with the loose edge of the leaf downward. The baking dish should be just large enough to hold all of the parcels easily —not packed too tightly —in a single layer.

4 **Baking the parcels.** Heat meat stock (recipe, page 164), as here, or the water in which the leaves were parboiled. Pour the liquid into the baking dish until the parcels are about half-submerged. Cover the dish with foil. Bake for about one hour in an oven preheated to 375° F. [190° C.]. Remove the foil and bake for 30 minutes more to reduce the liquid, basting the parcels every five to 10 minutes. Serve them on warmed plates, each portion moistened with a spoonful of sauce.

4 **Filling the shells.** Spoon stuffing into each zucchini shell. Place the zucchini in a shallow baking dish. Pour water into the dish to a depth of ⅛ inch [3 mm.]. Place the dish in a preheated 350° F. [180° C.] oven. Check the dish after about 15 minutes; if the bottom is dry, add more water.

5 **Adding cream.** In a small bowl, whisk flour and salt into heavy cream. Remove the zucchini from the oven after 25 minutes, or when they feel tender if pierced with a fork. Spoon the thickened cream over each shell (above) and return the dish to the oven for 10 minutes to heat the cream and brown the stuffing. If you like, sprinkle chopped fresh herbs —fennel leaves and parsley are shown —over the zucchini before serving them (inset).

Stratagems for Stretching Leftovers

Starchy root vegetables and such grains as rice or barley can stretch a small amount of leftover lamb into a satisfying main course by either of the strategies illustrated here. In the top demonstration, puréed potatoes blanket a blend of chopped lamb and partially cooked vegetables to create a shepherd's pie *(recipe, page 155)*. In the bottom demonstration, rice augments cubed lamb to produce a richly seasoned pilaf *(recipe, page 157)*. Both dishes may be based on leftover roasted or broiled lamb; the mixtures cook long enough to allow the lamb to become tender and juicy again after reheating has initially toughened it.

For the shepherd's pie, the lamb is combined with onions, carrots and peas, moistened with meat stock and topped with potato. The filling could, instead, be enriched with green beans, sliced parsnips, cubed artichoke bottoms or chunks of tomato. The topping might be puréed rutabagas or sweet potatoes.

Baking the pie slowly in the oven reheats the lamb while its flavor merges with the flavors of the other filling ingredients. The purée topping seals in the juices of the filling and gives the finished pie a crisp golden surface, or gratin.

For the pilaf, the lamb is flavored and reheated by sautéing it gently with pine nuts, raisins, dried currants and aromatic vegetables before it is incorporated into cooked rice. Other possible additions to the sauté include chopped ham or bacon, strips of green pepper and dried or fresh mushrooms.

To give it additional richness, the pilaf can be served with yogurt, as shown here, or with sour cream.

A Gratin Topped with Potato

1 Chopping lamb. Peel potatoes; immerse them in cold water to prevent them from discoloring while you work. Assemble vegetables — in this case, freshly shelled peas and finely chopped carrots and onions. Chop leftover lamb — here, from a roast leg. Place the chopped meat in a large bowl.

2 Mixing the filling. Sauté the onions in oil for about 10 minutes, until soft. Add them to the meat. Parboil the carrots for 10 minutes and the peas for five minutes, until nearly tender; drain and add them to the bowl. Add chopped parsley, and salt and pepper. Blend the ingredients with your hands.

A Background of Rice

1 Preparing ingredients. Assemble the ingredients — roast lamb, onion, tomatoes, dried currants, pine nuts, raisins and a garlic clove are shown. Chop the onion. Cut the cooked meat into small cubes. Scald the tomatoes in boiling water to loosen the skins; peel, seed and chop the tomatoes. Peel the garlic and chop it fine.

2 Cooking the meat. In a skillet, sauté the onion in oil for about five minutes. Add the pine nuts, tomatoes, raisins, currants, garlic and the cubes of lamb, and season with fresh or dried herbs. Cook the mixture gently, uncovered, for about 20 minutes, stirring occasionally.

3 **Preparing potatoes.** Slice the potatoes; boil them for 20 minutes, or until tender. Drain them and reserve the water. Purée the potatoes with a food mill or ricer, or push them through a sieve with a pestle. Stir in butter and enough cooking water to make a creamy purée. Season with nutmeg, salt and pepper.

4 **Assembling the pie.** Butter a baking dish. Put the meat-and-vegetable mixture in the dish. Heat stock, and add enough of it to the mixture to moisten all of the ingredients slightly. With a spatula or the back of a spoon, spread the puréed potatoes in an even layer over the meat and vegetables.

5 **Baking the pie.** Score the surface of the purée with a fork. Dot the surface with small pieces of butter. Place the dish in a preheated 375° F. [190° C.] oven and bake for about 45 minutes, until the surface of the purée develops a golden brown crust.

3 **Assembling the dish.** In a large sauté pan, cook rice in oil for three minutes, or until it whitens. Pour in boiling water, cover the pan and boil the rice for 15 minutes, or until it is just tender. Drain the rice and set the pan over low heat. Add the sautéed meat-and-onion mixture. With two forks, toss the mixture thoroughly to combine the ingredients.

4 **Serving.** Cook the pilaf, tossing the ingredients frequently, for two or three minutes, or until they are warmed through. Take the pan off the heat *(inset)* and serve the pilaf on warmed individual plates. Offer plain yogurt *(above)* separately, so that diners can spoon it onto the savory mixture themselves.

Moussaka: Lamb Layered with Vegetables

Layering finely chopped or ground lamb with sliced vegetables and baking them together can stretch a small amount of meat into an appealing main course. Before it is layered, the meat is sautéed briefly with chopped aromatic vegetables and herbs to imbue it with extra flavor. This preliminary cooking also reduces the excess moisture and fat of raw meat. However, because the final cooking is slow, you could also use leftover roasted, broiled or poached lamb, as well as the braised meat shown here.

Vegetables for slicing should be large and firm enough to form solid layers. Potatoes, eggplant and zucchini are used for a Greek moussaka in this demonstration *(recipe, page 151)*. Other choices include kohlrabi, celeriac or yellow squash.

Adding bread crumbs to the meat will lighten the layers, and eggs will bind them. A topping of sauce will prevent the uppermost layer from drying. Tomato sauce *(recipe, page 165)* will serve, but a mixture of egg with heavy cream or a cheese-flavored white sauce *(Step 8)* is more delicate and custard-like.

1 **Trimming vegetables.** Trim off both ends of zucchini and cut the zucchini lengthwise into slices ¼ inch [6 mm.] thick. Cut off the tips and stem ends of eggplants and slice the eggplants into ½-inch [1-cm.] rounds. Peel potatoes and drop them into cold water to prevent discoloring.

2 **Sautéing vegetables.** Pour a thin layer of oil into a skillet and set it over medium heat. Fry the zucchini and eggplant slices in small batches, cooking them for about five minutes on each side, or just until the slices are light brown. Add oil whenever the skillet looks dry. Drain the slices on paper towels.

6 **Layering the moussaka.** Butter a rectangular baking dish and sprinkle it with bread crumbs. Cut the potatoes into slices about ¼ inch [6 mm.] thick. Pat the slices dry with paper towels. Cover the bottom of the dish with a layer of overlapping potato slices. Cover the potato slices with half of the meat mixture.

7 **Completing the layers.** Neatly arrange the eggplant slices in a layer on top of the layer of meat. Cover the eggplant with the rest of the lamb mixture. Spread out the meat to make an even layer, taking care not to disturb the vegetables. Lay the strips of zucchini side by side on top of the meat layer.

3 **Preparing the meat.** Make crumbs from stale bread. Chop a large onion. Peel, seed and chop tomatoes. Cut lamb—in this case, leftover braised lamb—into small cubes, then chop the cubes fine. Chop fresh parsley. Peel and slice garlic cloves. Break eggs into a small bowl and beat them lightly.

4 **Sautéing the lamb.** In a sauté pan, stew the chopped onion in a little oil or butter until it is just soft. Add the meat and season the mixture with salt and pepper. Add the tomatoes, parsley and garlic. Allow the mixture to cook for about 10 minutes. Remove the pan from the heat and stir some of the bread crumbs into the meat mixture, then add the eggs.

5 **Cooking white sauce.** Melt butter over low heat. Stir in flour and cook for five minutes, stirring constantly, to make a roux. Pour in milk, whisking the mixture as you pour so that it blends smoothly. Increase the heat and continue whisking until the sauce comes to a boil. Then reduce the heat to very low and simmer for about 10 minutes.

3 **Making the topping.** Sieve ricotta cheese to make it smoother; add an egg to it. Grate Parmesan cheese and whisk it into the egg and ricotta. Pour in the white sauce and whisk the sauce-and-cheese mixture thoroughly. Season with salt. Spread the mixture over the meat and vegetables.

9 **Cooking the moussaka.** Sauté the remaining bread crumbs in butter until they are golden brown. Using a spoon, sprinkle the fried bread crumbs over the cheese topping *(inset)*. Bake the moussaka in a preheated 375° F. [190° C.] oven for about 45 minutes, until a golden brown crust forms. Remove the moussaka from the oven and let it settle for 10 minutes so that it becomes firmer and easier to cut into portions *(above)*.

A Spiraling Sheath for a Molded Moussaka

Like the simple moussaka that is demonstrated on the preceding pages, the elegant version shown here starts with finely chopped leftover lamb and slices of vegetable. In this case, the vegetable slices are arranged to line a deep charlotte mold, the lamb mixture is packed inside and the assembly is baked in a water bath, which prevents scorching. Unmolded for serving, the assembly reveals the swirling pattern formed by the slices.

The vegetable that encloses the meat must be flexible enough to be pressed against the sides of the mold. Eggplant slices, sautéed to soften them, are used here *(recipe, page 152)* but sliced zucchini or a parboiled leaf vegetable—chard, spinach or lettuce—would work as well.

The lamb can be combined with any number of flavorings—herbs, puréed tomato, mushrooms or lemon juice, for example. But dry bread crumbs and one or two eggs are essential: As the assembly bakes, the crumbs absorb excess liquid and the eggs set, making the mixture firm enough to be unmolded intact.

1 **Slicing eggplant.** Cut off both ends of eggplants to form cylinders that are as long as your mold is deep. Cut the cylinders lengthwise into slices that are about ¼ inch [6 mm.] thick. Set aside the first and last slices.

2 **Making strips for the sides.** Cut the eggplant slices lengthwise into strips about 1½ inches [4 cm.] wide for lining the sides of the mold. Set aside any leftover, undersized pieces.

5 **Filling the mold.** Finely chop leftover lamb and mix it with flavorings, eggs and dry bread crumbs *(page 77, Step 3)*. Add the chopped eggplant. Taking care not to displace the lining, spoon the meat mixture into the mold. Tap the bottom of the mold lightly against the work surface to settle the filling and expel air.

6 **Covering the mold.** Place the last of the eggplant strips over the meat mixture in a single layer. Cut a round of parchment paper to cover the top of the mold. Butter the paper, and lower and press it into position.

7 **Baking the assembly.** Place the mold on a trivet in a large, deep pot. Pour boiling water into the pot to reach two thirds of the way up the side of the mold. Bake in a preheated 350° F. [180° C.] oven for 40 minutes.

3 **Making shapes for the base.** Cut off the stem end of another eggplant. Cut the eggplant lengthwise into thin slices. Set aside the first and last slices. Make a cut from the rounded end of each remaining slice to the center, then cut across the slice *(above)* to make two quarter ovals. Trim them to a length equal to the radius of the mold.

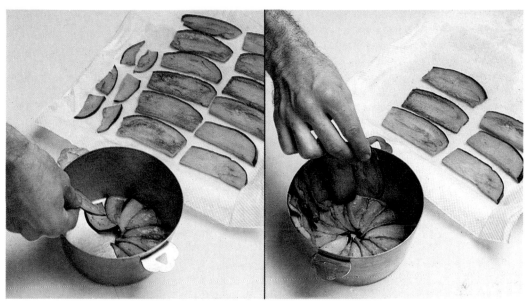

4 **Lining the mold.** Season all of the eggplant pieces and sauté them in oil — a small batch at a time — until they are browned on both sides. Drain them on paper towels. Place the quarter ovals on the bottom of the mold, overlapping each slice slightly *(above, left)*. Overlap the larger strips vertically against the sides of the mold and press them gently to stick them to the metal, aligning them where possible with the slices used to line the bottom *(right)*. From the pieces that were set aside, reserve the largest of the slices to top the mold; chop the rest fine.

8 **Unmolding the dish.** Remove the mold from the pot. Let it stand at room temperature for about 10 minutes; the assembly will become firmer and easier to unmold. Lift off the paper and invert a large plate on top of the mold. Carefully turn the mold and plate over together and lift away the mold.

9 **Slicing and serving.** For a colorful garnish, wash and dry sprigs of watercress. Tuck the stem ends of the watercress under the unmolded assembly. Slice the assembly into wedges and, if you like, serve each portion with tomato sauce *(page 26)*.

Double Cooking for a Textural Contrast

A dual cooking process—poaching followed by broiling—will turn lamb breast into a succulent delicacy. Lengthy poaching tenderizes the tough cut, and a brief exposure to high, direct heat gives it an appetizing, crusty surface.

Between the two cooking stages, the lamb should be boned. Leaving the bones in place during poaching provides gelatin, which helps keep the meat moist. After poaching, the bones slip easily and cleanly from the cooked meat.

While warm, the boned meat is soft and supple; as it cools it will stiffen into whatever shape is imposed on it. To create a flat surface for even broiling, the breast should be flattened underneath a weight. Before broiling, the meat is cut into serving-sized pieces. As demonstrated here, the pieces are dried and then can be given a coating of egg and cracker or bread crumbs, which will turn into a crisp crust under the broiler's intense, drying heat (recipe, page 147).

1 Preparing ingredients. Trim lamb breasts of excess fat. Dice turnips and chop onions. Cut celery and carrots into long, narrow strips, then cut across the strips to make dice. Cover the bottom of a roasting pan with some of the diced and chopped vegetables. Place the breasts on the vegetables.

2 Poaching the meat. Pour in water to almost cover the meat. Add the remaining vegetables and, if desired, such aromatics as garlic, thyme and bay leaf. Press foil against the meat and over the pan's rim to slow evaporation. Put the pan in a 375° F. [190° C.] oven. When the liquid boils, reduce the heat to 325° F. [160° C.].

5 Cutting the meat. When the meat has been flattened, remove the weights and the board; lift the breasts off the tray. Cut each breast into five or six triangles or rectangles of equal size. Pour the reserved poaching liquid into a saucepan, bring it to a boil over high heat, reduce the heat to low and let the liquid simmer gently.

6 Coating the pieces. Thoroughly dry each piece of lamb breast with paper towels. Sprinkle the pieces with salt and pepper, dip them into beaten eggs, then cover them with crumbs. Press the crumbs on gently so that they adhere evenly; let any excess crumbs drop off. Or, dip each piece into melted butter and then into bread crumbs.

7 Broiling the lamb. Place the pieces on a buttered baking sheet; broil them about 3 inches [8 cm.] from the heat source, basting with melted butter once or twice. Turn them after about five minutes, when the pieces are golden brown, and broil the other side. Baste them with more butter—just enough to be absorbed by the crumbs.

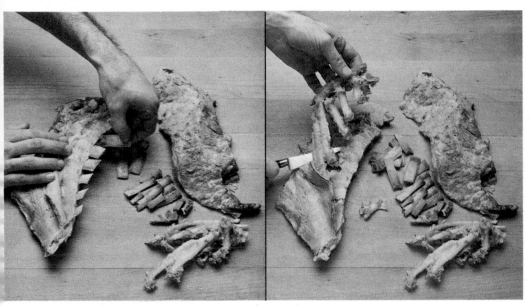

3 **Boning the breasts.** Simmer the breasts for two hours, or until they feel tender when prodded with the tip of a knife. Remove the roasting pan from the oven, lift out the meat and let it cool just enough to handle. Reserve the poaching liquid. To bone the lamb, first pull out the exposed rib tips with your fingers *(left)*; these small bones will slip out easily. Then use a sharp knife to cut away the breastbone from each breast *(right)* following the technique shown in the bottom demonstration on page 11, Step 2.

4 **Flattening the meat.** Spread out the boned breasts on a tray. Cover them with a board and place some weights on top — in this case, two food cans are used. Put the weighted meat into the refrigerator overnight.

8 **Serving.** Skimming repeatedly to cleanse it, simmer the reserved poaching liquid until it is reduced to a slightly creamy consistency *(page 60)*. Arrange the lamb pieces on a warmed platter *(left)*, adding a garnish of watercress, if you wish. Spoon some sauce beside the pieces when you serve *(inset)*.

A Versatile Combination of Puréed Lamb and Grain

Puréed or pounded lamb kneaded into the precooked, cracked wheat called bulgur yields a meaty paste that has many uses. Seasoned with lemon juice, chopped onion or mint, the paste—referred to in Lebanon as *kibbeh* and in Iraq as *kubbah*—can be eaten raw or may be fried or broiled until crisp. It may also serve as a component of an assemblage that offers a contrast in textures. Here, for example, a flavored purée of lamb that is not mixed with grain is sandwiched between layers of lamb-and-wheat paste. Baking gives the paste a firm texture; the lamb within remains moist and soft *(recipe, page 159)*.

Whatever the dish, both the cracked wheat and the lamb used to make the paste require careful preparation. The wheat is soaked in water so that it softens and swells; moisture that is not absorbed is squeezed out. All gristle and fat is meticulously removed from the meat so that it can be reduced to a smooth paste in a food processor, as here, or a mortar.

1 Soaking the wheat. Spill bulgur into a large mixing bowl and pour in about three times its volume of cold water. Skim off any film that forms on the surface. Let the bulgur soak for at least an hour, until most of the water is absorbed.

2 Puréeing lamb. Coarsely chop lamb—in this instance, from the sirloin end of a leg. Remove all fat and connective tissue from the meat. Using a food processor, grind the lamb—a small batch at a time—until it has the consistency of a smooth purée.

6 Making the paste. Knead the uncooked lamb and the bulgur until thoroughly blended into a thick paste. If you wish, add butter for a moister finished dish. Butter or oil a large rectangular baking dish. Put one half of the paste into the dish. With your finger tips, flatten the paste until it is spread evenly on the bottom of the dish.

7 Making layers. Scoop the sautéed lamb-and-onion mixture into the baking dish, distributing it evenly over the layer of uncooked lamb and bulgur. Spread the remaining half of the paste over the top. Smooth the surface with a spoon.

3 **Sautéing the lamb.** Slice onions paper-thin and sauté them in a little olive oil until soft. If you like, sprinkle in some pepper and turmeric. Add about two thirds of the puréed lamb. Stirring frequently, cook the mixture just until the meat loses its red color.

4 **Completing the filling.** Add dried currants and nuts — pine nuts, in this case — and correct the seasoning. Continue cooking for a moment, then remove the pan from the heat.

5 **Draining the bulgur.** Set a large strainer over a bowl; transfer the soaked bulgur to it. Scoop up the grain in your hand and squeeze out the excess water. Place the grain in another bowl and mix it with the uncooked puréed lamb.

8 **Scoring the surface.** With a knife, score the top diagonally to a depth of about ¼ inch [6 mm.], marking diamond-shaped serving portions. Place a small piece of butter in the center of each diamond to help prevent the surface from drying.

9 **Baking and serving.** Bake the *kibbeh* in a preheated 400° F. [200° C.] oven. After 30 to 40 minutes, if the surface of the *kibbeh* looks dry, baste with oil or melted butter. Cook for about 20 minutes more, until a golden crust forms. Serve the diamond-shaped portions of *kibbeh (inset)* with a green salad.

A Creamy Counterpoint for Fried Patties

Like the ubiquitous beef hamburger, a patty fashioned of raw ground lamb can simply be fried until it is browned outside and succulent within. However, cooking the patties in the two stages demonstrated here—frying them to brown and firm them, then baking them in a creamy custard to cook them through—produces a more savory dish of contrasting textures.

Any lean lamb is suitable for patties. To help keep the meat as fresh and juicy as possible, grind it at home—putting it once through the medium disk of a food grinder or chopping it in a food processor operated in short bursts.

The lamb can be seasoned with just salt and pepper or mixed with aromatic vegetables, herbs and ground spices (recipe, page 162). Bread crumbs or pieces of soaked-and-squeezed bread lighten the texture of the patties.

For the custard topping, the essential elements are eggs and milk or some milk-derived liquid—cream, sour cream or yogurt. During baking, juices seep from the patties to flavor the custard while it sets.

1 Preparing ingredients. Put pieces of crustless bread in a bowl of water to soften them. Assemble flavorings — here, flat-leafed parsley, onion, garlic and paprika. Trim the fat and connective tissue from lamb — in this instance, boned shoulder. Cut the meat into pieces and grind them in a food grinder or processor.

2 Combining ingredients. Place the ground meat in a mixing bowl and season it with salt, pepper and paprika. Chop the parsley, onion and garlic fine; add them to the lamb. Squeeze as much water as possible from the bread, then add it to the other ingredients and mix well.

6 Preparing the custard. Break eggs into a bowl, season them with a little salt and pepper, and whisk them lightly (above, left). Add plain yogurt, as in this demonstration, or sour cream, and a little of the liquid remaining in the skillet. Whisk again (right) until the ingredients are thoroughly blended.

7 Adding the topping. Pour the custard mixture over the patties. Color the remaining deglazing liquid with a little paprika and sprinkle the liquid onto the custard. Bake in a preheated 350° F. [180° C.] oven for about one hour.

3 Shaping patties. Take small handfuls of the meat mixture and shape each into a ball. Flatten out the balls between the palms of your hands to form neat, round patties that are about 1 to 1½ inches [2½ to 4 cm.] thick.

4 Frying patties. Set the patties in a skillet filmed with hot oil or fat, and sear them over medium to high heat for about three minutes, until the bottoms are browned and crisp. Flip each patty over with a spatula and brown it on the other side. Transfer the seared patties from the skillet to a gratin dish.

5 Deglazing the pan. Drain off the excess fat from the skillet. Add a splash of stock *(recipe, page 164)*, water or, as here, white wine. With a wooden spoon, scrape the bottom of the skillet to free the meaty deposits, and incorporate them into the liquid. Pour most of the liquid over the patties in the gratin dish, reserving a little liquid in the skillet.

8 Serving the dish. When the custard topping is firm to the touch and golden brown, remove the gratin from the oven and serve the patties immediately on warmed individual plates. Top each serving with some of the custard.

Deep-fried Nuggets Steeped in Spice

Because of its rich flavor and delicate texture, lamb rarely is deep fried. Yet Indian cooks use deep frying to give balls of raw ground lamb a crisp surface and moist interior. These meatballs, called *koftas*, are then cooked in a spicy curry sauce *(recipe, page 97)*.

To keep the lamb succulent, the meatballs are made small—no more than 1½ inches [4 cm.] across—so that they fry quickly. Before they are fried, the balls are coated with a batter of chick-pea flour and water. The batter firms on contact with the preheated oil, sealing in juices.

In this case, the meatballs enclose almonds for an extra crunch. The sauce is based on *ghee*, an Indian butter oil similar to clarified butter, and onions; it is seasoned with garlic, fresh ginger and ground spices—coriander, cumin, turmeric, cayenne pepper and *garam masala*, a spice blend containing cardamom, cinnamon, cloves and black pepper. Before the meatballs are added, the sauce is smoothed, and its fieriness tempered, by a generous addition of plain yogurt.

1 Forming the meatballs. Knead together ground lamb, chick-pea flour, egg, salt and pepper. Dipping your hands occasionally into cool water to prevent sticking, pick up walnut-sized pieces of the meat mixture and press them flat. Place a blanched and peeled almond in the center of each piece and form the meat into a ball around the nut.

2 Coating the meatballs. Mix chick-pea flour with just enough water to form a thick batter. Using your fingers, press a thin, even layer of this batter onto all sides of each meatball. Place the meatballs on a baking sheet or a piece of wax paper, and allow the coating to dry for about 15 minutes.

3 Frying. Pour oil into a saucepan or, as here, a wok to a depth of 3 inches [8 cm.]. Heat the oil until it registers 375° F. [190° C.] on a deep-frying thermometer. With a skimmer, lower a small batch of meatballs at a time into the oil. Turning the balls occasionally, fry them until golden brown—about five minutes. Drain on paper towels.

4 Making the sauce. Melt *ghee* or clarified butter in a skillet. Stir in chopped onion, garlic and fresh ginger, and cook over medium heat for two minutes. Add ground spices and stir until the onion browns—about 10 minutes. Stir in plain yogurt; add the meatballs and *garam masala*. Remove the pan from the heat and cover it tightly.

5 Reheating and serving. After the meatballs have steeped for one hour, reheat them in the sauce over low heat for about five minutes. Garnish the *koftas* and sauce with fresh sprigs of coriander. Serve immediately with boiled rice.

Anthology of Recipes

Drawing upon the cooking traditions and literature of more than 30 countries, the editors and consultants for this volume have selected 200 published lamb recipes for the Anthology that follows. The selections range from the simple to the elaborate—from broiled chops to a baron of lamb stuffed under the skin with scallions, mushrooms and herbs, roasted to succulence, crusted with crumbs and served with an orange-scented wine sauce.

Many of the recipes were written by world-renowned exponents of the culinary art, but the Anthology, spanning nearly 300 years, also includes selections from now rare and out-of-print books and from works never published in English. Whatever the sources, the emphasis is always on careful preparation of fresh, natural ingredients that blend harmoniously.

Since many early recipe writers did not specify amounts of ingredients, the missing information has been judiciously added. Where appropriate, clarifying introductory notes have also been supplied; they are printed in italics. Modern terms have been substituted for archaic language, but to preserve the character of the original recipes and to create a true anthology, the authors' texts have been changed as little as possible. Cooking times in older recipes may seem overlong by today's standards—and you may want to shorten them. Some instructions have necessarily been expanded, but where the directions still seem abrupt, the reader need only refer to the appropriate demonstrations in the front of the book.

For ease of use, the recipes are organized by cooking methods. Recipes for standard preparations—stock, velouté sauce and stuffings, for example—appear at the end of the Anthology. Cooking terms and ingredients that may be unfamiliar—including Oriental flavorings and sauces—are explained in the combined General Index and Glossary at the end of the book.

Apart from the primary components, all recipe ingredients are listed in order of use, with the customary U.S. measurements and the new metric measurements provided in separate columns. The metric quantities given here reflect the American practice of measuring such solid ingredients as flour or sugar by volume rather than by weighing them, as European cooks do.

To make the quantities simpler to measure, many of the figures have been rounded off to correspond to the gradations that are now standard on metric spoons and cups. (One cup, for example, equals precisely 240 milliliters; wherever practicable, however, a cup appears as a more readily measurable 250 milliliters—¼ liter.) Similarly, weight, temperature and linear metric equivalents are rounded off slightly. For these reasons, the American and metric figures are not equivalent, but using one set or the other will produce equally good results.

Grilling and Broiling

Perfect Grilled Lamb

Quartier d'Agneau Achevé

If desired, the lamb shoulder may be roasted in the oven and the chops cooked in the broiler.

To serve 8

4 to 6 lb.	lamb shoulder	2 to 3 kg.
8	lamb rib chops, cut about 1½ inches [4 cm.] thick	8
½ cup	lean salt pork, with the rind removed, blanched in boiling water for 5 minutes, drained, chopped and sautéed until golden	125 ml.
	salt and pepper	
3 tbsp.	chopped fresh parsley	45 ml.
4	scallions, chopped	4
¼ lb.	fresh mushrooms, finely chopped (about 1½ cups [375 ml.])	125 g.
	fine fresh bread crumbs	
2 tbsp.	butter, melted	30 ml.
	croutons *(recipe, page 167)*	
4 tbsp.	strained lemon juice (optional)	60 ml.

Mushroom sauce

¼ lb.	fresh mushrooms, chopped (about 1½ cups [375 ml.])	125 g.
2 tbsp.	butter	30 ml.
1 tbsp.	chopped fresh parsley	15 ml.
2 tbsp.	chopped scallions	30 ml.
2 tbsp.	flour	30 ml.
1 cup	meat stock *(recipe, page 164)*	¼ liter
½ cup	Champagne or white wine	125 ml.
	salt and freshly ground pepper	
3	egg yolks	3
½ cup	heavy cream	125 ml.
4 tbsp.	strained lemon juice	60 ml.

Put the lamb shoulder on a spit to roast.

Mix the cooked salt pork with the salt and pepper, parsley, scallions and mushrooms. Coat the chops on both sides with this mixture, and let the coating cool. For the sauce, melt the butter and cook the parsley, scallions and mushrooms in it until all of the mushroom liquid has evaporated. Sprinkle on the flour, and stir in the stock and Champagne or white wine. Season with salt and freshly ground pepper. Cook until the sauce is reduced and thickened. Remove the sauce from the heat.

When the shoulder is cooked, after about 40 minutes, remove it from the spit. Cut the meat off the bones and chop it coarse. Stir the chopped meat into the sauce mixture. Beat the egg yolks and cream together and stir them into the mixture; reheat the sauce without letting it boil. Add the lemon juice and keep the mixture warm.

Coat the chops with bread crumbs, making sure that all of the salt-pork mixture adheres, and grill them over coals for five to 10 minutes on each side, or until golden brown.

To serve, place the sauced, chopped meat in the center of a large, heated serving dish. Surround with croutons, then with the chops. You may sprinkle the chops with lemon juice if it is desired.

LE MANUEL DE LA FRIANDISE

Mutton Chops with Lemon and Shallots

Côtelettes de Mouton

To serve 6

6	mutton loin chops, cut 1½ inches [4 cm.] thick	6
3 tbsp.	fresh lemon juice	45 ml.
	salt and pepper	
	cayenne pepper	
12 tbsp.	butter, melted	180 ml.
3	shallots, very finely chopped	3
2 tbsp.	chopped fresh parsley	30 ml.

Sprinkle the chops on both sides with 2 tablespoons [30 ml.] of the lemon juice, some salt, pepper and cayenne pepper, and set them aside for 15 minutes. Brush the chops on both sides with some of the melted butter, and broil them about 4 inches [10 cm.] from the heat until done—about 18 minutes in all. Turn the chops once in the process and brush them again with more of the melted butter.

As soon as the chops have been turned and brushed, pour the remaining melted butter—approximately 8 tablespoons [120 ml.]—into a small saucepan. Add the shallots and cook over low heat for five to six minutes. Stir in the remaining lemon juice and the parsley. Season with salt, pepper and cayenne pepper.

When the chops are done, transfer them immediately to a heated platter. Pour the lemon-and-shallot butter over all and serve immediately.

MORTON G. CLARK
FRENCH-AMERICAN COOKING FROM NEW ORLEANS TO QUEBEC

Mutton Chops Broiled

To serve 4

4	mutton loin chops, cut about 1 inch [2½ cm.] thick	4
	salt and pepper	
4 tbsp.	butter	60 ml.

Trim the chops nicely, leaving only enough of the fat to make them palatable. Heat an iron griddle over high heat. Place the chops on it. After a minute or two, reduce the heat. Turn the chops frequently, taking care that the fork is not put into the lean part of the chop. When they are nearly cooked, after about 10 minutes, season them with salt and pepper. Remove from the griddle, spread a little fresh butter over each chop and send them to table upon very hot plates.

JOSEPHINE DAVID
EVERY-DAY COOKERY FOR FAMILIES OF MODERATE INCOME

Charcoal-broiled Lamb

Agneddu Arrustutu 'nta Braci

To serve 8

4 lb.	lamb, cut into 8 chops or slices, each about 1 inch [2½ cm.] thick	2 kg.
1	sprig rosemary	1
	Garlic marinade	
8	garlic cloves, crushed	8
1½ cups	white wine	375 ml.
½ cup	olive oil	125 ml.
6 tbsp.	fresh lemon juice	90 ml.
1 tsp.	dried oregano	5 ml.
8	fresh sage leaves, chopped	8
2 tsp.	chopped rosemary leaves	10 ml.
	salt and pepper	

Combine all of the ingredients of the marinade in a large bowl. Add the pieces of lamb and let them marinate for 30 minutes, turning them from time to time. Drain the marinated pieces of lamb and place them on a grill over hot coals. As the surfaces dry, moisten the pieces with a sprig of rosemary that has been dipped in the marinade. When the first side is cooked, in about 10 minutes, put the lamb back into the bowl of marinade. Then return the pieces to the grill and cook the other side for five to 10 minutes. Serve hot.

PINO CORRENTI
IL LIBRO D'ORO DELLA CUCINA E DEI VINI DI SICILIA

Lamb Chops with Thyme

Kuzu Pirzolasi

To serve 4

8	lamb chops, cut 1½ inches [4 cm.] thick and trimmed of excess fat	8
1	medium-sized onion	1
1 tsp.	salt	5 ml.
2 tbsp.	olive oil	30 ml.
1 tbsp.	chopped fresh thyme	15 ml.
	parsley sprigs	

Grate the onion and sprinkle the salt over it. Leave for 10 minutes. Squeeze the onion between your palms to extract the juice. Add the juice to the olive oil. Lay the chops on wax paper. Rub the onion-juice mixture onto both sides of the chops. Sprinkle the thyme on both sides. Cover the chops with wax paper and leave them for two hours.

Grill, preferably over hot coals, placing the chops 3 inches [8 cm.] from the heat. Grill for five minutes on each side. Arrange the chops on a platter; garnish with parsley.

NEŞET EREN
THE ART OF TURKISH COOKING

Skewered Lamb, Tartar-Style

Schaschliks à la Tatare

To serve 4

1 lb.	boneless leg of lamb, sliced thick	½ kg.
	salt and pepper	
	grated nutmeg	
1 tsp.	thyme	5 ml.
1	bay leaf, crumbled	1
¼ cup	oil	50 ml.
1	onion, sliced	1
¼ lb.	fresh pork fatback or salt pork with the rind removed, blanched in boiling water for 5 minutes, drained, thinly sliced and cut into 1½-inch [4-cm.] squares	125 g.
¼ lb.	uncooked cured ham, thinly sliced and cut into 1½-inch [4-cm.] squares	125 g.

Place the lamb in a dish containing a mixture of salt and pepper, nutmeg, thyme, bay leaf, oil and onion. Turn to coat the lamb well. After two hours, remove the lamb from this marinade. Thread the pieces of lamb onto skewers, alternating them with pork fatback or salt pork and ham. Grill the skewered meat over hot coals for five to 10 minutes.

A. PETIT
LA GASTRONOMIE EN RUSSIE

Grilled Skewered Lamb and Vegetables

Şaşlik

These are traditionally accompanied by a salad of chopped onions, cucumbers, tomatoes and parsley, moistened with lemon juice.

	To serve 4	
1½ lb.	boneless lamb sirloin, cut into 1½-inch [4-cm.] cubes	¾ kg.
2	lamb kidneys, peeled, halved lengthwise, inner core of fat removed, and halved crosswise	2
8	fresh button mushrooms, stems trimmed off flush with the caps	8
8	small tomatoes	8
1	large green or red pepper, halved, seeded, deribbed and cut into 1½-inch [4-cm.] squares	1
8	small boiling onions or shallots	8

Thread the meats and vegetables onto eight flat-bladed skewers, alternating the meats with the vegetables. Grill them over hot coals for about 15 minutes, turning the skewers several times during cooking.

NEZIH SIMON
TURKISH COOKERY

Spiced Skewered Mutton

Quaah

	To serve 3	
½ lb.	boneless lean mutton, cut into pieces 1 inch [2½ cm.] square and ¼ inch [6 mm.] thick	¼ kg.
½ lb.	boneless fat mutton, cut into pieces 1 inch [2½ cm.] square and ¼ inch [6 mm.] thick	¼ kg.
1	leek, chopped	1
2	small onions, chopped	2
1 tbsp.	finely chopped fresh chervil	15 ml.
1 tsp.	salt	5 ml.
1 tsp.	ground cumin	5 ml.
1 tsp.	ground ginger	5 ml.
1 tsp.	freshly ground black pepper	5 ml.
1 tsp.	cayenne pepper	5 ml.

In a mortar pound together the leek, one onion, the chervil and the salt. Mix this in a plate with the pieces of lean and fat meat. Crush the remaining onion and spread it over all. Add

the cumin, ginger, pepper and cayenne. Mix the whole well, then put the meat on skewers, a piece of fat and lean alternately. There is sufficient for nine skewers. Set these over charcoal or under a broiler, turning frequently for 10 minutes, when the meat should be ready to eat.

JOHN, FOURTH MARQUIS OF BUTE (EDITOR)
MOORISH RECIPES

Mutton Kebabs

Sate Madoera

	To serve 4	
1 lb.	boneless lean mutton, cut into ¾-inch [2-cm.] cubes	½ kg.
4	garlic cloves, chopped	4
1 tsp.	ground ginger	5 ml.
1 tsp.	pepper	5 ml.

Grind the garlic, ginger and pepper to a paste and rub this mixture well into the meat. Leave for at least two hours. The meat will exude some liquid.

Drain the pieces of meat and thread them onto skewers. Brushing the meat occasionally with the marinade, grill for about five minutes over low heat, then for five to 10 minutes more over the hottest part of the fire.

BEB VUYK
GROOT INDONESISCH KOOKBOEK

Azerbaijan Skewered Meatballs

Kebab Aserbeidschan

Serve these quickly browned meatballs with country-style bread and red wine and, if you wish, with a garnish of thin lemon slices and crushed barberries. Gourmets will also enjoy having tartar or walnut sauce presented as a dip.

	To serve 6	
2 lb.	ground lean lamb	1 kg.
2	medium-sized onions, finely chopped	2
2	eggs	2
2 tbsp.	fresh lemon juice	30 ml.
1 tbsp.	chopped fresh thyme	15 ml.
	salt and pepper	
¾ cup	dry bread crumbs	175 ml.
	oil	
	finely cut chives	

Mix the lamb thoroughly with the onions and eggs. Season with the lemon juice, thyme, salt and pepper. Form into about 20 small balls, dip these in bread crumbs and thread them onto skewers, five balls per skewer. Paint with oil, and grill the meatballs on a baking sheet set under a preheated broiler for about eight minutes, turning the meatballs once. Serve them sprinkled with chives.

LILO AUREDEN
DAS SCHMECKT SO GUT

Ground Meat Kebabs

Kefta

In Morocco, all kebabs are grilled over embers. To reach the ember stage, the charcoal must be lighted at least 30 minutes in advance.

To serve 4

1 lb.	ground lean lamb	½ kg.
¼ lb.	beef suet or marrow, chopped	125 g.
¾ cup	chopped fresh parsley	175 ml.
¾ cup	chopped fresh coriander	175 ml.
1	onion, chopped	1
1½ tsp.	ground cumin	7 ml.
1 tbsp.	paprika	15 ml.
¼ tsp.	cayenne pepper	1 ml.
1 tsp.	ground cinnamon (optional)	5 ml.
2 tbsp.	chopped fresh mint (optional)	30 ml.
	salt	

Mix all of the ingredients together and put the mixture through the food grinder twice. Knead the mixture well with your hands and let it rest for about one hour.

Lightly moisten your hands, take a lump of the mixture the size of an egg and mold it around a skewer, shaping it into a sausage 4 to 5 inches [10 to 13 cm.] long. Make sure the meat sticks well at each end, so that it will not turn around the skewer during cooking. Repeat with the remaining mixture; you will have 12 to 16 kebabs on separate skewers.

Grill over coals or broil under a preheated broiler, turning the skewers once or twice for about 10 minutes, depending on the desired degree of doneness. The outside should be well browned, but do not let the meat dry out.

LATIFA BENNANI SMIRES
LA CUISINE MAROCAINE

Frying

Mutton Chops

To serve 6

6	mutton chops	6
6	sprigs parsley, finely chopped	6
2	shallots, finely chopped	2
	salt	
	cayenne pepper	
1 tbsp.	olive oil	15 ml.
½ cup	fine dry bread crumbs	125 ml.
4 tbsp.	butter	60 ml.

Combine the parsley and shallots with small quantities of salt and cayenne pepper, and mix all together in the oil; cover the chops on both sides with these ingredients, shake them in the bread crumbs, and fry in fresh butter, turning them until quite done.

MRS. RUNDELL
MODERN DOMESTIC COOKERY

Lamb with Olives

Agnello con le Olive

To serve 4

12	small lamb rib chops	12
½ cup	flour	125 ml.
7 tbsp.	olive oil	105 ml.
1	small piece fresh hot chili	1
	salt	
1 cup	pitted ripe olives, preferably Mediterranean-style black olives, coarsely chopped	¼ liter
¼ tsp.	oregano	1 ml.
3 tbsp.	fresh lemon juice	45 ml.

Lightly flour the chops. In a large skillet, heat the oil with the chili, then remove the chili. Brown the chops on both sides over high heat. Season with salt, and add the olives, oregano and lemon juice. Bring to a boil and serve very hot.

STELLA DONATI (EDITOR)
IL GRANDE MANUALE DELLA CUCINA REGIONALE

Lamb Chops with Vegetables and Eggs
Chouchouka

	To serve 6	
6	lamb rib chops, cut 1 inch [2½ cm.] thick	6
5 tbsp.	olive oil	75 ml.
8	medium-sized green or red peppers, halved, seeded, deribbed and cut into strips	8
3	onions, chopped	3
3	garlic cloves	3
12	medium-sized tomatoes, peeled, seeded and coarsely chopped	12
1	medium-sized eggplant, peeled and diced	1
	salt and pepper	
	cayenne pepper	
6	eggs	6

In a large, heavy pan, heat the oil and sauté the chops for five minutes on each side. Remove the chops from the pan. Add the peppers and cook for 10 minutes. Add the onions and garlic, and cook for five minutes more. Add the tomatoes and the eggplant. Season with salt, pepper and cayenne pepper. Cook the vegetables, uncovered, over very low heat for one hour, or until all excess liquid has evaporated and the mixture is reduced to a thick purée. Five minutes before serving, return the chops to the pan and spoon the purée over them. One at a time, break the eggs into a bowl and slide them into the pan. Cook for five minutes, or until the whites are set.

IRÈNE AND LUCIENNE KARSENTY
LA CUISINE PIED NOIR

Lamb Chops with Parmesan Cheese
Côtelettes d'Agneau à la Parmesane

	To serve 4	
4	lamb rib chops, cut 1 inch [2½ cm.] thick, chined and trimmed of excess fat	4
10 tbsp.	butter	150 ml.
⅔ cup	freshly grated Parmesan cheese	150 ml.
2	eggs, lightly beaten	2
½ cup	fresh bread crumbs	125 ml.
	tomato sauce *(recipe, page 165)* (optional)	

Melt 4 tablespoons [60 ml.] of the butter and dip the chops into it. Coat them with Parmesan cheese. Dip the chops into the eggs, then coat them with bread crumbs.

Melt the remaining butter in a skillet, add the chops, and fry over medium high heat for about four minutes on each side, or until they are just pink in the center and nicely browned on the outside. Serve plain or with tomato sauce.

OFFRAY AINÉ
LE CUISINIER MÉRIDIONAL

Creole Chops
Côtelettes Panées Créoles

	To serve 4	
8	lamb or kid rib chops, cut about ½ inch [1 cm.] thick	8
3	limes or lemons, 1 sliced into rounds, the juice of 2 strained	3
2	garlic cloves, chopped	2
4	scallions, chopped	4
	salt and pepper	
3	eggs	3
2 tbsp.	milk	30 ml.
3 tbsp.	flour	45 ml.
3½ cups	dry bread crumbs	875 ml.
2 tbsp.	oil	30 ml.
	chopped fresh parsley	

Mix the lime or lemon juice, garlic, scallions, and salt and pepper. Place the chops in this mixture, turn them over and let them marinate for one hour. Pat the chops dry with towels. Beat the eggs with the milk. Dip both sides of each chop into the flour, then into the egg mixture and finally into the bread crumbs.

Heat the oil in a large skillet, add the chops and fry over medium heat for about four minutes on each side, or until well browned and cooked through. Serve garnished with the lime or lemon slices and chopped parsley.

CHRISTIANE ROY-CAMILLE AND ANNICK MARIE
LES MEILLEURES RECETTES DE LA CUISINE ANTILLAISE

Lamb with Olives, Abruzzi-Style

Agnello con Olive all'Abruzzese

To serve 4

1½ lb.	boneless leg or loin of baby lamb, cut into 4 thick slices	¾ kg.
7 tbsp.	olive oil	105 ml.
2 tbsp.	flour	30 ml.
	salt and pepper	
1 cup	ripe olives (preferably Mediterranean-style olives), pitted and coarsely chopped	¼ liter
¼ tsp.	oregano	1 ml.
2 tbsp.	finely chopped green pepper	30 ml.
1½ tbsp.	fresh lemon juice	22 ml.

Heat the oil in a skillet. Flour the lamb slices lightly, and brown in the oil on both sides over high heat for up to five minutes. Sprinkle the lamb with salt and drain off any excess fat. Reduce the heat and add the olives, oregano, green pepper and lemon juice. Cook over medium heat for a few minutes, until the lamb is just pink in the center. Arrange the slices of meat on a heated serving platter, and spoon the garnish over the top.

WAVERLEY ROOT
THE BEST OF ITALIAN COOKING

Spanish Fried Lamb

Corderito à la Chilindrón

In 18th Century Spanish, "chilindrón" means a collection or assemblage. This dish may also be made with any cut of lamb suitable for stewing—shoulder, neck or breast.

To serve 6 to 8

one 12 lb.	baby lamb, cut into serving pieces	one 6 kg.
	salt and freshly ground pepper	
¾ cup	oil	175 ml.
1	large garlic clove	1
10 oz.	smoked ham, diced	300 g.
1	onion, chopped	1
6	large green or red peppers, broiled until the skin blisters, skinned, halved, seeded and cut into large pieces	6
6	medium-sized tomatoes, peeled and chopped	6

Season the lamb with salt and pepper. In a large, heavy casserole, preferably earthenware, heat the oil and fry the garlic clove until lightly browned. Remove the garlic clove from the oil and put in the lamb; add the ham and onion. Stir the ingredients with a perforated spoon and, when the onion begins to brown, add the peppers. Stir again a few times before adding the tomatoes. Fry until the lamb is cooked, about one and one half hours, keeping in mind that the result should have a dry consistency. It should be like a fried dish rather than a stew. Serve from the casserole.

MARIA DOLORES COMAS
LO MEJOR DE LA COCINA ESPAÑOLA

Lamb Sauté with Pesto

Petit Sauté d'Agneau au Pistou

To serve 4

1 lb.	lamb eye of loin, cut into 1-inch [2½-cm.] slices	½ kg.
4 tbsp.	butter	60 ml.
8	small boiling onions	8
2	medium-sized carrots, cut into oval shapes	2
1	medium-sized turnip, cut into oval shapes	1
2	large artichoke bottoms, quartered and cut into oval shapes	2
½ cup	freshly shelled peas	125 ml.
½ cup	green beans, cut into 1-inch [2½-cm.] pieces	125 ml.
3 to 4 tbsp.	lamb stock (recipe, page 164)	45 to 60 ml.
Pesto		
1 cup	fresh basil leaves	¼ liter
2 tbsp.	finely chopped fresh pork fat	30 ml.
1	garlic clove, roughly chopped	1
3 to 4 tbsp.	olive oil	45 to 60 ml.

For the pesto, chop the basil, fat and garlic together until very fine. Pound in a mortar, working in the olive oil until a smooth paste is formed.

Melt half of the butter, add the vegetables, cover and cook over low heat—shaking the pan occasionally—for 10 to 15 minutes, or until the vegetables are just tender.

Heat the remaining butter and quickly sauté the pieces of lamb, keeping them pink inside. Add the vegetables and cook together for a minute or two, adding the lamb stock, a spoonful at a time, to make a light sauce.

Little by little, add the pesto to the pan, shaking to incorporate it and to form a smooth sauce. Serve immediately.

ROBERT COURTINE
MES REPAS LES PLUS ÉTONNANTS

Sautéed Lamb with Scallions

To serve 4

½ lb.	boneless lean lamb, very thinly sliced	¼ kg.
2 tbsp.	soy sauce	30 ml.
½ tsp.	salt	2 ml.
1 tbsp.	rice wine or dry sherry	15 ml.
½ tsp.	ground white pepper	2 ml.
½ cup	peanut oil	125 ml.
1 tbsp.	black vinegar	15 ml.
1 tbsp.	sesame-seed oil	15 ml.
3 tbsp.	sliced garlic	45 ml.
½ lb.	scallions, halved lengthwise, then cut crosswise into diagonal pieces including 2 inches [5 cm.] of the green tops	¼ kg.

Place the lamb in a bowl with 1 tablespoon [15 ml.] of the soy sauce, the salt, wine, pepper and 2 tablespoons [30 ml.] of the peanut oil. Marinate for at least 15 minutes.

Mix together the remaining soy sauce, the black vinegar and the sesame-seed oil. This is the seasoning sauce.

Heat the remaining peanut oil in a wok or skillet. When it is very hot, add the garlic first, then the lamb. Stir fry over high heat for 10 seconds. Add the scallions and the seasoning sauce. Continue to stir fry until thoroughly heated, then serve immediately.

FU PEI MEI
PEI MEI'S CHINESE COOK BOOK

Sliced Leg of Lamb with Fresh Glazed Onions

Civet de Gigot aux Oignons Frais Confits

To serve 6

6 lb.	leg of lamb, cut lengthwise into 6 large slices	3 kg.
16 tbsp.	butter (½ lb. [¼ kg.]), 8 tbsp. [120 ml.] softened and cut into small pieces	240 ml.
2 tbsp.	finely chopped shallots	30 ml.
5 cups	red wine (Cabernet or Brouilly)	1¼ liters
1	bouquet garni, including rosemary	1
1¼ lb.	small boiling onions	⅔ kg.
	salt and pepper	
1 tbsp.	superfine sugar	15 ml.
4 tbsp.	oil	60 ml.

Melt 4 tablespoons [60 ml.] of the butter in a large saucepan and cook the shallots until they are soft. Do not let them

brown. Add the wine and the bouquet garni, and reduce the liquid, over medium heat, to two thirds of its original volume. Strain and set this sauce aside in the saucepan.

Place the onions in a deep skillet and add enough water to come one third of the way up their sides. Dot with 4 tablespoons of the butter and add salt, pepper and the sugar. Cook uncovered over medium heat until the water has evaporated, leaving only the butter. Shake the pan from time to time. Reduce the heat, and glaze and brown the onions. Meanwhile, heat a little oil in a large skillet and sauté the lamb slices for about five minutes, leaving them rare. Keep them warm, without prolonging the cooking, on a heated serving platter. Salt and pepper lightly.

To finish the sauce, bring it back to a boil and add salt and pepper. Then remove it from the heat and, little by little, stir in the softened butter pieces.

Arrange the very hot onions around the lamb on the serving platter, spoon a little sauce over everything and serve on hot plates, with the rest of the sauce in a sauceboat.

MADELEINE PETER
FAVORITE RECIPES OF THE GREAT WOMEN CHEFS OF FRANCE

Flash-fried Lamb with Scallions

Cong-bao Yang-rou

This recipe is from Shantung Province in North China. The lamb should be sliced very thin and cooked quickly.

To serve 4

¾ lb.	boneless lean lamb, sliced ⅛ inch [3 mm.] thick	375 g.
½ cup	peanut oil	125 ml.
3 or 4	small garlic cloves, thinly sliced	3 or 4
3 or 4	scallions, cut crosswise into 3-inch [7½-cm.] pieces and sliced lengthwise into thin shreds	3 or 4
2 tbsp.	soy sauce	30 ml.
1 tbsp.	vinegar	15 ml.
1 tbsp.	sesame-seed oil	15 ml.
Soy marinade		
2 tbsp.	peanut oil	30 ml.
2 tbsp.	rice wine or dry sherry	30 ml.
2 tbsp.	soy sauce	30 ml.
½ tsp.	salt	2 ml.
½ tsp.	ground Szechwan pepper	2 ml.

Make the marinade, first heating the 2 tablespoons [30 ml.] oil in a wok or a large frying pan until hot. Put the oil into a small bowl and add the other marinade ingredients. Mix with the lamb slices and marinate for at least 15 minutes.

Mix the seasonings in a cup or small bowl.

Heat ½ cup [125 ml.] peanut oil (or other vegetable oil) in the wok or large frying pan until very hot. Add the garlic slices and stir fry for a few seconds. Pour the excess marinade off the lamb and then add the lamb slices to the oil; the slices are cooked as soon as they turn white. To keep the oil very hot and cook the lamb very quickly, cook a few slices at a time, removing and draining each batch as it cooks. When all of the lamb slices have been cooked, return the previously cooked portions to the wok.

Keeping the heat high, add the scallion shreds and seasonings. Give all of the ingredients a good stir. Remove to a serving dish and serve hot.

ROBERT A. DELFS
THE GOOD FOOD OF SZECHWAN: DOWN-TO-EARTH CHINESE COOKING

Lamb with Pepper, Mushrooms and Scallions

Jingisukan-yaki

To serve 4

1 lb.	boneless lean lamb, thinly sliced	½ kg.
3	green peppers, quartered, seeded and deribbed	3
10	mushrooms, sliced	10
5	scallions, cut into 1-inch [2½-cm.] lengths, green tops included	5
	oil	

Soy seasoning

1	garlic clove, finely chopped	1
1 tsp.	finely chopped fresh ginger	5 ml.
¼ tsp.	cayenne pepper	1 ml.
1 tsp.	grated lemon peel	5 ml.
⅓ cup	soy sauce	75 ml.
¼ cup	rice wine or dry sherry	50 ml.
1 tbsp.	sugar	15 ml.
1 tbsp.	fresh lemon juice	15 ml.
2 tbsp.	finely chopped scallion	30 ml.

Arrange the lamb slices, peppers, mushrooms and scallion pieces attractively on a large platter. Mix together all of the seasoning ingredients and place the mixture in a small bowl.

On the dining table, heat a small amount of oil in a sukiyaki pan over a burner, then add about half of the lamb, peppers, mushrooms and scallions. Turn and cook for several minutes, then add half of the seasoning mixture. Continue cooking until the peppers are barely tender.

Let the diners help themselves from the pan. When the pan is nearly empty, add the remaining lamb, vegetables and seasoning mixture. Turn and cook similarly.

JOHN D. KEYS
JAPANESE CUISINE

Hot or Deviled Lamb

Agnello "all'Arrabbiata" o alla Diavola

To serve 4 to 6

2 lb.	boneless lean lamb, cubed	1 kg.
	salt and pepper	
¼ tsp.	cayenne pepper	1 ml.
½ cup	oil	125 ml.
2	garlic cloves, chopped	2
2 tsp.	chopped fresh rosemary	10 ml.
1 cup	white wine	¼ liter

Season the meat with salt, pepper and cayenne, and brown it in a frying pan with the oil, garlic and rosemary. Cook over high heat, shaking the pan frequently to avoid sticking.

When the lamb is golden brown, add the wine and cook uncovered until the wine evaporates. Serve immediately.

NICE CORTELLI LUCREZI
LE RECETTE DELLA NONNA

Lamb Noisettes with Tarragon

Noisettes d'Agneau à l'Estragon

This recipe is from the Charles Barrier restaurant at Tours. Lamb noisettes are small round slices cut from the boned rib, loin or leg. The lamb should be served with buttered noodles, cooked al dente.

	To serve 4	
8	lamb noisettes, cut about 1 inch [2½ cm.] thick	8
	salt and pepper	
3 tbsp.	peanut oil	45 ml.
4 tbsp.	butter	60 ml.
⅓ cup	Madeira	75 ml.
2 tbsp.	coarsely chopped fresh tarragon	30 ml.
¼ cup	*crème fraîche*	50 ml.

Salt and pepper both sides of the noisettes. Heat the oil and half of the butter in a sauté pan and, when very hot, add the lamb and cook the noisettes for about three minutes on each side. The lamb should be pink inside. Take the noisettes out of the pan, set aside and keep them warm.

Quickly drain off the oil and melt the remaining 2 tablespoons [30 ml.] of butter in the pan; pour in the Madeira. Add the tarragon and *crème fraîche*. Boil this sauce to reduce its volume slightly, and pour through a fine sieve over the meat.

ANTHONY BLAKE AND QUENTIN CREWE
GREAT CHEFS OF FRANCE

Zucchini and Lamb Croquettes with Dill, Turkish-Style

	To serve 6	
1 lb.	ground lean lamb	½ kg.
1 tsp.	salt	5 ml.
1 lb.	zucchini, grated	½ kg.
3	sprigs fresh dill, 2 chopped	3
1	large onion, grated	1
¼ cup	cream cheese, softened	50 ml.
2	eggs	2
	pepper	
2 tbsp.	flour	30 ml.
2 tbsp.	olive oil	30 ml.
1	lemon, cut into 6 wedges	1

In a strainer, sprinkle the salt on the zucchini and let it drain over a bowl until liquid forms—about 30 minutes. Squeeze out the excess moisture. Mix the zucchini with the lamb, chopped dill, onion, cream cheese, eggs, and pepper to taste. Add the flour and form the mixture into 12 round patties. Heat the oil in a skillet and fry the croquettes over medium heat for about five minutes on each side—or until brown on both sides. Serve hot, decorated with the lemon wedges and the remaining dill sprig.

SHERYL LONDON
EGGPLANT AND SQUASH: A VERSATILE FEAST

Moroccan Meatballs

Boulettes à la Viande

Accompany this dish, if you wish, with a tomato sauce (recipe, page 165).

	To serve 6 to 8	
½ lb.	ground lean lamb	¼ kg.
2	medium-sized potatoes, boiled, peeled and mashed	2
2	eggs, beaten	2
½ cup	chopped fresh parsley	125 ml.
2	onions, finely chopped	2
¼ tsp.	freshly ground black pepper	1 ml.
½ tbsp.	cayenne pepper	7 ml.
	salt	
¼ cup	flour	50 ml.
1 cup	olive oil	¼ liter

Work together the meat, potatoes, eggs, parsley, onions, pepper, cayenne pepper and salt. Form the mixture into balls the size of eggs. Flatten them slightly and roll them in flour.

Heat the oil until it is very hot but not smoking, and fry the meatballs in it for 10 to 15 minutes, turning them several times, until they are golden brown. Serve very hot.

AHMED LAASRI
240 RECETTES DE CUISINE MAROCAINE

Almond-stuffed Meatballs in Curry Sauce

Kofta

The besan called for in this recipe is chick-pea flour. It is available where Indian foods are sold. Many Indian-food stores also carry karhais, which are round- or flat-bottomed pans similar to Chinese woks.

To serve 4

1 lb.	boneless lean lamb, ground twice	½ kg.
16	almonds, blanched and peeled	16
1	egg	1
6 tbsp.	besan	90 ml.
½ tsp.	salt	2 ml.
¼ tsp.	freshly ground black pepper	1 ml.
2 tbsp.	water	30 ml.
	vegetable oil for deep frying	
¼ cup	ghee	50 ml.
½ cup	finely chopped onions	125 ml.
1 tsp.	finely chopped garlic	5 ml.
1 tbsp.	finely chopped fresh ginger	15 ml.
½ tsp.	ground coriander	2 ml.
½ tsp.	ground cumin	2 ml.
½ tsp.	turmeric	2 ml.
¼ tsp.	cayenne pepper	1 ml.
1 cup	plain yogurt	¼ liter
½ tsp.	garam masala	2 ml.
	fresh coriander sprigs	

Place the almonds in a bowl, pour in enough boiling water to cover them by about 1 inch [2½ cm.], and let them soak for two hours. Drain the almonds and discard the water.

In a deep bowl, combine the lamb, egg, 3 tablespoons [45 ml.] of the *besan,* and the salt and black pepper. Knead vigorously with both hands, then beat with a spoon until the mixture is smooth. Divide the lamb into 16 equal portions. Pat each portion into a flat round, place an almond in the center, and then shape the meat into a ball that completely encloses the nut. Make a thick, smooth batter with the remaining 3 tablespoons of *besan* and the 2 tablespoons [30 ml.] of water. With your fingers or a pastry brush, spread the batter evenly on all sides of each meatball, or *kofta.* Arrange the *koftas* side by side on a sheet of wax paper.

Pour 2 cups [½ liter] of vegetable oil into a 10-inch [25-cm.] *karhai* or 12-inch [30-cm.] wok, or pour 2 to 3 inches [5 to 8 cm.] of oil into a deep fryer. Heat the oil until it reaches a temperature of 375° F. [190° C.] on a deep-frying thermometer. Deep fry the *koftas* five or six at a time, turning them about with a slotted spoon, for about five minutes, or until richly browned. As they brown, transfer them to a plate.

In a heavy 3- to 4-quart [3- to 4-liter] saucepan, heat the *ghee* over medium heat until a drop of water flicked into it sputters instantly. Add the onions, garlic and ginger, and stir for two minutes, then add the ground coriander, cumin, turmeric and cayenne pepper. Stirring constantly, cook over medium to low heat for 10 minutes, or until the onions are golden brown.

Stir in the yogurt, mix thoroughly, and add the *koftas.* Turn them about with a spoon until they are coated with yogurt, sprinkle the top with the *garam masala,* and cover the pan tightly. Remove the pan from the heat and, without removing the cover, let the *koftas* steep for about one hour in the flavorful sauce.

Just before serving, return the pan to low heat and, stirring gently, simmer for five minutes, or until the *koftas* and sauce are hot. Sprinkle with fresh coriander and serve at once from a heated deep platter.

FOODS OF THE WORLD/THE COOKING OF INDIA

Spicy Meatballs

El Kefta

To serve 6

2 lb.	boneless mutton, including about ½ lb. [¼ kg.] fat, finely chopped or ground in a food grinder	1 kg.
½ tbsp.	chopped fresh parsley	7 ml.
1½ tbsp.	finely chopped fresh chervil	22 ml.
14 tbsp.	butter	210 ml.
1	onion, finely ground	1
½ tsp.	ground saffron	2 ml.
½ tsp.	pepper	2 ml.
½ tsp.	ground ginger	2 ml.
½ tsp.	ground cumin	2 ml.
1 tsp.	cayenne pepper	5 ml.
¼ tsp.	salt	1 ml.
1 cup	water	¼ liter

Mix the parsley and ½ tablespoon [7 ml.] of the chervil with the meat. Roll this into balls about ½ inch [1 cm.] in diameter. Put the remaining ingredients into a cooking dish and fry until the butter is melted.

Put in the meatballs and cook over medium heat for about 15 minutes, or until firm.

Serve the meatballs in a deep platter with the liquid in which they were cooked.

JOHN, FOURTH MARQUIS OF BUTE (EDITOR)
MOORISH RECIPES

Roasting

Stuffed Foresaddle of Lamb

Punjeno Jagnje

To serve 8 to 10

one 18 lb.	foresaddle of lamb	one 9 kg.
	salt	
1	lamb liver	1
2	bunches scallions, finely chopped	2
7 tbsp.	lard or rendered lamb fat	105 ml.
8	thick slices firm-textured white bread with the crusts removed, cut into small cubes	8
½ cup	raw short-grain rice, parboiled until just tender (about 12 minutes) and drained	125 ml.
	freshly ground pepper	
2 or 3	fresh mint leaves, chopped	2 or 3
2 tbsp.	chopped fresh parsley	30 ml.

Season the lamb with salt and let it stand.

Drop the liver into boiling water and simmer for six to eight minutes, or until the liver becomes lighter in color and firm. Drain, cool and then dice the liver.

Brown the scallions with the diced liver in 1 tablespoon [15 ml.] of the lard or lamb fat. Fry the bread cubes separately in another tablespoon of the fat until golden brown.

Mix the rice, liver, scallions and fried bread. Season well with salt and pepper. Add the chopped herbs. Stuff this mixture into the rib cavity of the lamb. Gather the flaps of meat over the rib opening and sew up the cavity. Then brush the lamb all over with melted lard or lamb fat. Roast in a preheated 350° F. [180° C.] oven for about three hours, or until thoroughly done. Baste often with hot water and melted fat.

Carve the lamb, arranging the slices on a large heated platter. Garnish with the stuffing and serve at once.

SPASENIJA-PATA MARKOVIĆ (EDITOR)
VELIKI NARODNI KUVAR

The Two Hind Quarters of Lamb with Sweet Herbs

This 18th Century dish may also be prepared with a leg of lamb, as in the demonstration on pages 44-45, in which case the amounts of ingredients for the stuffing should be halved.

To serve 12 to 16

one 18 lb.	baron of lamb, fell loosened from the flesh without tearing	one 9 kg.
½ lb.	lean salt pork with the rind removed, blanched in boiling water for 5 minutes, drained and finely chopped	¼ kg.
1 cup	chopped fresh parsley	¼ liter
6	scallions, chopped	6
	salt and pepper	
2 tbsp.	fines herbes	30 ml.
1 tbsp.	mixed spices	15 ml.
8 tbsp.	butter, softened	120 ml.
1½ cups	chopped fresh mushrooms	375 ml.
½ lb.	sliced bacon (optional)	¼ kg.
⅔ cup	dry bread crumbs	150 ml.
2 cups	meat stock (recipe, page 164) or white wine	½ liter
5	shallots, chopped	5
about 1 cup	bitter-orange juice, or sweet-orange juice and lemon juice mixed	about ¼ liter
2	garlic cloves, finely chopped (optional)	2

Mix together the chopped salt pork, parsley, scallions, salt and pepper, fines herbes, spices, butter and mushrooms. Put the mixture between the fell and the flesh of the lamb, and tie up the fell to keep in the stuffing. If desired, wrap the lamb with slices of bacon, then in parchment paper or foil. Place the lamb on a spit set over a drip pan and cook it in front of a hot fire for about two hours or until the juices run almost clear. Alternatively, sear the lamb in a pan for 10 minutes in a preheated 450° F. [230° C.] oven, then reduce the heat to 350° F. [180° C.]. Allow about 10 to 15 minutes a pound [½ kg.] depending on how well done you like the meat.

Remove the paper or foil and bacon, if used. Sprinkle the lamb with the bread crumbs and roast for a further 10 minutes, or until the coating browns lightly. Transfer the lamb to a serving platter.

Deglaze the drip pan or the roasting pan by pouring in the stock or wine, adding the shallots, and stirring over high heat until all of the drippings are dissolved and the sauce is slightly reduced. Correct the seasoning, stir in the orange juice or mixture of orange and lemon juice, and the garlic, if used. Serve the sauce with the lamb.

VINCENT LA CHAPELLE
THE MODERN COOK

Stuffed Kid

Caprettu Chinu

Caciocavallo and provolone are firm gourd-shaped Italian cheeses, often with a light, smoky flavor.

This old recipe is common to both Sicily and Calabria. In Maletto and Bronte, in the northeast of Sicily, the pasta or rice in the stuffing is replaced by a tomato risotto or a risotto flavored with pork sausage and wild fennel.

To serve 8		
one 12 lb.	kid, skinned and boned, heart, liver and kidneys chopped	one 6 kg.
1 tbsp.	lard	15 ml.
	olive oil (optional)	
	salt and pepper	
Pasta stuffing		
8 to 10 cups	small shell pasta or 4 to 6 cups [1 to 1½ liters] raw unprocessed rice	2 to 2½ liters
14 oz.	prosciutto, cut into small pieces	400 g.
14 oz.	fresh *caciocavallo* or provolone cheese, diced	400 g.
7 oz.	ground veal or chicken	200 g.
1	onion, sliced	1
	olive oil	
¼ cup	chopped fresh parsley	50 ml.
	salt and pepper	
8	eggs, hard-boiled and quartered	8

To prepare the stuffing, boil the pasta or rice in salted water until it is *al dente*. Drain. In a bowl, mix the pasta or rice with the ham, cheese and veal or chicken. Fry the onion in a little oil until barely soft. Add the kid's heart, liver and kidneys and fry gently until brown, then stir the onion mixture into the pasta or rice mixture. Add the parsley; season with salt and pepper. Use this stuffing to fill the stomach cavity of the kid. Arrange the quartered eggs in the stuffing, taking care not to break them.

Sew up the kid with strong white thread. Smear the kid with the lard, place in a roasting pan, and cook in a preheated 400° F. [200° C.] oven for just over one hour, or until done. Alternatively, the stuffed kid can be charcoal-grilled, but it must be brushed continuously with the oil, salt and pepper. It will take about one hour to grill.

PINO CORRENTI
IL LIBRO D'ORO DELLA CUCINA E DEI VINI DI SICILIA

Marinated Kid

Chevreau à la Marinade

To serve 8		
one 12 lb.	kid, prepared for roasting	one 6 kg.
2	onions, sliced	2
2	carrots, sliced	2
	salt and pepper	
	mixed spices	
¼ cup	vinegar	50 ml.
1 cup	white wine	¼ liter
¼ cup	oil	50 ml.
1	bay leaf	1
1 tbsp.	crumbled dried thyme or mixed herbs	15 ml.
3	sprigs parsley	3
4 tbsp.	butter	60 ml.
1	lemon, sliced	1
	croutons *(recipe, page 167)*	

Combine the onions, carrots, salt and pepper, spices, vinegar, wine, oil and herbs. Place the kid in this marinade, cover, and refrigerate for 24 hours, turning the meat and spooning the marinade over it several times. Drain the kid and pat it dry with paper towels. Strain the marinade and reserve it for basting.

Place the kid in a roasting pan, smear the butter over the surface, and put in a preheated 350° F. [180° C.] oven. Roast for about 15 minutes, then baste with the fat in the pan. After about 45 minutes, begin basting with the marinade. Roast for one and one half to two hours in all. When the meat is done, serve it on a large platter garnished with lemon slices and croutons.

GASTON DERYS
LES PLATS AU VIN

Leg of Lamb

Lammkeule

Serve this with small roast potatoes, braised whole tomatoes and mint sauce.

To serve 4 to 6

6 lb.	leg of lamb	3 kg.
1½ tbsp.	salt	22 ml.
1 tsp.	freshly ground black pepper	5 ml.
1 tbsp.	chopped fresh rosemary or 1 tsp. [5 ml.] crushed dried rosemary	15 ml.
4 tbsp.	butter, melted	60 ml.

Preheat the oven to 450° F. [230° C.]. Mix the salt, pepper and rosemary with the melted butter, and use the mixture to coat the meat as evenly as possible all over. Place the lamb in a shallow roasting pan and sear in the oven for 20 minutes. Reduce the heat to 350° F. [180° C.] and roast for 40 to 60 minutes, or until the lamb is done to your taste.

DOROTHEE V. HELLERMANN
DAS KOCHBUCH AUS HAMBURG

Stuffed Leg of Easter Lamb

Pierna de Cordero Pascual Rellena

To serve 6 to 8

one 3 lb.	boneless leg of lamb	one 1½ kg.
¼ lb.	very finely chopped mushrooms (about 1 cup [¼ liter])	125 g.
1 tsp.	fresh lemon juice	5 ml.
2 tbsp.	butter	30 ml.
	salt	
1 lb.	ground pork	½ kg.
½ cup	dry sherry	125 ml.
¼ tsp.	mixed dried herbs	1 ml.
¼ cup	flour	50 ml.
3 tbsp.	oil	45 ml.
	hot water	

Sprinkle the mushrooms with the lemon juice. Sauté them in the butter for about 10 minutes; season with salt.

Mix the ground pork with half of the sherry and the herbs. Add the cooked mushrooms. Place this stuffing in the cavity of the boned leg and sew or tie up the meat with string to enclose the stuffing. Sprinkle the meat with salt and dust it lightly with flour, brushing off any excess.

Put the lamb in a roasting pan with the oil and the remaining sherry. Roast in a preheated 325° F. [160° C.] oven for one and one half hours, or until the meat is cooked through. Turn the lamb several times during the roasting and baste with the pan juices. If necessary, add a little hot water to the pan juices to provide more basting liquid.

To serve, remove the string and slice the lamb. Degrease the pan juices and serve them in a sauceboat.

SIMONE ORTEGA
MIL OCHENTA RECETAS DE COCINA

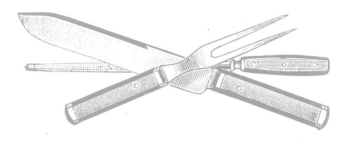

Crying Leg of Lamb

To serve 8

6 to 9 lb.	leg of lamb	3 to 4½ kg.
¼ cup	olive oil	50 ml.
6	garlic cloves, 2 cut into slivers and 4 chopped	6
1 tbsp.	chopped rosemary	15 ml.
2 tbsp.	chopped thyme	30 ml.
	salt and pepper	
12	medium-sized potatoes (3 lb. [1½ kg.]), peeled and thinly sliced	12
3 tbsp.	butter, diced	45 ml.

Preheat the oven to 425° F. [220° C.].

Rub the leg of lamb with the oil. Make small, deep gashes in the lamb and poke the garlic slivers into the gashes. Dust the leg all over with the chopped herbs and sprinkle it with salt and pepper.

Layer the potatoes in a large buttered roasting pan longer than the length of the lamb. Sprinkle the layers with salt, pepper, the chopped garlic and the butter. Set the dish on the bottom shelf of the oven. Place the lamb on a second oven rack, directly above the potatoes so the drippings will fall onto the potatoes. This is how the recipe received its name.

Roast for one and one half hours or to the desired degree of doneness, reducing the heat if the potatoes brown too quickly. Stir up the potatoes once or twice during cooking. To serve, carve the meat and arrange it on top of the potatoes.

THE VOLUNTEERS OF THE AMERICAN HOSPITAL OF PARIS
AND ELIZABETH W. ESTERLING
LE COOKBOOK

Leg of Lamb Cooked like Venison

Gigot de Mouton en Chevreuil

To serve 6 to 8

6 lb.	leg of lamb, trimmed of excess fat	3 kg.
2 tbsp.	salt	30 ml.
1 cup	red wine vinegar	¼ liter
2	medium-sized onions, sliced	2
⅓ cup	chopped fresh parsley	75 ml.
4	sprigs thyme	4
9	whole cloves	9
18	juniper berries, bruised	18
	freshly ground pepper	
6 cups	red wine	1½ liters
¼ lb.	fresh pork fatback, cut into lardons	125 g.
1 cup	heavy cream	¼ liter

With a larding needle, pierce the leg in about 20 places to allow the marinade to penetrate. Rub half of the salt all over the leg. Put it in a deep oval dish just large enough to hold it.

In a small saucepan, heat the vinegar to the boiling point and pour it over the lamb. Refrigerate overnight, basting the leg occasionally. Take the leg out of the vinegar and dry it. Mix the onions, parsley, thyme, cloves, juniper berries and the remaining salt. Pour all of the vinegar out of the dish and place half of the onion mixture in the dish. Put in the leg and cover with the other half of the onion mixture. Sprinkle with pepper and pour on the wine to cover. Cover and marinate in the refrigerator for six to eight days. Turn the lamb every morning and evening; baste it several times a day.

On the day you wish to serve the lamb, remove it from the marinade and dry it. Strain the marinade and set it aside. Using a larding needle, lard the lamb on both sides with the lardons. Place the leg on a spit over a drip pan or, if you wish to roast it in the oven, place it on a rack in a roasting pan. Roast in a preheated 400° F. [200° C.] oven or in front of a hot fire for 30 minutes. Then begin basting frequently with the strained marinade. Cook for about another 30 minutes, or longer for well-done meat, basting often. Five minutes before the end of the cooking time, spoon the cream over the lamb; it will run into the pan and blend with the marinade.

Transfer the lamb to a heated serving platter. Scrape the pan so that all adhering bits dissolve in the sauce, which should be creamy and smooth and the color of a coffee custard. Strain the sauce into a sauceboat and serve.

ÉDOUARD NIGNON (EDITOR)
LE LIVRE DE CUISINE DE L'OUEST-ÉCLAIR

Roast Lamb Marinated in Lemon Juice

Pieczén Barania "Na Dziko"

To serve 6

3 lb.	leg of lamb, excess fat removed	1½ kg.
3 tbsp.	water	45 ml.
3 tbsp.	fresh lemon juice	45 ml.
15	juniper berries, lightly pounded	15
15	peppercorns	15
15	small dried chilies	15
1	garlic clove, crushed to a paste	1
	salt	
2 tbsp.	flour	30 ml.
2 tbsp.	butter	30 ml.
2	onions, sliced	2
2 or 3	dried mushrooms, soaked in warm water for 30 minutes and drained	2 or 3
½ cup	red wine	125 ml.
¼ cup	sour cream	50 ml.
3	fresh mushrooms, sliced, or dried mushrooms, soaked in warm water for 30 minutes, drained and sliced (optional)	3

Bring the water and lemon juice to a boil with 10 each of the juniper berries, peppercorns and chilies. Pour this marinade over the meat. Turn the meat in the marinade, rubbing it in lightly. Cover and refrigerate overnight.

The next day, drain the meat and rub it with the crushed garlic and salt. Let the meat stand for one hour, then dust it with the flour.

Heat the butter in a roasting pan and brown the meat in it on all sides. Roast the meat in a preheated 375° F. [190° C.] oven, basting frequently with its own juices.

After 30 minutes, add to the pan the onions and whole dried mushrooms, the remaining juniper berries, peppercorns and chilies, and the wine. Cover and return to the oven. After 60 to 80 minutes, the meat should be well done. (If the cooking liquid evaporates, add some boiling water from time to time.)

When the meat is tender, coat it with the sour cream, cover again and cook for a further five minutes. Slice the meat, not too thinly, and arrange it on a heated serving dish. Sieve the cooking liquid, add the sliced mushrooms if using, reheat the liquid and pour it over the meat. Serve with rice, beets and creamed potatoes.

MARIA LEMNIS AND HENRYK VITRY
W. STARO-POLSKIEJ KUCHNI I PRZY POLSKIM STOLE

Kid with Lemon

Capretto al Limone

To serve 4

3 lb.	kid loin, sirloin or leg roast	1½ kg.
2	garlic cloves, chopped	2
1 tbsp.	chopped fresh rosemary	15 ml.
1 tbsp.	chopped fresh sage	15 ml.
1	bay leaf, crumbled	1
	salt	
½ cup	olive oil	125 ml.
6 tbsp.	fresh lemon juice	90 ml.
3	lemons, sliced	3
2 tsp.	peppercorns	30 ml.

Mix the garlic and herbs with a little salt and rub the meat with this mixture. Place the meat in a bowl and pour on the oil. Sprinkle with the lemon juice and coat with the lemon slices and peppercorns. Cover the bowl and marinate in the refrigerator for two days, turning the meat several times.

Drain the meat and place it in a roasting pan. Brown it over high heat, season with salt and place in a preheated 450°F. [230°C.] oven. Roast for one hour, or until the meat is tender, basting occasionally with the marinade.

Alternatively, spit-roast the meat over a charcoal fire.

STELLA DONATI (EDITOR)
IL GRANDE MANUALE DELLA CUCINA REGIONALE

Lemon-roasted Lamb

To serve 6 to 8

6 lb.	leg of lamb	3 kg.
2	lemons	2
1	large garlic clove, slivered	1
1 tbsp.	Dijon mustard	15 ml.
¼ tsp.	ground ginger	1 ml.
2 tbsp.	olive oil	30 ml.
	salt and freshly ground pepper	

Peel each lemon, keeping the peel in one long strip. Reserve the lemons. Cut each strip of peel into thirds lengthwise (you should have three long strips of peel from each lemon).

Without breaking the parchment-like fell, lightly score the surface of the lamb with crosshatched diagonal lines spaced at 1½-inch [4-cm.] intervals. Using a larding needle, make small incisions along the score marks at 1-inch [2½-cm.] intervals. Thread one long strip of lemon peel into the eye of a larding needle; insert the needle into one incision, bring it under one section of fell and over the next as you pull

it through. Continue to weave the lemon peel along the score marks; repeat with the remaining strips of peel.

Make rows of 10 small incisions with an ice pick or sharp knife between the rows of lemon peel, and insert the garlic slivers in the incisions. Place the lamb in a roasting pan. Squeeze the reserved lemons and combine their juice with the remaining ingredients. Spoon half of this mixture over the lamb and refrigerate for two hours.

Preheat the oven to 450°F. [230°C.]. Roast the lamb for 15 minutes. Reduce the heat to 325°F. [160°C.]. Roast the lamb for 10 to 12 minutes per pound [½ kg.] for rare meat, 15 minutes for medium-rare—basting with the remaining lemon-juice mixture every 10 minutes.

BERT GREENE
BERT GREENE'S KITCHEN BOUQUETS

Leg of Lamb, Breton-Style

Gigot Bretonne

To serve 5 or 6

3 to 4 lb.	leg of lamb, shank half	1½ to 2 kg.
1 or 2	garlic cloves, cut into slivers	1 or 2
1 cup	dried white kidney beans or marrow beans, soaked overnight and drained	¼ liter
1	carrot, diced	1
1	small onion, diced	1
1	whole clove	1
1 tsp.	salt	5 ml.
1 tbsp.	finely chopped fresh parsley	15 ml.

Add to the beans the carrot, onion, whole clove, salt and enough water to cover the beans completely; bring to a boil, reduce the heat, and simmer until tender, about one hour. Drain the beans.

Meantime, cut gashes in the lamb in several places, and insert the slivers of garlic. Set the lamb, with a meat thermometer inserted in the thickest part, in a preheated 450°F. [230°C.] oven. Sear the meat for 15 minutes, then reduce the heat to 325°F. [160°C.]. After the lamb has been in the oven for half an hour, spoon off excess fat from the pan in which it is roasting. Add the beans to the pan around the meat. Roast for 30 minutes longer. Remove the lamb to a warmed platter when the desired temperature is reached. Skim off any excess fat, add the parsley to the beans, and serve the beans with the lamb.

BETTY WASON
BRIDE IN THE KITCHEN

Roast Lamb with Garlic Sauce

Gigot des Alpilles à la Crème d'Ail

In Provence, the tradition of cooking a leg of lamb stuck with garlic cloves is as old as the tradition of sheepherding. Yet some gourmets accuse the garlic of giving a bitter taste to the meat. Here is a recipe that overcomes the problem: The garlic is made into an accompanying sauce.

	To serve 6 to 8	
6 to 9 lb.	leg of lamb	3 to 4½ kg.
5 tbsp.	butter, softened	75 ml.
	salt and pepper	
10	garlic cloves	10
1 cup	meat stock (recipe, page 164)	¼ liter
2 tbsp.	puréed tomato	30 ml.

Spread the leg of lamb with the butter and put it in a baking dish. Roast in a preheated 400° F. [200° C.] oven for 15 minutes per pound [½ kg.] of meat. Season with salt and pepper halfway through the cooking time.

While the lamb is cooking, prepare the garlic. Bring a pan of water to a boil, add the garlic cloves and parboil them for three to four minutes. Remove the garlic cloves, cool them under cold water and drain. In a mortar, pound the garlic to a purée. Transfer the purée to a saucepan.

When the lamb is roasted, set it on a serving platter. Add to the garlic purée the stock, the roasting juices and the puréed tomato. Season with salt and pepper, and cook over high heat for five minutes to reduce the sauce.

Serve the leg of lamb accompanied by the piping hot sauce in a sauceboat.

IRÈNE LABARRE AND JEAN MERCIER
LA CUISINE DU MOUTON

Leg of Lamb with Garlic

Gigot de Mouton à l'Ail

	To serve 6 to 8	
6 to 9 lb.	leg of lamb	3 to 4½ kg.
3	garlic bulbs, the cloves separated and peeled	3
	salt	
½ cup	meat stock (recipe, page 164)	125 ml.

Roast the leg of lamb on a spit or in a preheated 350° F. [180° C.] oven for about one to one and a quarter hours.

Meanwhile, bring a large pan of water to a boil and throw in the garlic cloves and a little salt. After four to five minutes, drain the garlic cloves. Put them in a small saucepan with the stock and cook them gently until they are tender—about five minutes.

Place the leg of lamb on a serving dish, deglaze the roasting pan with a little of the stock, pour the deglazing liquid into the remaining stock to make a sauce, and serve the garlic cloves and sauce with the lamb.

CHARLES DURAND
LE CUISINIER DURAND

Leg of Lamb with Parsley and Bread Crumbs

Gepersilleerde Schapebout

Serve the meat with green beans, asparagus, fried tomatoes and watercress.

	To serve 6 to 8	
6 to 9 lb.	leg of lamb	3 to 4½ kg.
6 tbsp.	butter, melted, or lamb stock (recipe, page 164)	90 ml.
1 cup	fresh white bread crumbs	¼ liter
½ cup	chopped fresh parsley	125 ml.
1	shallot, chopped	1
1	leek, trimmed to 1 inch [2½ cm.] above the white part and chopped	1
3 tbsp.	prepared mustard	45 ml.

Place the lamb in a roasting pan and roast in a preheated 350° F. [180° C.] oven for about one hour, basting often—first with the butter or lamb stock, then with the pan juices.

Mix together the bread crumbs, parsley, shallot and leek. Remove the meat from the oven and coat it first with the mustard, then with the bread-crumb mixture. Return the meat to the oven for another 30 minutes, or until the topping is golden.

ONS KOOKBOEK

Leg of Lamb, Mexican-Style

Pierna de Carnero a la Mexicana

	To serve 6 to 8	
6 to 9 lb.	leg of lamb	3 to 4½ kg.
2	garlic cloves	2
1 tbsp.	oregano	15 ml.
¼ tsp.	ground cumin (optional)	1 ml.
1 tbsp.	chili powder	15 ml.
2 tbsp.	vinegar	30 ml.
3 tbsp.	olive oil	45 ml.
	salt and pepper	

Mash the garlic, oregano and cumin, if using, into a paste; add the chili powder and mix well. With a sharp-pointed knife, make incisions in the leg of lamb, and fill the incisions with the paste. Pour the vinegar and oil over the meat, season the lamb and refrigerate overnight.

Roast, uncovered, in a preheated 350° F. [180° C.] oven for one to one and one half hours, or until the desired degree of doneness is reached.

ELENA ZELAYETA
ELENA'S SECRETS OF MEXICAN COOKING

Greek-Style Leg of Lamb

Lammkeule nach Griechischer Art

To serve 6 to 8

6 to 9 lb.	leg of lamb	3 to 4½ kg.
1 quart	buttermilk, lightly salted	1 liter
3	bay leaves	3
3	whole cloves, partially crushed	3
4	juniper berries, partially crushed	4
6	black peppercorns, partially crushed	6
3	garlic cloves, finely chopped	3
12	slices lean bacon	12
1 cup	red wine	¼ liter
20	fresh sage leaves	20
2 tbsp.	butter	30 ml.
¼ cup	flour	50 ml.
1 tbsp.	puréed tomato	15 ml.
	salt and pepper	
	paprika	
½ cup	heavy cream, whipped and sweetened with 1 tsp. [5 ml.] sugar	125 ml.

Place the meat in a mixture of the buttermilk, bay leaves, cloves, juniper berries and peppercorns. Cover the meat, refrigerate it and let it marinate for two days, turning the meat occasionally in the marinade.

Remove the meat and strain the marinade. Dry the meat, rub it with the garlic and wrap it with the bacon. Roast for 35 minutes in a preheated 425° F. [220° C.] oven, basting frequently with the wine and pan juices. About 10 minutes before the end of the cooking time, remove the bacon and cover the lamb with the sage leaves.

Meanwhile, melt the butter in a saucepan, stir in the flour and brown it lightly. Stir in 1 cup [¼ liter] of the marinade, and cook and stir until the sauce is thickened. Add the puréed tomato and season with salt, pepper and paprika.

When the meat is done, transfer it to a heated platter and add the pan juices to the sauce. Cook, skimming to degrease, until the sauce is of the desired consistency. Remove the pan from the heat and stir in the cream. Serve the meat accompanied by the sauce in a heated sauceboat.

LILO AUREDEN
WAS MÄNNERN SO GUT SCHMECKT

Roast Lamb with Coffee

To serve 6

5 lb.	leg of lamb	2½ kg.
	salt and pepper	
	dry mustard	
	ground rosemary	
Coffee sauce		
1 cup	strong black coffee	¼ liter
2 tbsp.	cream	30 ml.
2 tbsp.	sugar	30 ml.
3 tbsp.	brandy	45 ml.

Salt and pepper the lamb, and dust it all over with the mustard. Pat some ground rosemary into the top of the lamb. Combine the ingredients for the sauce.

Roast the lamb in a preheated 300° F. [150° C.] oven for 18 minutes to the pound if your intention is to have it well done, or for 12 minutes if you like it pink. While the lamb is in the oven, baste it frequently with the sauce. Transfer the lamb to a warm serving tray and let it stand for 20 minutes before carving.

JANET E. C. WURTZBURGER (EDITOR)
PRIVATE COLLECTIONS: A CULINARY TREASURE

Baker's Wife's Lamb

Le Gigot Boulangère

To serve 6 to 8

6 to 9 lb.	leg of lamb, the shank stuck with a garlic clove	3 to 4½ kg.
2 tbsp.	cold water	30 ml.
	salt and pepper	
4 tbsp.	butter, melted	60 ml.
6 to 8	medium-sized potatoes, very thinly sliced	6 to 8
1	onion, thinly sliced	1
1	garlic clove, chopped	1
1	bay leaf	1
2	sprigs thyme	2
	boiling water, lightly salted	

Pour the cold water into a shallow fireproof earthenware dish and put in the lamb. Salt the lamb and sprinkle it with half of the melted butter. Put in a preheated 425° F. [220° C.] oven for 20 minutes, basting from time to time. Meanwhile, mix the potatoes, onion, garlic, bay leaf and thyme. Season the mixture with salt and pepper.

After 20 minutes, transfer the lamb to a plate and cover to keep it warm. Spread the potato mixture in the baking dish, add enough salted boiling water to come just to the top of the potatoes, and place the dish over medium heat. When the water comes to a boil, put the lamb on top of the potatoes, sprinkle with the remaining melted butter, and return the dish to the oven. Roast for at least another 20 minutes, turning the leg of lamb twice. The potatoes will be tender in 20 minutes, but the dish should continue to cook until the lamb is done—that is, still pink inside.

To serve, carve the lamb and arrange the slices in an overlapping circle on the potatoes. Serve in the baking dish.

PAUL BOUILLARD
LA GOURMANDISE À BON MARCHÉ

Roast Lamb Stuffed with Ham

Pieczén Barania Nadziewana Szynką

To serve 4 to 6

2 lb.	boneless lamb shoulder or leg of lamb, excess fat removed, pounded until thin and roughly square	1 kg.
	salt and pepper	
2	garlic cloves, lightly crushed	2
7 tbsp.	butter	105 ml.
½ cup	sour cream	125 ml.
	Ham stuffing	
5 oz.	boiled ham, coarsely ground in a food grinder or processor (about 1 cup [¼ liter])	150 g.
2	thick slices stale, firm-textured bread, crusts removed, soaked in milk and squeezed dry	2
4 tbsp.	finely chopped beef marrow, or butter	60 ml.
1	small onion, finely chopped and sautéed in 1 tbsp. [15 ml.] butter until soft	1
¼ lb.	mushrooms, thinly sliced (about 1 cup [¼ liter]) and sautéed with the onion (optional)	125 g.
1 tsp.	finely chopped fresh parsley	5 ml.
1	large egg	1

Dust the meat with salt and pepper, and rub it with the garlic. Combine all of the stuffing ingredients, kneading with your hands until the stuffing has a uniform consistency. Spread the stuffing over the inside of the meat, roll it up

tightly, and tie it in several places with cotton thread. The tied meat should have the shape of a rolling pin.

In a heavy casserole, brown the meat on all sides in the butter. Then cover and roast in a preheated 375° F. [190° C.] oven for one hour, or until the meat is tender, basting occasionally with the sour cream.

MARIA LEMNIS AND HENRYK VITRY
W. STARO POLSKIEJ KUCHNI I PRZY POLSKIM STOLE

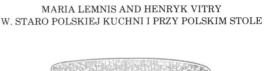

Roast Baby Lamb or Kid

Abbacchio o Capretto al Forno

Either red or white wine may be used in this dish. White wine will give a more delicate flavor and is to be preferred with kid. Serve the meat with roast potatoes and a salad dressed with oil and lemon. If you wish to cook the potatoes with the meat, add another 7 tablespoons [105 ml.] of butter and eight peeled potatoes, cut into large pieces, to the pan 30 minutes before the meat is done.

To serve 4 to 6

4 lb.	baby lamb or kid roast (shoulder, rib or loin)	2 kg.
¾ cup	oil	175 ml.
	salt	
1 tsp.	whole cloves	5 ml.
2 tsp.	juniper berries	10 ml.
1 tsp.	ground cinnamon	5 ml.
	pepper	
7 tbsp.	butter	105 ml.
1	onion, chopped	1
1¼ cups	wine	300 ml.

The day before cooking the meat, place it in a roasting pan, rub it with the oil and season with salt. Cut small slits in the meat, and push in the cloves and juniper berries. Sprinkle with cinnamon and pepper, cover the pan, refrigerate, and let the meat marinate, turning it over after a few hours.

Three hours before serving time, add the butter and onion to the pan. Place in a preheated 375° F. [190° C.] oven and immediately reduce the heat to 325° F. [160° C.]. When the top of the meat is golden brown, turn the roast over. When the meat is browned on all sides, begin basting with the wine. Cook for a total of three hours, then serve very hot.

FRANCA FESLIKENIAN
CUCINA E VINI DEL LAZIO

Shoulder of Lamb with Rice and Apricot Stuffing

The original version of this recipe calls for a single lamb shoulder cut in the English style with part of the ribs and the top of the shank and breast attached. Such a shoulder can be boned to form a natural pocket for stuffings. For American cooks, the best substitute is two boned shoulders joined to make a cushion shape, as demonstrated on pages 66-67. The techniques of boning lamb shoulder appear on pages 12-13.

To serve 6

two 5 to 6 lb.	lamb shoulders, boned	two 2½ to 3 kg.
	salt and pepper	
4 tbsp.	butter, melted	60 ml.

Rice and apricot stuffing

1 cup	raw unprocessed long-grain rice	¼ liter
¼ lb.	dried apricots (about 1½ cups [375 ml.]), soaked in hot water for 2 hours, drained and chopped	125 g.
2 tbsp.	seedless raisins, soaked in hot water for 15 minutes and drained	30 ml.
2 tbsp.	halved blanched almonds	30 ml.
½ tsp.	ground cinnamon	2 ml.
½ tsp.	ground coriander	2 ml.
½ tsp.	ground ginger	2 ml.
	salt and black pepper	

Lay the lamb shoulders boned side up and season them with salt and pepper.

Boil the rice in plenty of boiling, salted water for about 15 minutes, or until almost cooked. Drain well and mix with the remaining stuffing ingredients. Spread some of the mixture on top of one shoulder, cover with the other shoulder and sew the shoulders together with a needle and thread.

Brush with some of the melted butter; roast the lamb in a preheated 375° F. [190° C.] oven for 30 minutes per pound [½ kg.]—stuffed weight—plus 20 minutes. When it is done, remove it to a heated serving platter.

Pour the fat from the pan juices, then mix in the remaining rice mixture to reheat over low heat for about five minutes. Add the remaining butter if necessary to moisten. Arrange this around the lamb, cut away the thread and serve.

JANE GRIGSON
ENGLISH FOOD

Stuffed Lamb Shoulder with Eggplant

Arni Yemisto me Melitzana

To serve 4

4 to 6 lb.	lamb shoulder, boned	2 to 3 kg.
1	large eggplant, peeled and thinly sliced	1
	salt and pepper	
1½ cups	olive oil	375 ml.
1	onion, grated	1
1	garlic clove, crushed to a paste	1
1 tsp.	dried mint, finely crumbled	5 ml.
1 tbsp.	chopped fresh parsley	15 ml.
1 cup	white wine	¼ liter
½	lemon, juice strained, shell reserved	½
8	small potatoes, parboiled for 5 minutes	8
½ tsp.	oregano	2 ml.

Season the eggplant slices with salt and pepper, and use 1 cup [¼ liter] of the olive oil to brown them lightly until almost, but not quite, tender; drain them on paper towels.

In another skillet, lightly brown the onion, garlic, mint and parsley in 2 tablespoons [30 ml.] of the olive oil.

Lay the lamb shoulder flat—boned side upward—and spread the sautéed onion mixture over the meat. Season with salt and pepper, and arrange the eggplant slices on top. Roll and tie the lamb; place in a roasting pan and pour half of the wine over the lamb. Brown the rolled lamb in a preheated 450° F. [230° C.] oven for 15 minutes; then reduce the heat to 300° F. [150° C.] and roast for one and three quarters hours for pink lamb; two and one quarter hours for well-done meat. Baste the lamb frequently with a mixture of the remaining oil and the lemon juice, using the lemon shell, pierced with a fork, as a basting brush.

About 30 minutes before the lamb is done, add the parboiled potatoes to the pan. Sprinkle them lightly with salt, pepper and oregano, and baste them with the pan juices.

When the lamb is cooked, remove it to a warmed platter and skim the fat from the pan juices. Add to the juices the remaining ½ cup [125 ml.] wine, salt and pepper to taste, and simmer this sauce for several minutes. Cut the lamb roll into slices 1 inch [2½ cm.] thick; place the slices on the platter surrounded by the potatoes. Serve accompanied with the sauce and a crisp salad.

EVA ZANE
GREEK COOKING FOR THE GODS

Roast Saddle of Lamb with Herbs

Selle d'Agneau Rôti aux Aromates

For instructions on the preparation and carving of a saddle of lamb — a double-loin roast — see pages 34-35.

To serve 6

one 3 to 3½ lb.	saddle of lamb, all fat removed	one 1½ to 1¾ kg.
2	garlic cloves	2
1 tsp.	mixed dried herbs (thyme, savory, oregano and marjoram)	5 ml.
¼ cup	olive oil	50 ml.
	salt and freshly ground pepper	
⅓ cup	white wine or water	75 ml.
2 tbsp.	butter, diced (optional)	30 ml.

Rub the surfaces of the bones and meat with the garlic cloves. Sprinkle the herbs lightly on all surfaces, most sparingly on the underside, and coat with olive oil, rubbing and patting with your hands to ensure an even distribution. Just before roasting, sprinkle the underside of the apron and the fillet with salt and pepper, and roll the aprons under so that the two rolls touch. The rolls may be skewered together crosswise or the roast held in shape by a couple of rounds of string, but this is not essential.

Place the roast in a heavy, shallow baking dish of just the right size to hold it (otherwise, the drippings risk burning) and count a maximum of 10 minutes per pound [½ kg.] of roasting time (30 minutes in this instance) in a preheated 425° F. [220° C.] oven. After 10 minutes, turn the heat down to 325° F. [160° C.]; salt and pepper the roast at this time. Baste with the pan juices during the last 10 minutes or so and, after roasting is done, leave the meat in its roasting pan in a warm but not hot place for 10 to 15 minutes so that the meat may relax. Given all these precautions, the meat should be neither rare nor gray in color, but rose throughout.

Transfer the roast to a heated platter (or, better, a carving board with a well for collecting the juices). Skim off the fat from the roasting pan, place the pan over high heat, pour in the wine or water, and reduce by about two thirds, stirring and scraping with a wooden spoon to dislodge and dissolve all caramelized adherences. Remove from the heat and swirl in the butter if desired; this transforms the clear juice into a light-bodied velvety sauce.

Send the roast to the table with the vegetable garnishes and sauce separately. Carve the meat so that each person has a slice of the eye of the loin, a section of fillet and a piece of apron. Serve on heated plates, and pass the sauceboat only when the carving has been finished and the resultant juices added to the sauce.

RICHARD OLNEY
THE FRENCH MENU COOKBOOK

Crown Roast of Lamb

If you wish to cook the lamb until well done, you may fill the central cavity of the crown before roasting with one of the stuffing mixtures on page 166. However, if you prefer your lamb pink, fill its cavity after roasting, but use a cooked mixture. Among the author's suggestions for a cooked filling are broiled lamb kidneys, rice or bulgur pilaf with toasted nuts, chestnut purée garnished with whole chestnuts, small buttered Brussels sprouts mixed with chestnuts, new peas or a mixture of peas and small onions, or sautéed mushrooms tossed with fresh herbs and cream.

To serve 6

2	lamb rib roasts (6 small chops each), bone ends trimmed of fat and meat	2
	freshly ground pepper	
½ tsp.	chopped fresh tarragon	2 ml.
1	garlic clove, halved (optional)	1
4 tbsp.	butter, 2 tbsp. [30 ml.] softened and 2 tbsp. melted, or 2 tbsp. olive oil and 2 tbsp. melted butter	60 ml.
	salt	

Curve the two racks of lamb so that their ends touch, forming a ring with the bones sticking up. Tie string around the outside to hold the crown together.

Season the meat with pepper and tarragon and, if you like, rub it with the cut sides of the garlic. Place the crown on a rack in a shallow roasting pan. Crumple a piece of foil into a ball large enough to fill the middle of the crown so it will hold its shape while roasting.

Rub the meat well with the softened butter or the olive oil and roast in a preheated 375° F. [190° C.] oven for about 30 to 35 minutes for pink lamb; baste it with melted butter twice during that time. It is best to gauge the cooking time by the size of the chops: About nine to 10 minutes for each pound [½ kg.] of lamb is generally right, but the eye of the meat differs so much in size that this can only be approximate.

Salt the meat well before removing it from the oven. Transfer the crown to a hot platter and remove the string and foil. Fill the crown with one of the fillings given above. Garnish the platter with watercress or with cooked artichoke bottoms filled with béarnaise sauce. To serve, carve into chops, allowing two per person.

JAMES A. BEARD
JAMES BEARD'S AMERICAN COOKERY

Rack of Lamb with Anise and Sweet Garlic

Cooking the cloves of garlic in their skins makes them tender and sweet. The quantity of garlic seems staggering at first, but the flavor is mild. Have a butcher trim the meat from the ends of the rib bones and be sure the chine bone is sawed through so you can carve the chops after cooking.

To serve 4		
2	8-rib racks of lamb	2
	coarse salt	
	freshly ground pepper	
2¼ tsp.	anise seeds	11 ml.
2	garlic bulbs, the cloves separated but not peeled	2
½ tbsp.	sugar	7 ml.
2 tbsp.	red wine vinegar	30 ml.

Season each rack of lamb with coarse salt, pepper and 1 teaspoon [5 ml.] of anise seeds. Place the racks of lamb in one roasting pan if you have a large one, or use two smaller ones. (Do not set the lamb on a roasting rack.) Strew the garlic around the lamb, and roast in a preheated 425° F. [220° C.] oven for 45 minutes for rarish lamb or 55 minutes for medium. Remove the meat from the oven and place it on a carving board to rest.

With a slotted spoon, remove the garlic cloves from the roasting pan (or pans) and pop the flesh out of the skins into a small skillet. Add the remaining anise seeds, along with the sugar and vinegar. Bring to a boil and reduce rapidly until the sugar and liquid turn viscous and syrupy, and coat the garlic. Season with salt and pepper.

Slice the racks into chops. Serve three to four chops per person on warmed plates. Spoon some garlic and sauce around the chops and serve.

MICHÈLE URVATER AND DAVID LIEDERMAN
COOKING THE NOUVELLE CUISINE IN AMERICA

Guard of Honor

The techniques of assembling a lamb Guard of Honor are shown on pages 38-39.

Once the meat has been skewered, you can push some herb stuffing into the cavity, but the stuffing has a tendency to fall out in a messy way unless the mixture is made very stiff with egg—and most people prefer a light, crumbly stuffing. I prefer to fill the cavity after cooking with small new potatoes, separately cooked, or with mushrooms. Guard of Honor can be served with all of the usual things for lamb,

but the best thing is stuffed tomatoes, which should be placed around the meat on its serving dish.

To serve 7 or 8		
1	double rib lamb roast, cut into 2 racks along the backbone, chined and the bones left long	1
	salt and pepper	
2 tsp.	chopped fresh thyme or crushed dried rosemary	10 ml.

Turn the racks skin side up and remove about 1½ inches [4 cm.] of skin and fat from the ends of the bones; scrape them free of meat as well as you can. Score the skin in stripes or in diamond shapes.

Rub in salt, pepper, and the thyme or rosemary. Now stand the racks up on their thick sides, skin side out, and push them together so that the exposed bones cross each other alternately. The assembly will bristle like a military row of crossed swords.

Skewer the racks together at the base. Protect the exposed bones from burning with a piece of foil pressed into place over them. Roast in a preheated 375° F. [190° C.] oven for one and one half hours. To carve, cut down between the chops, allowing two per person.

JANE GRIGSON
ENGLISH FOOD

Roasted Rack of Lamb

Lamsrug uit de Oven

Serve this with new potatoes sprinkled with parsley, and boiled green peas.

To serve 2		
1	6-rib lamb roast	1
2 tbsp.	Dijon mustard	30 ml.
	salt and pepper	
2 tsp.	chopped fresh rosemary	10 ml.
⅓ cup	fine fresh bread crumbs	75 ml.
3 tbsp.	chopped fresh parsley	45 ml.
2	garlic cloves, chopped	2
2 tbsp.	olive oil	30 ml.
4 tbsp.	butter, 2 tbsp. [30 ml.] melted, 2 tbsp. diced	60 ml.
⅔ cup	meat stock *(recipe, page 164)*, heated	150 ml.

Rub the roast with the mustard. Sprinkle with salt, pepper and rosemary. Mix the bread crumbs with the parsley, garlic, and salt and pepper. Cover the meat with this mixture, pressing it in firmly. Put the meat in a shallow roasting pan.

Combine the olive oil with the melted butter and dribble the mixture over the meat.

Roast the meat in a preheated 350° F. [180° C.] oven for 45 minutes to one hour, depending on the degree of doneness you want. Transfer it to a warmed platter. Pour the stock into the pan; add the diced butter. Heat, stirring, until the pan juices blend into the stock and the butter thickens the sauce slightly. Pour the sauce around the meat and serve.

HUGH JANS
VRIJ NEDERLAND KOOKBOEK

Lamb Cutlets in Paper

Costolette di Agnello al Cartoccio

Cutlets may be sliced from boned rib, eye of the loin, sirloin or leg. The slices of prosciutto or other cooked ham should be trimmed to match the length and breadth of the cutlets. The author suggests foil may be used instead of parchment paper.

To serve 4

4	boneless lamb cutlets, cut ¼ inch [6 mm.] thick	4
2 tsp.	salt	10 ml.
¼ tsp.	freshly ground black pepper	1 ml.
3	dried mushrooms, soaked in warm water for 30 minutes, drained and chopped	3
2 tbsp.	olive oil	30 ml.
¾ cup	chopped onions	175 ml.
⅛ tsp.	grated nutmeg	½ ml.
2 tbsp.	melted butter	30 ml.
8	thin slices prosciutto or cooked ham	8

Season the lamb cutlets with 1½ teaspoons [7 ml.] of the salt and all of the pepper. Set aside. Heat the oil in a skillet; sauté the onions for five minutes; mix in the mushrooms, nutmeg and the remaining salt. Cook over very low heat for 10 minutes. Cool for five minutes.

Cut four pieces of parchment paper, each large enough to completely enclose a cutlet. Brush each piece of paper with the butter, place a slice of ham on it, spread the ham with the onion mixture, place a cutlet over it and cover the cutlet with another slice of ham. Bring up the edges of the paper and seal the edges. Place the parcels on a baking sheet. Bake in a preheated 350° F. [180° C.] oven for 45 minutes. Slit the paper, and serve the lamb from the parcels.

ROMEO SALTA
THE PLEASURES OF ITALIAN COOKING

Herbed Lamb Shanks

To serve 4

four 1 ½ lb.	lamb shanks	four ¾ kg.
2	garlic cloves, cut lengthwise into slivers	2
2 tsp.	thyme	10 ml.
2 tsp.	marjoram	10 ml.
½ tsp.	grated nutmeg	2 ml.
½ tsp.	cayenne pepper	2 ml.
2 tsp.	salt	10 ml.
1	onion, sliced and separated into rings	1
1	lemon, thinly sliced	1

Place the shanks on a large piece of brown paper or foil; with a sharp knife, make a few small incisions in each shank and insert a garlic sliver in each incision. Sprinkle thyme, marjoram, nutmeg, cayenne pepper and salt over the shanks. Place a few onion rings and a slice of lemon on each shank, fold the paper or foil over the shanks to seal them, and place the parcel on a baking sheet. Bake in a preheated 375° F. [190° C.] oven for one hour. Serve piled high on a dish.

BABETTE HAYES
TWO HUNDRED YEARS OF AUSTRALIAN COOKING

Roast Breast of Lamb with Potatoes

Petto di Agnello in Forno

To serve 4

1½ to 2 lb.	lamb breast, cut into pieces 2 inches [5 cm.] wide	¾ to 1 kg.
7	medium-sized potatoes, cut into strips	7
	salt and coarsely ground black pepper	
8	juniper berries, crushed	8
2 tsp.	finely chopped fresh rosemary	10 ml.
3	garlic cloves, finely chopped	3
¼ cup	olive oil	50 ml.
¾ cup	water	175 ml.

Place the potatoes in the bottom of a deep baking dish and season with salt and pepper. Place the pieces of lamb on top and sprinkle with the juniper berries, rosemary and garlic. Season with salt and pepper, and pour the oil and water over the lamb. Cover with a closely fitting lid and place in a preheated 350° F. [180° C.] oven. After 45 minutes, remove the lid and increase the heat to 425° F. [220° C.]. Cook for 20 minutes more, or until the meat has become brown. Turn it over gently and let the other side brown. Serve immediately.

SAVINA ROGGERO
COME SCEGLIERE E CUCINARE LE CARNI

Lamb Bandit-Style
Arni Kleftiko

To serve 4

2 lb.	boneless lean lamb, cubed	1 kg.
½ cup	olive oil	125 ml.
1	garlic clove, finely chopped	1
3 tbsp.	fresh lemon juice	45 ml.
1	large onion, finely chopped	1
½ cup	dry sherry	125 ml.
1½ tsp.	oregano	7 ml.
	salt and pepper	
1	tomato, sliced	1
¼ lb.	feta cheese	125 g.
2 tbsp.	butter	30 ml.

Mix the lamb well with the olive oil, garlic, lemon juice, onion, sherry, 1 teaspoon [5 ml.] of the oregano, and salt and pepper to taste.

Brush four sheets of aluminum foil or parchment paper with olive oil and arrange a portion of the meat mixture in the center of each sheet. On each portion place a tomato slice; sprinkle the cheese over the meat, season with a pinch of oregano and place two pats of butter on top. Fold the foil or parchment paper over the mixture and crimp the edges tightly to seal. Bake the packets in a preheated 375° F. [190° C.] oven for one hour.

EVA ZANE
GREEK COOKING FOR THE GODS

Roast Lamb with Oregano
Agneddu 'nfurnatu cu Riganu

This is an old recipe from the mountains of northern Sicily.

To serve 4

2½ lb.	baby lamb, cut into small pieces	1¼ kg.
1 cup	olive oil	¼ liter
	salt and pepper	
4	medium-sized onions, very thinly sliced	4
¼ cup	chopped fresh oregano	50 ml.

Place the pieces of lamb in a roasting dish, season with the oil, salt and pepper, and onions, and sprinkle the oregano

over all in an even layer. Place in a preheated 300° F. [150° C.] oven and, after 15 minutes, increase the oven temperature to 325° F. [160° C.]. After a further 15 minutes, increase the oven temperature to 350° F. [180° C.]. During cooking, baste the pieces of lamb occasionally with oil from the bottom of the roasting dish. After a further 30 minutes, the lamb will be golden brown and crisp.

PINO CORRENTI
IL LIBRO D'ORO DELLA CUCINA E DEI VINI DI SICILIA

Lamb Roll
Rotolo di Agnello

To serve 4 or 5

1¼ lb.	ground lean lamb	⅔ kg.
2	thick slices firm-textured white bread with crusts removed, soaked in milk and squeezed dry	2
1	egg	1
2 tbsp.	freshly grated Parmesan cheese	30 ml.
	salt	
4	large thin slices Emmentaler cheese	4
⅓ cup	dried mushrooms (preferably cepes), soaked in warm water for 30 minutes, drained, chopped and cooked in 1 tbsp. [15 ml.] butter until soft	75 ml.
2 tbsp.	butter, melted	30 ml.

In a bowl, mix the meat with the bread, egg, Parmesan and salt. Gather the mixture into a ball and pound it repeatedly and vigorously against the bottom of the bowl to knead it. On a damp cloth, spread out the meat mixture to a finger's thickness. Cover with the slices of Emmentaler cheese, then with the cooked mushrooms. Roll up the meat and, with damp hands, seal the edges.

Transfer the roll to a well-greased baking dish, setting the joined edge down. Bake in a preheated 350° F. [180° C.] oven for about one hour, basting the roll occasionally with the melted butter.

LISA BIONDI (EDITOR)
350 RICETTE DI CUCINA LEGGERA

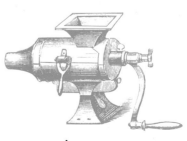

Poaching, Braising and Stewing

Provençal Lamb

Rot de Bif di Agnello alla Provenzale

To serve 12

8 to 10 lb.	baron of baby lamb, legs tied together	4 to 5 kg.
¼ lb.	fresh pork fatback, cut into strips	125 g.
	salt and pepper	
1 tbsp.	mixed spices	15 ml.
½ lb.	fatty ham, thinly sliced	¼ kg.
½ lb.	veal scallops, thinly sliced and pounded flat	¼ kg.
6	onions, 2 sliced, 4 chopped	6
6	whole cloves	6
5	carrots, 1 sliced, 4 chopped	5
1	bouquet garni, including 3 bay leaves	1
1	garlic clove (optional)	1
1¼ cups	white wine	300 ml.
2 quarts	meat stock (recipe, page 164)	2 liters
3	egg yolks	3
¾ cup	freshly grated Parmesan cheese	175 ml.
¾ cup	dry bread crumbs	175 ml.

Roll the strips of fatback in salt and the spices, and use them to lard the lamb. Cover the bottom of a pan with the ham, put in the lamb and add the veal, sliced onions, cloves, sliced carrot, bouquet garni, and garlic, if using. Cover and braise gently for one hour, basting with the wine and a little stock. Add salt and pepper. When the lamb is almost cooked, transfer it to a roasting pan. Strain the cooking liquid into a bowl.

Skim the fat from the cooking liquid, mix the fat with the egg yolks and use this mixture to glaze the lamb. Mix the cheese and bread crumbs and use them to coat the lamb. Place in a preheated 400° F. [200° C.] oven and cook for 30 minutes more, or until the lamb reaches the desired degree of doneness and the coating is a beautiful golden brown.

Meanwhile, put the cooking liquid in a saucepan with the remaining stock and the chopped onions and carrots. Simmer for 30 minutes, or until the vegetables are tender. This broth may be served as a first course, followed by the lamb.

IPPOLITO CAVALCANTI, DUCA DI BUONVICINO
CUCINA TEORICO-PRATICA

Daube Avignonnaise

The technique of larding is shown on pages 58-59.

To serve 6 to 8

3 to 4 lb.	boneless leg of lamb	1½ to 2 kg.
9	onions, 1 stuck with 2 whole cloves, 2 sliced and 6 coarsely chopped	9
2	sprigs parsley	2
8	garlic cloves	8
	salt	
	fresh pork fatback, cut into lardons, soaked in Cognac and rolled in chopped parsley	
1	carrot, sliced	1
¼ cup	olive oil	50 ml.
1 tsp.	thyme	5 ml.
1	bay leaf	1
	red wine	
1	pig's foot, split	1
3 or 4	slices salt pork with the rind removed, blanched in boiling water for 5 minutes, drained and diced	3 or 4
	orange peel	

Ask the butcher for the bones from the lamb and for one or two extra. Place the bones in a pot with the onion stuck with cloves, one parsley sprig and two whole garlic cloves. Add 2 quarts [2 liters] of water and cook down to a good broth. Season with salt to taste.

In the meantime, cut the lamb in good-sized pieces. Lard each piece with one or two lardons. Combine the sliced onions and carrot, olive oil, thyme, bay leaf, the remaining parsley, three crushed cloves of garlic, and wine almost to cover. Marinate the lamb for several hours or overnight in this marinade.

Make a bed of the chopped onions in a heavy, deep casserole. Add half of the pig's foot, then half of the marinated meat, more onions, the salt pork, the remaining meat and the rest of the pig's foot. Add the orange peel, strain the marinade and add the seasonings, onions, carrots and garlic from it and the three remaining garlic cloves. Add enough of the broth to cover. Seal the casserole with flour-and-water paste and cook very slowly on the stove or in a 275° F. [140° C.] oven for three to four hours. Serve with rice and a salad.

THE EDITORS OF HOUSE & GARDEN
HOUSE & GARDEN'S NEW COOK BOOK

English-Style Leg of Lamb
Gigot à l'Anglaise

Serve this dish with steamed new potatoes and a creamed purée of turnips.

To serve 6 to 8

6 to 9 lb.	leg of lamb	3 to 4½ kg.
about 2 quarts	meat stock *(recipe, page 164)*	about 2 liters
2 tbsp.	butter	30 ml.
¼ cup	flour	50 ml.
2	egg yolks, lightly beaten	2
½ cup	heavy cream	125 ml.
2 tbsp.	capers, rinsed	30 ml.

In a large pan, bring the stock to a boil and put in the leg of lamb. Reduce the heat, cover partially and simmer for 15 minutes for each pound [½ kg.] of meat. When the lamb is cooked, remove it and set it on a heated platter.

In a small pan, melt the butter, stir in the flour and cook until lightly colored. Stir in about 2 cups [½ liter] of the stock in which the lamb was cooked. Stirring constantly, simmer until the sauce is smooth and lightly thickened. Remove the sauce from the heat. Mix the egg yolks with the cream and stir them into the sauce. Return the sauce to the heat for a minute or two to thicken it, without letting it come to a boil. Stir in the capers and serve the sauce with the lamb.

MME. ELISABETH
500 NOUVELLES RECETTES DE CUISINE

Leg of Lamb with Shallots
Gigot aux Échalotes

As accompaniments for this dish, serve boiled and puréed dried beans, whole poached chestnuts, and a dandelion or endive salad with croutons.

To serve 8

6 to 9 lb.	leg of lamb, trimmed well and the shank bone sawed short	3 to 4½ kg.
4 tbsp.	rendered goose fat	60 ml.
1 lb.	shallots	½ kg.
½ lb.	fresh pork rind, in 1 piece	¼ kg.
1	bouquet garni	1
about 6 cups	meat stock *(recipe, page 164)*	about 1½ liters

Melt the goose fat and in it brown the leg of lamb on all sides. Remove the lamb and cook the shallots in the fat until soft

and golden. Line a heavy casserole with the pork rind, placed fat side down. Place the lamb on the pork rind and surround the lamb with the shallots. Add the bouquet garni. Cover with the stock.

Bring to a boil, cover, and simmer gently for four to five hours. At the end of this time the shallots will be reduced to a purée and the lamb will be surrounded by a creamy, aromatic sauce. Discard the bouquet garni. Slice the lamb and arrange the slices on a heated platter, surrounded by the sauce. Cut the pork rind into small squares and scatter it over the slices of lamb.

ZETTE GUINAUDEAU-FRANC
LES SECRETS DES FERMES EN PÉRIGORD NOIR

Lamb in a Piquant Sauce, Basque-Style
Cordero con Salsa Picante

To serve 4

3 to 4 lb.	leg of baby lamb	1½ to 2 kg.
⅓ cup	oil	75 ml.
1	large onion, halved	1
4	carrots, sliced	4
4	potatoes, thickly sliced	4
1	ripe tomato, thickly sliced	1
1	apple, peeled, cored and thickly sliced	1
	salt	
¾ cup	meat stock *(recipe, page 164)*	175 ml.
2	garlic cloves	2
2 tbsp.	vinegar	30 ml.
2 tbsp.	chopped fresh parsley	30 ml.

Heat 4 tablespoons [60 ml.] of the oil in a sauté pan. Add the onion, carrots, potatoes, tomato and apple, and then the lamb. Season with salt. Cook over fairly high heat for about 20 minutes, turning the lamb from time to time and stirring the vegetables until all are well browned. Spoon off any fat that accumulates. Add the stock, cover, then cook over low heat for approximately one and one half hours, or until the meat is tender.

Remove the meat from the pan and cover it to keep it warm. In a small skillet, fry the garlic in the remaining oil until lightly browned. Add the vinegar and parsley, and cook for another minute or two. Add the garlic mixture to the lamb cooking juices, stir well, and press this sauce through a sieve. Slice the lamb and pour the sauce over it.

ANA MARÍA CALERA
365 RECETAS DE COCINA VASCA

Leg of Lamb with Parsley Sauce

Gigot à la Persillade

To serve 8

6 to 9 lb.	leg of lamb	3 to 4½ kg.
about 2 quarts	meat stock (recipe, page 164)	about 2 liters
1	bouquet garni	1
1	bunch parsley, stems removed	1
	salt and pepper	

Place the leg of lamb in an oval pot of just the size to hold it. Cover the meat with stock, add the bouquet garni and bring to a boil. Cover the pot and simmer for about one and one half hours, turning the leg occasionally.

Remove the lamb and discard the bouquet garni. Degrease the stock in the pot and boil it vigorously to reduce it to a syrupy glaze. Put the lamb back into the pot and turn it in the glaze to cover all sides, taking care it does not stick. Remove to a warmed serving platter.

Meanwhile, blanch the parsley in boiling water for seven minutes. Drain, plunge into cold water, drain again, and press the parsley dry with your hands. Chop it fine.

Pour a little more stock into the pot, and boil and stir until all of the glaze is dissolved. Add the parsley to this sauce, season, and serve with the lamb.

MENON
LA CUISINIÈRE BOURGEOISE

Leg of Lamb, Country-Style

Perna de Carneiro á Camponesa

To serve 8

6 to 9 lb.	leg of lamb	3 to 4½ kg.
12	garlic cloves, halved	12
3	onions, coarsely chopped	3
3	carrots, sliced	3
2 oz.	fresh pork fatback or salt pork with the rind removed, blanched in boiling water for 5 minutes, drained and finely chopped	60 g.
2 tbsp.	lard	30 ml.
	salt and pepper	
1	bay leaf	1
1 cup	white wine	¼ liter

Using the point of a sharp knife, make 24 small, deep slits in the leg of lamb and push the garlic halves into them. Put the onions, carrots, and pork fatback or salt pork into a large casserole with the lard, salt and pepper, and bay leaf; place over medium heat. When the lard is melted and very hot, put in the lamb and brown it on all sides. Pour in the wine and enough water to cover the meat; bring the liquid to a boil, cover the casserole and place it in a preheated 325° F. [160° C.] oven. Cook for three hours, or until the lamb is tender.

Transfer the lamb to a warmed platter. Degrease the cooking liquid, then reduce it over high heat until it has the consistency of a sauce. Sieve the sauce, and pour it over the lamb as the leg is carved.

BERTHA ROSA-LIMPO
O LIVRO DE PANTAGRUEL

Marinated Leg of Lamb

Gigot de Mouton à la Friande

This recipe is adapted from an 18th Century French book written for professional chefs —and published anonymously.

To serve 8

6 to 9 lb.	leg of lamb	3 to 4½ kg.
¼ lb.	fresh pork fatback, cut into lardons	125 g.
	salt	
	mixed spices	
¼ cup	olive oil	50 ml.
3	unpeeled garlic cloves, lightly crushed	3
3	whole cloves	3
2 or 3	sprigs thyme	2 or 3
2	bay leaves	2
2 or 3	sprigs basil	2 or 3
2 or 3	sprigs parsley	2 or 3
3	scallions, thinly sliced	3
3	shallots, thinly sliced	3
1½ cups	white wine	375 ml.
⅓ cup	meat stock (recipe, page 164)	75 ml.

Roll the lardons in salt and mixed spices, and use them to lard the leg of lamb. Mix the oil, garlic, cloves, thyme, bay leaves, basil, parsley, scallions and shallots, and rub the mixture over the lamb. Cover the lamb and marinate it in the refrigerator for 24 hours.

Place the lamb and its marinade in a deep pan. Add the wine. Cover, and cook over very low heat or in an oven preheated to 325° F. [160° C.] for four to five hours, or until the meat is tender, turning it occasionally and basting it regularly. Remove the lamb from the pan, degrease the cooking liquid and strain it. Add the stock and reduce by boiling over high heat until the sauce reaches the desired consistency. Serve the sauce poured over the carved lamb.

LE MANUEL DE LA FRIANDISE

Poached Leg of Lamb

Gigot à la Ficelle

The volatile oils in chilies may irritate your skin. Wear rubber gloves when handling them.

To serve 6

2½ to 3 lb.	boneless leg of lamb, rolled and tied, the bones reserved	1¼ to 1½ kg.
5	garlic cloves, 1 cut into slivers, 4 lightly crushed	5
1	bay leaf	1
1 tbsp.	tarragon	15 ml.
4 tbsp.	freshly ground black pepper	60 ml.
3	dried red chilies	3
2 tbsp.	salt	30 ml.

Anchovy sauce

12	oil-packed flat anchovy fillets, finely chopped	12
12	black Italian or Greek olives, pitted and finely chopped	12
1 or 2	small fresh chilies, stemmed, seeded and finely chopped	1 or 2
1	garlic clove, finely chopped	1
2 tbsp.	olive oil	30 ml.
1 tsp.	fresh lemon juice	5 ml.
1 tsp.	grated lemon peel	5 ml.

In a large kettle, combine the lamb bones and all of the seasonings with enough water to cover the leg of lamb. Bring the water to a boil and cook for one hour over medium heat.

Stud the lamb with the slivers of garlic. Roll the lamb in a linen towel or cloth and tie it securely. Now place the wrapped leg of lamb in the kettle, tying the cloth to the handles of the kettle so the lamb will not rest on the bottom, or place the lamb on a rack set inside the kettle. Bring the liquid to a boil and then reduce it to a simmer. Allow approximately 15 minutes per pound [½ kg.] of boned weight for rare lamb. Remove the lamb from the kettle, unwrap it and set it on a warmed platter. Combine ½ cup [125 ml.] of the cooking liquid with the ingredients for the sauce, and stir well over medium heat until the mixture is fairly smooth and heated through. Correct the seasoning. The sauce should be very hot and the anchovy flavor should be quite pronounced.

Serve the lamb with the sauce, tiny new potatoes sprinkled with parsley, and peas that have been flavored with a little chopped parsley and chives.

THE EDITORS OF HOUSE & GARDEN
HOUSE & GARDEN'S NEW COOK BOOK

Leg of Lamb with Garlic Cloves and Bread Sauce

As an alternative to the standard roast leg of lamb, the British frequently boil or braise the leg. The following hearty presentation, with garlic and a classic English bread sauce, stretches the expensive meat so that a half leg will easily feed six to eight people. The dish should be accompanied simply with boiled new potatoes, tossed in parsley butter.

To serve 6 to 8

4 lb.	leg of lamb, sirloin or shank half, trimmed of excess fat	2 kg.
1	onion, sliced	1
1	large carrot, sliced	1
1 tbsp.	mixed dried herbs	15 ml.
2 tbsp.	olive oil	30 ml.
2 tbsp.	flour	30 ml.
1½ cups	dry white wine	375 ml.
1½ cups	water	375 ml.
2	large garlic bulbs, cloves separated but not peeled	2
	salt and pepper	
1	bouquet garni of parsley, bay leaf, celery and a 2-inch [5-cm.] strip of orange peel	1
¾ cup	fresh bread crumbs	175 ml.
2 tbsp.	butter	30 ml.

Choose a covered fireproof casserole just large enough to hold the lamb and place the meat in it. Scatter the onion, carrot and herbs over the lamb, and dribble the olive oil over all. Cover the casserole, place it over medium-low heat and cook for 30 minutes, turning the meat over after 15 minutes.

Lift the lamb out onto a platter and sprinkle the flour over the onion and carrot. Stir over heat for three to four minutes until a soft, light gold roux has formed. Whisk in the wine and water, bring to a simmer, then strain the sauce through a sieve into a bowl. Press the vegetables well to release all juices.

Return the lamb to the casserole and pour the strained sauce over it. Place the unpeeled garlic cloves around the lamb. Season, and add the bouquet garni. Either place the casserole in a preheated 350° F. [180° C.] oven for one hour, or continue cooking on top of the stove with the casserole tightly covered and the liquid at the barest simmer.

Remove the lamb to a serving platter. Fish out and discard the bouquet garni, and lift out the garlic cloves with a slotted spoon. Scatter the garlic over the lamb and place the meat in a warming oven. Skim off any fat accumulated on the surface of the sauce and bring the sauce to a boil. Throw in the bread crumbs and let them cook at a good pace for 10 minutes. Stir in the butter for gloss, and taste for seasoning.

Serve out slices of lamb (each with several garlic cloves) and place the bread sauce on the side. The diners can either suck out the mild garlic purée from the cloves' interiors or they can press out the soft garlic with a fork and mash the purée and the sauce into their potatoes.

JUDITH OLNEY
COMFORTING FOOD

Leg of Lamb with Its Flavor Enhanced

Membre de Mouton à la Fidelle

This recipe is adapted from a book published in the 17th Century when cockscombs were a widely used garnish for foods. Although the cockscombs may be omitted from the dish, adventurous cooks will still find them available at butchers specializing in freshly killed poultry. To prepare them for cooking, prick them all over with a needle and rinse them under cold running water. Drop them into a pan of cold water, bring to a simmer, then drain them. Rub the cockscombs between cloth towels to remove their skins, then soak them in cold water until they are completely white.

To serve 8

6 to 9 lb.	leg of lamb, trimmed of excess fat and lightly beaten with a mallet to tenderize it	3 to 4½ kg.
¼ lb.	fresh pork fatback, cut into small strips	125 g.
1 cup	meat stock *(recipe, page 164)*	¼ liter
	salt and pepper	
1	bouquet garni	1
¾ cup	flour, mixed to a paste with about ⅓ cup [75 ml.] water and a few drops of oil	175 ml.
½ lb.	fresh mushrooms, sliced	¼ kg.
2 tbsp.	butter	30 ml.
1 tbsp.	flour	15 ml.
¼ lb.	calf's sweetbreads, soaked in cold water for 1 hour, blanched for 2 minutes in boiling water, drained, plunged into cold water, trimmed of tubes, fat and superficial membranes, and diced	125 g.
8	cockscombs, blanched	8
¼ cup	capers, rinsed and drained	50 ml.
3 tbsp.	fresh lemon juice	45 ml.

Lard the leg of lamb with the strips of pork fatback. Place the leg in an oval earthenware casserole with the stock, salt, pepper and bouquet garni. Roll the flour-and-water paste into a long cylinder, fit it around the rim of the casserole and put on the lid, pressing to make an airtight seal. Place the casserole in a 300° F. [150° C.] oven for four to five hours.

Sauté the mushrooms in the butter, sprinkle on the flour, and add the sweetbreads, cockscombs and capers. When the lamb is cooked, pour off the cooking liquid, strain and degrease it, and stir it into the mushroom mixture. Pour this sauce over the lamb, cover, and simmer gently for about 30 minutes. Add the lemon juice to the sauce and correct the seasoning. Slice the leg of lamb and serve it with the sauce.

PIERRE DE LUNE
LE NOUVEAU CUISINIER

Braised Lamb with Chicory

Braisé d'Agneau à la Chicorée

To serve 12

two 4 to 6 lb.	lamb shoulders, boned	two 2 to 3 kg.
14 tbsp.	butter	210 ml.
2	sprigs thyme	2
	salt and pepper	
1	large thin slice fresh pork fat	1
about ⅔ cup	meat stock *(recipe, page 164)*	about 150 ml.
4 or 5	heads chicory, cored	4 or 5
3	lemons, quartered	3

Place 2 tablespoons [30 ml.] of butter, a sprig of thyme and a sprinkling of salt inside each shoulder; roll and tie the shoulders separately. Line a large, heavy casserole with the pork fat; add 7 tablespoons [105 ml.] of butter and ⅓ cup [75 ml.] of stock. Put in the shoulders, cover and cook over high heat for four to five minutes, or until the pork fat sizzles. Reduce the heat and continue to braise the meat, turning it occasionally, for one and one half hours, or until well done. If the juices begin to dry up, moisten the meat occasionally with a few spoonfuls of water or stock.

Meanwhile, fill a large nonreactive pot with salted water and bring to a boil, add the chicory, and cook for 20 minutes. Drain thoroughly, then chop it fine. Sauté the chicory in the remaining 3 tablespoons [45 ml.] of butter for about 10 minutes, and season it with salt and pepper.

Transfer the shoulders to a large, warmed serving dish. Add a little more stock to the casserole, stir well to deglaze the casserole, strain the liquid, and spoon off excess fat from its surface. Spoon some of the cooking liquid over the chicory and serve it in a warmed deep vegetable dish with the lamb. Pass the remaining cooking liquid in a sauceboat and accompany the dish with the lemon quarters.

JEANNE SAVARIN (EDITOR)
LA CUISINE DES FAMILLES

Rumanian Lamb or Mutton Stew
Ragout de Mouton ou d'Agneau Roumain

To serve 8

4 lb.	lamb or mutton shoulder and breast	2 kg.
2	large onions, coarsely chopped	2
2	eggplants, peeled and thickly sliced	2
4	zucchini, peeled and thickly sliced	4
6	tomatoes, peeled, seeded and quartered	6
	salt and pepper	
1	bouquet garni	1
2	celery ribs, chopped	2
1	garlic clove, crushed to a paste	1
8	medium-sized potatoes, quartered	8
	chopped fresh parsley	

Place the lamb in a large oval casserole and brown it in a preheated 400° F. [200° C.] oven for 15 minutes, without adding any fat. Turn the pieces to brown them all over. Add the onions and cook for another 10 minutes.

Add the eggplant, zucchini, tomatoes, salt and pepper, bouquet garni, celery and garlic. Mix all of the ingredients together without adding any liquid. Cover the casserole, reduce the oven temperature to 350° F. [180° C.] and cook for one hour. Add the potatoes, cover again and cook one hour, or until everything is tender. Remove the bouquet garni.

To serve, shake the dish so that the cooking juices mix together and thicken. Pour the stew into a deep serving dish. Sprinkle with the chopped parsley.

JEANNE SAVARIN (EDITOR)
LA CUISINE DES FAMILLES

Shoulder of Lamb with Turnips
Hammelschulter mit Weissen Rüben

To serve 4 to 6

1 to 2 lb.	rolled boneless lamb shoulder	½ to 1 kg.
4 tbsp.	butter	60 ml.
1 tbsp.	flour	15 ml.
1½ cups	meat stock (recipe, page 164)	375 ml.
	salt and pepper	
	ground allspice	
4	medium-sized turnips, cut into pieces	4

Brown the lamb on all sides in half of the butter. Add the flour to the pan juices. When the flour has browned, pour in the stock and bring to a boil. Season with salt, pepper and allspice. Reduce the heat and simmer gently for two hours.

Meanwhile, melt the remaining butter in a saucepan and add the turnips. Cover and cook for 15 minutes, stirring occasionally, until the turnips are golden. Add the turnips to the meat and simmer for about half an hour, until the meat and turnips are tender. Place the meat in a serving dish and surround it with the turnips. Degrease and strain the cooking liquid, and pour it over the meat and turnips.

ELIZABETH SCHULER
MEIN KOCHBUCH

Catalan Lamb Shoulder
Épaule de Mouton à la Catalane

To serve 6

6 to 8 lb.	lamb shoulder, boned and rolled, with 2 garlic cloves inside if desired	3 to 4 kg.
	salt and pepper	
2 tbsp.	lard	30 ml.
2	slices ham	2
1	large onion, coarsely chopped	1
2	carrots, coarsely chopped	2
2 tbsp.	flour	30 ml.
1 cup	dry white wine	¼ liter
about 1 cup	water or chicken stock (recipe, page 164)	about ¼ liter
2	bay leaves	2
3	sprigs thyme	3
2 tbsp.	chopped fresh parsley	30 ml.
3	garlic cloves, 2 chopped, 1 parboiled for 2 minutes and drained	3
1	strip dried orange peel	1
3 tbsp.	dry bread crumbs (optional)	45 ml.

Rub the lamb with salt and pepper. Melt the lard in a heavy casserole. Add the ham, onion, carrots and the lamb. Basting with the hot lard, brown the meats over medium heat. Then cover the casserole, reduce the heat and cook for 30 minutes.

Remove the lamb and ham from the casserole. Stir in the flour and let it brown over medium heat. Add the wine and the water or chicken stock, mix all together well and bring to a boil. Strain this sauce.

Return the lamb to the casserole and add the sauce, bay leaves, thyme, parsley, chopped and parboiled garlic, and the orange peel. Cover and cook for 20 to 25 minutes, or until the lamb is tender. Just before removing the pan from the heat, dice the ham and add it. If the sauce is too thin, thicken it by stirring in the bread crumbs.

MARIE-THÉRÈSE CARRÉRAS AND GEORGES LAFFORGUE
LES BONNES RECETTES DU PAYS CATALAN

Stuffed Shoulder of Lamb

Épaule de Mouton Farcie

The original version of this recipe requires a single lamb shoulder, cut in the French manner to include parts of the rib and shank. Two square-cut lamb shoulder roasts provide a suitable substitute for American cooks. To prepare fresh chestnuts, cut a cross through the shell on the flat side of each nut, parboil the nuts for 10 minutes, then shell and peel them.

To serve 8 to 12

two 4 to 6 lb.	lamb shoulders, boned, the bones and trimmings reserved	two 2 to 3 kg.
	salt and pepper	
7 tbsp.	butter	105 ml.
½ lb.	boiling onions	¼ kg.
¼ lb.	salt pork, diced	125 g.
1	bouquet garni, including 1 celery rib	1
1 cup	white wine	¼ liter
48	fresh chestnuts, peeled and skinned	48
20	small fresh mushrooms	20
12	*chipolata* sausages, browned in butter	12

Simple lamb stock

	reserved lamb bones and trimmings	
2 tbsp.	butter	30 ml.
1	onion, quartered	1
1	carrot, quartered	1
1 tbsp.	flour	15 ml.
about 1 quart	water	about 1 liter
2 tbsp.	puréed tomato	30 ml.

Pork and onion stuffing

1 lb.	finely ground pork	½ kg.
2 tbsp.	finely chopped onion, sautéed in butter	30 ml.
1 tbsp.	chopped fresh parsley	15 ml.
1	egg, beaten	1

For the stock, melt the butter, and brown the bones and trimmings from the meat with the onion and carrot. Sprinkle with flour, cover with water and add the puréed tomato. Bring to a boil, then reduce the heat, partially cover, and simmer for at least one hour. Strain and degrease the stock.

Season the boned surfaces of the lamb shoulders with salt and pepper. Combine the stuffing ingredients and spread them over the boned surface of one shoulder. Cover the stuffing with the second shoulder, boned side down, and sew the shoulders together. Place the lamb in a roasting pan.

Melt 4 tablespoons [60 ml.] of the butter, pour it over the lamb, season, and roast in a 400° F. [200° C.] oven for 20 minutes. Sauté the boiling onions in 2 tablespoons [30 ml.] of the butter until lightly browned. Blanch the salt pork for one minute in boiling water, then drain it and brown it in the remaining butter.

Transfer the meat to a casserole and add the sautéed onions and salt pork. Put in the bouquet garni and the white wine. Cook over high heat until the wine is reduced to half its original volume, then add 1 cup [¼ liter] of the stock.

Cover the casserole and place in a 350° F. [180° C.] oven. After 40 minutes, remove the bouquet garni and add the chestnuts and mushrooms. Cover, and return to the oven for 35 minutes. Add the sausages and cook for another 15 minutes. Degrease before serving.

GASTON DERYS
LES PLATS AU VIN

Poached Lamb with Dill Sauce

Fårbog med Dillsås

The Swedes love mutton or lamb in dill. Serve this with boiled potatoes and a green salad.

To serve 6

2 lb.	lamb shoulder roast	1 kg.
	hot water	
2	bay leaves	2
2	whole cloves	2
1	unpeeled onion, halved	1
	salt and pepper	
1 tbsp.	butter	15 ml.
1 tbsp.	flour	15 ml.
2	egg yolks	2
½ cup	heavy cream	125 ml.
¼ cup	finely cut fresh dill	50 ml.
1 tbsp.	fresh lemon juice	15 ml.

Place the lamb in a saucepan and cover with hot water. Bring to a boil and skim. Stick the bay leaves and cloves into the onion halves and add them to the pan. Season to taste with salt and pepper. Cover, and simmer over low heat for one and one half hours, or until the meat comes loose from the bones. Bone and slice the meat, spoon a little of the cooking liquid over it and keep it warm.

Melt the butter, stir in the flour and add about 1 cup [¼ liter] of the cooking liquid. Stirring constantly, cook until a smooth, thick sauce is formed. Remove from the heat. Beat the egg yolks with the cream and gradually stir the mixture into the sauce. Add the dill and lemon juice. Pour the sauce over the meat and serve it immediately.

LILO AUREDEN
DAS SCHMECKT SO GUT

Lamb Stuffed with Couscous

Quartier de Mouton Farci au Couscous

To serve 10 to 12

6 to 9 lb.	lamb shoulder with the rib roast attached	3 to 4½ kg.
14 tbsp.	butter	210 ml.
	salt and pepper	
2	large onions, grated	2
½ tsp.	ground saffron	2 ml.
¼ cup	honey	50 ml.
2-inch	stick cinnamon	5-cm.

Couscous stuffing

2 lb.	couscous	1 kg.
1 tbsp.	oil	15 ml.
	salt	
1 cup	orange-flower water	¼ liter
24 tbsp.	butter (¾ lb. [350 g.]), melted	360 ml.
3 cups	sugar	¾ liter
5 cups	seedless raisins, soaked in warm water for 15 minutes and drained	1¼ liters
2½ tbsp.	ground cinnamon	35 ml.
1 lb.	almonds (about 3 cups [¾ liter]), blanched, peeled, fried in 2 cups [½ liter] of oil until browned, drained, and coarsely crushed in a mortar	½ kg.

First prepare the couscous stuffing. Pour 5 quarts [5 liters] of water into the bottom of a *couscoussier* or into a large saucepan, and bring to a boil. Sprinkle the couscous with the oil, pour it into the top section of the *couscoussier* or into a cheesecloth-lined steaming basket, and place it over the boiling water. Let the couscous steam for 30 minutes.

Turn the couscous into a wide, shallow bowl and toss and crush it lightly to remove any lumps. Let it cool, salt it and sprinkle it with 2 tablespoons [30 ml.] of orange-flower water, 3 tablespoons [45 ml.] of melted butter and 6 tablespoons [90 ml.] of sugar. Mix well. Leave for 15 minutes, then return it to the *couscoussier* or steaming basket and set it over the boiling water again.

When steam appears above the surface of the couscous, remove it from the heat and again toss it and sprinkle with the same quantities of orange-flower water, butter and sugar. Leave for 15 minutes before returning it to the heat. Repeat this operation six more times, allowing the couscous to rest for 15 minutes between each steaming.

The last time, place the raisins in the *couscoussier* or basket beneath the couscous. When steam appears above the surface of the couscous, turn the couscous and raisins into

the bowl, toss to separate the grains, and add the ground cinnamon and the fried almonds.

Gently loosen the parchment-like fell covering of the shoulder of lamb by sliding your hand under it, being careful not to tear it. Stuff the shoulder under the fell with about half of the couscous mixture, pushing the couscous down as far as possible. Sew the opening together carefully.

Melt the butter in a large pan and put in the lamb, fell side up. Season with salt and pepper, add the onions and saffron, and pour in 1 quart [1 liter] of water.

Cover the pan and place over low heat. After 30 minutes, turn the meat over gently, taking care not to pierce the stuffed part. Baste from time to time with the cooking liquid. The meat is done when it detaches easily from the bone, after three to three and one half hours. At this point, add the honey and the cinnamon stick to the cooking liquid. Cook, uncovered, until the sauce thickens slightly. Then take the pan off the heat.

About 30 minutes before serving time, remove the meat from the pan, put it in a baking dish, and place in a preheated 425° F. [220° C.] oven until the surface is nicely browned. Reheat the remaining couscous over boiling water. Reheat the sauce and remove the cinnamon stick.

Put the meat on a warmed serving dish, pour the sauce over it, and serve, accompanied by small bowls of the extra couscous.

AHMED LAASRI
240 RECETTES DE CUISINE MAROCAINE

Boiled Lamb Shoulder for Cold Cuts

Bok Tek Yeune Yook

For the buffet table, arrange the lamb slices on a platter garnished with lettuce, cucumber spears and red cherries.

To serve 10 to 20

4 lb.	rolled boneless lamb shoulder	2 kg.
3 quarts	water	3 liters
1 cup	sliced white radishes	¼ liter
2 tbsp.	oil	30 ml.
4	slices fresh ginger	4
2	garlic cloves	2
2 tbsp.	salt	30 ml.
2 tbsp.	sugar	30 ml.
2 tbsp.	dark soy sauce	30 ml.
1 tbsp.	peppercorns	15 ml.
½ tsp.	anise extract	2 ml.
1	cinnamon stick	1

Bring the water to a boil, add the radish slices and boil for 10 minutes. Add the lamb and boil for 15 minutes more. Reserve the cooking liquid, set the lamb aside separately to drain, and discard the radish slices.

Wash the cooking vessel thoroughly. Add the oil and heat to a sizzle. Then add the ginger and garlic, and brown. Now add the lamb and brown well on all sides, then add the reserved liquid and all of the other ingredients. Bring to a boil, cover and simmer for one hour, or until tender. Remove from the heat and refrigerate the lamb overnight in the liquid.

To serve, drain the lamb and cut it into very thin slices.

ARTHUR LEM AND DAN MORRIS
THE HONG KONG COOKBOOK

Stuffed Shoulder of Lamb in the Style of Berry

Épaule de Mouton Farcie à la Mode du Berry

Berry, a province in Central France, is famous for producing high-quality lamb and mutton.

To serve 6 to 8

4 to 6 lb.	lamb shoulder, boned	2 to 3 kg.
	salt	
3	leeks, white parts only	3
2	celery ribs	2
1	bouquet garni	1
1	onion, stuck with 1 whole clove	1
2	carrots, halved lengthwise	2
1 lb.	celeriac, quartered	½ kg.
3	large potatoes, peeled and quartered	3
7 tbsp.	butter	105 ml.
	pepper	
	Pork and garlic stuffing	
½ lb.	finely ground pork	¼ kg.
1	garlic clove, finely chopped	1
1	egg	1
1 tsp.	chopped fresh parsley	5 ml.
¾ cup	fresh bread crumbs, soaked in meat stock *(recipe, page 164)* and squeezed dry	175 ml.
1	onion, chopped and sautéed in butter until soft	1
	salt and pepper	
1 tsp.	mixed spices	5 ml.

In a bowl, mix together all of the stuffing ingredients. Stuff the shoulder with the mixture, filling the cavities. Roll and tie the meat so that the stuffing is completely enclosed.

Place the stuffed shoulder in a deep oval casserole and just cover it with water. Add 1 tablespoon [15 ml.] of salt for each quart [1 liter] of water used. Slowly bring the liquid to a boil, skimming off any scum. Add the leeks, celery, bouquet garni, onion and carrots. Reduce the heat, cover the casserole, and simmer for one and one quarter hours. Then add the celeriac and simmer for 25 minutes longer. Add the potatoes and continue cooking until the potatoes are just done.

With a slotted spoon, remove all of the vegetables; purée them through a sieve. In a sauté pan, cook the vegetable purée over high heat, stirring constantly. When the purée has a firm, dry consistency, remove it from the heat and stir in the butter. Salt the purée to taste and grind in a generous amount of pepper. If the purée is stiff, beat in several spoonfuls of the cooking liquid.

Remove the string from the shoulder and place the meat on an oval serving dish. Pour several spoonfuls of the cooking liquid over it. Serve the shoulder with the rest of the cooking liquid in a sauceboat and the vegetable purée in a vegetable dish.

PAUL BOCUSE
THE NEW CUISINE

Dill Meat Fricassee

Serve this dish with boiled potatoes and green beans.

To serve 4

2 lb.	lamb shoulder or loin roast	1 kg.
	salt	
8	white peppercorns	8
1	small carrot	1
1	leek, cut into pieces	1
	Dill sauce	
3 tbsp.	finely cut dill	45 ml.
2 tbsp.	butter	30 ml.
2 tbsp.	flour	30 ml.
1 tbsp.	fresh lemon juice	15 ml.
1	egg yolk	1
⅓ cup	heavy cream	75 ml.

Place the meat in a saucepan. Measure and add enough cold water to cover the meat. Add 2 teaspoons [10 ml.] of salt for each quart [1 liter] of water. Bring to a boil. Skim thoroughly. Add the peppercorns, carrot and leek. Cover the saucepan and let the meat simmer over low heat until tender, one to one and one half hours. Strain the cooking liquid. Keep the meat hot.

For the sauce, melt the butter and add the flour. Stir in about 1¼ cups [300 ml.] of the cooking liquid. Stirring constantly, let the sauce cook until thickened. Add the lemon juice and dill. Blend the egg yolk and cream. Remove the sauce from the heat and add the egg mixture. The sauce must not be allowed to boil again or it will curdle. Cut the meat into pieces or slices, and serve with the sauce.

SWEDISH RECIPES

Braised Lamb Sirloin

Carbonade

To serve 6

3 lb.	lamb sirloin roast	1½ kg.
¼ lb.	fresh pork fatback, cut into lardons	125 g.
	salt and pepper	
	mixed spices	
2 oz.	lean salt pork, with the rind removed, blanched in boiling water for 5 minutes, drained and chopped	60 g.
1	carrot, sliced	1
1	onion, stuck with 1 whole clove	1
about 2 cups	boiling meat stock (recipe, page 164) or water	about ½ liter
4 to 5	medium-sized turnips, blanched in salted water for 5 minutes and drained	4 to 5
2 tbsp.	butter	30 ml.

Roll the pork lardons in salt, pepper and mixed spices; use them to lard the lamb. Cook together in a casserole the salt pork, carrot and onion. After about five minutes, put in the lamb and brown it on all sides over medium heat. Add stock or water to come two thirds of the way up the sides of the lamb. Cover, and cook over low heat for about one hour.

Cook the turnips in the butter for five to 10 minutes, until they are lightly glazed. Add them to the casserole and cook for another 20 to 30 minutes, until both the lamb and the turnips are tender. Degrease the cooking liquid, correct the seasoning and serve.

OFFRAY AINÉ
LE CUISINIER MÉRIDIONAL

Breast of Mutton Stewed with Celery

To serve 4

3 to 4 lb.	mutton or lamb breast	1½ to 2 kg.
	salt and pepper	
	grated nutmeg	
1¼ cups	water	300 ml.
1	large bunch celery, trimmed and cut into large pieces	1
1	garlic clove, finely chopped	1
1 tbsp.	flour	15 ml.
3 tbsp.	fresh lemon juice	45 ml.
¼ tsp.	ground saffron	1 ml.

Put the meat in a heavy pan with the salt, pepper, nutmeg and water. Put in the celery and the garlic. Cover and let the mixture simmer nicely until tender, about one and one half hours. Transfer the breast and celery to a heated platter. Skim off all the fat from the gravy in the pan. In a bowl, rub the flour with the lemon juice and ground saffron, add it to the gravy a little at a time, and stir well until the gravy is thickened. Serve the gravy with the meat.

MRS. J. ATRUTEL
AN EASY AND ECONOMICAL BOOK OF JEWISH COOKERY

Lamb Breast Stuffed with Chestnuts

Poitrine de Mouton Farcie aux Châtaignes

For the method of boning a lamb breast, see the demonstration on pages 10-11. The technique of stuffing a breast is shown on pages 40-41.

To serve 6 to 8

3 to 5 lb.	lamb breast, boned for stuffing	1½ to 2½ kg.
2 tbsp.	lard	30 ml.
2	carrots, quartered	2
2	onions, quartered	2
1	bouquet garni	1
	salt and pepper	
2½ cups	meat stock (recipe, page 164) or water	625 ml.
Chestnut stuffing		
½ lb.	fresh chestnuts	¼ kg.
	boiling stock or water	
¼ lb.	fresh pork fat, chopped	125 g.
½ lb.	boneless beef, lamb or pork, chopped	¼ kg.
	salt and pepper	
	mixed spices	
1	onion, chopped and sautéed in lard	1
1 tbsp.	chopped fresh parsley	15 ml.

To make the stuffing, slit the chestnuts with a sharp knife, broil them for five minutes, shell and peel them, and cook for 15 minutes in stock or water. Mix the chestnuts with the other stuffing ingredients and use the mixture to fill the pocket of the lamb. Sew up the opening.

Heat the lard in a fireproof casserole and brown the lamb on all sides. Add the carrots, onions and bouquet garni; season with salt and pepper. Pour on the stock or water, cover, and braise gently for two hours, or until the lamb is tender.

PROSPER MONTAGNÉ (EDITOR)
MANUEL DU BON CUISTOT ET DE LA BONNE MÉNAGÈRE

Stuffed Breast of Lamb

Poitrine de Mouton Farcie

The techniques for boning a breast of lamb are demonstrated on pages 10-11.

To serve 6

4 to 6 lb.	lamb breast, boned for stuffing	2 to 3 kg.
2 to 3 quarts	salted water	2 to 3 liters
2	carrots	2
1	turnip	1
2	leeks	2
1	onion, stuck with 2 or 3 whole cloves	1
1	bouquet garni	1
	pepper	
¼ cup	raw unprocessed long-grain rice (optional)	50 ml.

Meat and rice stuffing

½ lb.	ground pork	¼ kg.
½ lb.	ground beef	¼ kg.
¼ cup	raw unprocessed long-grain rice, parboiled in salted water for 8 to 10 minutes and drained	50 ml.
1 cup	chopped spinach	¼ liter
1 tbsp.	butter or oil	15 ml.
2	garlic cloves	2
2 or 3	sprigs parsley	2 or 3
2	slices firm-textured white bread, soaked in milk and squeezed dry	2
1	egg yolk	1
	salt and pepper	
	grated nutmeg	

To prepare the stuffing, mix the pork, beef and rice. Sauté the spinach in the butter or oil for 10 minutes. Chop the garlic and parsley together. Add the spinach, garlic, parsley and bread to the meat mixture. Add the egg yolk and season with salt, pepper and nutmeg. Knead all of the ingredients thoroughly with your hands.

Loosely fill the pocket in the breast of lamb with the stuffing; do not overfill it or it will burst during cooking. Sew up the edges of the breast so that it forms a cushion shape. Bring the salted water to a boil, and add the vegetables, bouquet garni and pepper. Put in the stuffed breast, skim, cover and simmer gently for two and one half hours, or until the meat is tender.

Remove the stuffed breast and strain the cooking liquid to use as a broth. If you wish, cook the remaining ¼ cup [50 ml.] of rice in the broth before serving it. Slice the meat and serve it separately, hot or cold.

IRÈNE LABARRE AND JEAN MERCIER
LA CUISINE DU MOUTON

Shanks with Garlic

Souris aux Aulx

The technique of braising lamb shanks in their own juices is demonstrated on page 60.

To serve 4

four ½ lb.	lamb shanks, trimmed of outside fat	four ¼ kg.
	salt	
3 tbsp.	olive oil	45 ml.
15 to 20	garlic cloves, unpeeled	15 to 20
½ tsp.	finely crumbled mixed dried herbs	2 ml.
½ cup	dry white wine	125 ml.
	pepper	

Use, if possible, a heavy tin-lined copper pan of just a size to hold the shanks easily. It should have a tight-fitting lid.

Salt the shanks and brown them lightly in the oil. Toss in the garlic, cover, and cook over very low heat, turning the shanks occasionally, for one and one half hours or longer to be very tender. Use a fireproof pad if necessary—the shanks should only very gently stew in their own juices. In heavy copper their natural juices will hold for about one hour—in other metals, for a much shorter time. When the juices have evaporated and the shanks begin to sizzle in fat, begin to add a spoonful of water from time to time so that a film of liquid remains always in the bottom of the pan. Sprinkle with the herbs after about one hour's time.

As the meat approaches the desired tenderness, stop moistening with water so that all the liquid will evaporate. When the meat begins to sizzle again in pure fat, remove it to a plate. Pour off the fat and deglaze the pan with the white wine, scraping and stirring with a wooden spoon to dissolve all caramelized adherences. Press the liquid and garlic through a sieve to strain out the garlic skins, return the liquid to the pan, reduce it to the staccato bubbling stage, and return the meat to the pan—there should be only enough sauce to coat the pieces. Grind over pepper to taste.

RICHARD OLNEY
SIMPLE FRENCH FOOD

Lemon Lamb Shanks

To serve 4 to 6

4 to 6	lamb shanks	4 to 6
1	garlic clove	1
1 tsp.	salt	5 ml.
½ tsp.	black pepper	2 ml.
3 tbsp.	flour	45 ml.
1 tsp.	paprika	5 ml.
2 tbsp.	shortening	30 ml.
½ cup	chicken stock *(recipe, page 164)*	125 ml.
1	bay leaf	1
4	peppercorns	4
2 tbsp.	grated lemon peel	30 ml.
1 cup	fresh lemon juice	¼ liter
	lemon wedges	

Cut the garlic clove into four to six pieces and insert the pieces into gashes made in the shanks. Season the shanks with salt and pepper. Roll the meat in the flour, combined with the paprika.

Brown the shanks in the shortening in a heavy skillet or Dutch oven. Add all of the remaining ingredients except the lemon wedges.

Cover and simmer until the meat is tender, two to two and one half hours. Turn the shanks occasionally during cooking and add more stock, if necessary. Serve garnished with the lemon wedges.

JEAN HEWITT
THE NEW YORK TIMES LARGE TYPE COOKBOOK

Braised Lamb Shanks with Lentils

To serve 4

4	lamb shanks	4
2 tbsp.	butter or olive oil	30 ml.
	salt and pepper	
2	garlic cloves	2
1	sprig thyme	1
½ cup	water or meat stock *(recipe, page 164)*	125 ml.
1½ cups	dried lentils	375 ml.
1	onion, stuck with 2 whole cloves	1
1	bay leaf	1

Sear the lamb shanks in the butter or olive oil until nicely browned. Add salt and pepper, one garlic clove, the thyme

and the ½ cup [125 ml.] of water or stock. Cover and simmer over low heat for one hour, adding more liquid if necessary.

Meanwhile, place the lentils in a saucepan with enough water to cover them by 1 inch [2½ cm.]. Add the onion, bay leaf, the remaining garlic clove and 1½ teaspoons [7 ml.] of salt. Cover, and let the lentils simmer until just tender but not mushy, about one hour. Do not let them boil.

Combine the lentils and lamb shanks in a casserole and cover with the lentil liquid and whatever liquid is left from the shanks. Place in a preheated 350° F. [180° C.] oven for 30 minutes, or until the lamb is tender. Add more water or stock if the casserole cooks dry.

JAMES A. BEARD
THE FIRESIDE COOK BOOK

Pumpkin and Lamb Shanks with Mint

This Armenian dish should be served over hot rice or steamed bulgur.

To serve 6

3 lb.	lamb shanks, cut into 2-inch [5-cm.] pieces	1½ kg.
	salt and pepper	
2	garlic cloves, finely chopped	2
1½ quarts	water	1½ liters
3 cups	puréed tomato	¾ liter
¼ cup	fresh lemon juice	50 ml.
2½ to 3 lb.	pumpkin, halved, seeded, cut into 2-inch [5-cm.] squares and peeled	1 to 1½ kg.
1	green pepper, halved, seeded, deribbed and cut into 1-inch [2½-cm.] squares	
¼ cup	chopped fresh mint leaves, or 2 tbsp. [30 ml.] crushed dried mint	50 ml.

In a large pot, sprinkle the salt, pepper and garlic over the lamb and sauté over low heat until lightly browned on all sides. Add the water and bring to a boil. Skim froth from the top as it accumulates. Add the tomato and the lemon juice, and simmer for one and one half hours, or until the meat is partially tender and can be separated from the bones.

Lift out the meat with a slotted spoon and cool. Strain the liquid in the pan and cool until the fat rises to the surface. Skim with a spoon. Remove the meat from the bones and put the meat back into the pot with the liquid.

Add the pumpkin and green pepper, and bring to a boil. Reduce the heat and simmer for one hour, until the pumpkin and meat are tender. Add more salt, pepper and lemon juice, if necessary. Add the mint and cook for one minute.

SHERYL LONDON
EGGPLANT AND SQUASH: A VERSATILE FEAST

Baked Lamb Chops with Potatoes

Costolette d'Agnello in Tortiera

To serve 6

12	baby lamb chops	12
1	onion, sliced	1
1	leek, chopped	1
1	garlic clove, chopped	1
5	fresh tomatoes, peeled, seeded and chopped, or canned tomatoes, drained and chopped	5
	salt and freshly ground black pepper	
6	potatoes, sliced	6
1 tbsp.	chopped fresh oregano or 1 tsp. [5 ml.] dried oregano	15 ml.
2 tbsp.	lard, cut into small dice	30 ml.
½ cup	meat stock (recipe, page 164)	125 ml.

Coat the inside of a heavy casserole with lard. Mix the onion, leek, garlic and tomatoes, and stew half of this mixture in the casserole until the vegetables are soft. Arrange the lamb chops on top. Sprinkle with a little more of the vegetable mixture. Season with salt and pepper. Cover the lamb with the potatoes and add the rest of the vegetable mixture. Sprinkle with the oregano, and a little salt and pepper. Dot with the diced lard. Add the stock, cover, and cook in a pre-heated 375° F. [190° C.] oven for 45 minutes. Uncover and cook for about 15 minutes more. The lamb and potatoes must be completely tender.

FRANCO LAGATTOLLA
THE RECIPES THAT MADE A MILLION

Mutton Chops with Tomatoes

If mutton chops are not obtainable, lamb shoulder-blade chops or shoulder-arm chops may be substituted.

To serve 4

4	mutton chops, cut 1 inch [2½ cm.] thick and trimmed of excess fat	4
3 or 4	large tomatoes, sliced	3 or 4
1	onion, chopped	1
	salt and pepper	
1 cup	water	¼ liter
3 tbsp.	fresh lemon juice	45 ml.
	cayenne pepper (optional)	
	chopped fresh parsley	

Put the mutton chops in a heavy pan with the tomatoes, onion, salt and pepper, and water. Cook the mixture over low heat until the chops are tender, about one hour. Take out the chops and let them drain well. Then purée the tomatoes, onion and cooking liquid through a sieve; the resulting gravy will be quite thick. Stir in the lemon juice. (A little cayenne pepper is always an improvement to the tomatoes.) Turn the chops in the gravy. Return the chops and the gravy to the pan and reheat them; bring to a boil before you dish them up, sprinkled with a little chopped parsley.

MRS. J. ATRUTEL
AN EASY AND ECONOMICAL BOOK OF JEWISH COOKERY

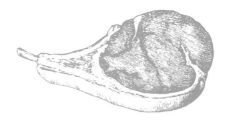

Mariner's Lamb Chops

Hammel Koteletten nach Seemansart

Hamburg parsley root is the fleshy, parsnip-shaped root of a hardy variety of parsley. If it is unavailable, substitute a small parsnip.

To serve 4

4	lamb rib chops, cut 1 inch [2½ cm.] thick and the flesh lightly flattened with a mallet	4
	salt and pepper	
1 tbsp.	butter	15 ml.
½ cup	white wine	125 ml.
½ cup	meat stock (recipe, page 164)	125 ml.
12	small boiling onions	12
¼ lb.	lean salt pork with the rind removed, blanched in boiling water for 5 minutes, drained and finely chopped	125 g.
1	carrot, finely chopped	1
1	Hamburg parsley root, finely chopped	1
1 tbsp.	finely chopped fresh savory	15 ml.
2 tbsp.	finely chopped fresh parsley	30 ml.
1 tbsp.	tarragon vinegar	15 ml.

Sprinkle the chops with salt and pepper, and fry them in the butter until lightly browned. Pour the wine and stock over the chops, add the boiling onions, cover the pan and simmer for 30 minutes.

Add the salt pork, carrot, parsley root, savory, parsley and vinegar, correct the seasoning and simmer for another 10 minutes, or until the chops and vegetables are tender.

FRED METZLER AND KLAUS OSTER
AAL BLAU UND ERRÖTHETES MÄDCHEN

Mutton Chops Braised with Ham

Côtelettes de Mouton Amoureuses

The technique of larding is demonstrated on pages 58-59.

To serve 6

6	mutton chops, cut 2 inches [5 cm.] thick	6
2 oz.	fresh pork fatback, cut into lardons	60 g.
2 tbsp.	butter	30 ml.
3 or 4	sprigs parsley	3 or 4
3 or 4	sprigs savory	3 or 4
¼ lb.	ham, cut into julienne	125 g.
2	onions, sliced	2
2	carrots, diced	2
1	parsnip, diced	1
2 tbsp.	olive oil	30 ml.
1 cup	Champagne or white wine	¼ liter
½ cup	meat stock *(recipe, page 164)*	125 ml.

Lard the chops with the pork fatback. Sauté them gently in the butter with the parsley and savory for about 15 minutes.

Meanwhile, cook the ham, onions, carrots and parsnip in the oil until the vegetables are just tender. Transfer the chops to the pan with the ham and vegetables. Deglaze the sauté pan with the Champagne or wine, and pour the deglazing liquid and the stock over the meats and vegetables. Simmer until the chops are cooked and the sauce is reduced, about 15 minutes. Transfer the chops to a warmed serving platter. Degrease the sauce and spoon it over the chops.

LE MANUEL DE LA FRIANDISE

Lancashire Hot Pot

To serve 6

6	mutton or lamb chops	6
1	bay leaf	1
7 tbsp.	lard	105 ml.
	flour	
	salt and pepper	
6	onions, chopped	6
6	medium-sized carrots, chopped	6
6	medium-sized potatoes, thickly sliced	6
12	live oysters, shucked (optional)	12
	boiling water	
	sugar	

Make a big brown flameproof earthenware pot with a fitted lid "right hot" over low heat or in a 350° F. [180° C.] oven. Put a bay leaf and 1 tablespoon [15 ml.] of the lard in the pot.

Meanwhile, flour and pepper the chops, then fry them brown on both sides in 2 tablespoons [30 ml.] of the lard. Take them out and pack them into the pot standing on their heads, thin ends up. If the chops came with kidneys attached, put them in too. Fry the onions in 2 tablespoons of the lard and pack them among the chops. Flour the carrots, then brown in the remaining lard and pack them among the onions. Put the potatoes on top, overlapping them like slates on a roof. Add pepper and salt as you go, and if you can get some oysters (do not fry these) put them under the potatoes.

Now take the fat you have fried all in, thicken it with flour and stir until brown, pour in boiling water and stir until this gravy is well cooked. Season it with pepper and salt, and then a good sprinkle of sugar (do not leave this out).

Pour in the gravy till it comes to the level of the potatoes, put on the lid and bake in a 350° F. [180° C.] oven for two hours. Shortly before dinner, take off the lid, raise the oven heat to 375° F. [190° C.] and get the potatoes "right brown."

JOAN POULSON
OLD LANCASHIRE RECIPES

Kid Stew

Civet de Chevreau

For this Italian dish, the quantity of meat may be increased if desired; kid contains a high proportion of bone.

To serve 4

2½ lb.	kid, cut into serving pieces	1¼ kg.
½ cup	oil	125 ml.
⅓ cup	chopped onion	75 ml.
5	garlic cloves, chopped	5
1¼ cups	freshly grated Parmesan cheese	300 ml.
7	sprigs parsley, tied together	7
½ cup	red wine	125 ml.
5	medium-sized potatoes, diced	5
2 cups	meat stock *(recipe, page 164)* or salted water	½ liter
	salt and pepper	

In a heavy pot, heat the oil and cook the onion until it is golden. Add the pieces of kid. When the meat is lightly browned, add the garlic, cheese and parsley. Stir in the wine and allow it to reduce by two thirds. Add the potatoes and stock or salted water. Season with salt and pepper. Cook for 25 to 30 minutes, or until the meat is tender.

Transfer the meat and potatoes to a warmed serving platter. Strain the sauce and pass it separately in a sauceboat. For a family meal, the dish may be served in the cooking pot.

PIERRE ANDROUET
LA CUISINE AU FROMAGE

Neck of Lamb with Quinces and Okra

Collier d'Agneau aux Coings et Gombos

	To serve 6	
3 lb.	lamb neck slices	1½ kg.
7 tbsp.	butter	105 ml.
5	onions, thinly sliced	5
1 tsp.	pepper	5 ml.
½ tsp.	salt	2 ml.
½ tsp.	ground saffron	2 ml.
1½ quarts	water	1½ liters
2 lb.	quinces, peeled, halved or quartered, and seeded (about 1 quart [1 liter])	1 kg.
2	tomatoes, peeled, seeded and chopped	2
1 lb.	okra, stemmed (about 2 cups [½ liter])	½ kg.

Put the lamb in a large pan with the butter, one of the onions, the pepper, salt, saffron and water. Bring to a boil, cover partially, and cook over medium heat for one hour.

Add in turn the quinces, the remaining onions, the tomatoes and finally the okra. Reduce the heat and simmer for 20 to 25 minutes, or until the meat and vegetables are tender. Put the meat in the center of a serving dish and the quinces around the edge. Pour the okra and the sauce over all.

FETTOUMA BENKIRANE
LA NOUVELLE CUISINE MAROCAINE

Irish Stew

It is quite wrong to cook carrots with this stew as the long cooking will leave them insipid. They should be cooked separately and served with the stew. The traditional accompaniment for an Irish stew is pickled red cabbage. This gives a suitable crunch to the dish and adds color.

	To serve 6	
3 lb.	lamb neck slices, trimmed of excess fat and cut through the bone into serving pieces	1½ kg.
12	medium-sized potatoes, 8 left whole and 4 thinly sliced, or 4 large mealy potatoes, thinly sliced, and 12 whole small new potatoes	12
4	large onions, sliced	4
	salt and pepper	
1	sprig thyme	1
2 cups	water	½ liter

Into a heavy pot put the thinly sliced potatoes, then a layer of sliced onions and then the pieces of lamb. Season well with salt. Add the thyme and another layer of sliced onions. Cover with the whole potatoes. Season again and add the water.

Cover the pot with foil and with a very tight-fitting lid. Cook in a preheated 350° F. [180° C.] oven for two and one half hours or simmer gently over low heat on top of the stove for the same time. Correct the seasoning. The thinly sliced potatoes at the bottom of the pot should dissolve and thicken the juice, while the potatoes on top retain their shape. This stew is very easy on the digestion.

MONICA SHERIDAN
MY IRISH COOK BOOK

Provencal Braised Lamb

La Carbounade

	To serve 6	
6	large lamb slices, cut about 1 inch [2½ cm.] thick from the sirloin end of the leg	6
6	garlic cloves, sliced	6
½ lb.	lean salt pork with the rind removed, blanched in boiling water for 5 minutes, drained, one quarter cut into lardons and the rest chopped	¼ kg.
2 tbsp.	olive oil	30 ml.
	salt and pepper	
	grated nutmeg	
1	bay leaf	1
12	boiling onions	12
1 lb.	tender baby carrots	½ kg.
1 lb.	tender baby turnips	½ kg.
1	celery heart	1
1	tomato, peeled and seeded	1
½ cup	white wine	125 ml.
6	small artichokes, trimmed, chokes removed, placed in water with lemon juice to prevent blackening	6

Using a small, sharp knife, cut slits in the lamb slices. Insert the slices of garlic and the lardons into the slits.

In a large, heavy casserole, heat the olive oil and sauté the chopped salt pork until it begins to brown. Over brisk heat, brown the lamb a few slices at a time, turning the slices until they are golden on both sides. Season with salt, pepper and a little nutmeg. Add the bay leaf, onions, carrots, turnips, celery and tomato, and sauté for a few minutes, stirring with a wooden spoon. Add the wine. Drain the artichokes and add them. Cover the casserole tightly and simmer the mixture over low heat for one and one half to two hours, or until the meat is tender.

IRÈNE LABARRE AND JEAN MERCIER
LA CUISINE DU MOUTON

Stuffed Lamb Steaks
Gefüllte Lammsteaks
To serve 4

four ½ lb.	boneless lamb leg steaks, cut about ¼ inch [6 mm.] thick and lightly flattened with a mallet	four ¼ kg.
1	garlic clove, crushed to a paste	1
1 tbsp.	chopped fresh rosemary	15 ml.
1 tbsp.	thyme	15 ml.
	salt and pepper	
4	thin slices feta cheese	4
4	slices bacon	4
½ cup	flour	125 ml.
3 tbsp.	lard or butter	45 ml.
½ cup	meat stock *(recipe, page 164)*, hot	125 ml.
½ cup	wine	125 ml.

Season the steaks with garlic, rosemary, thyme and pepper. Place a slice of cheese and a slice of bacon on each steak. Fold the steaks over and fasten them with wooden picks. Season the outsides of the steaks with the herbs and salt, and dip the steaks in the flour. Heat the lard or butter, and fry the steaks until brown. Add the stock and wine. Cover the pan and simmer gently for 20 minutes, or until the lamb is tender.

HEDWIG MARIA STUBER
ICH HELF DIR KOCHEN

Lamb Tenderloins in White Sauce
Filetti d'Agnello in Blanchette
The original version of this recipe calls for verjuice, the juice of unripe grapes. Vinegar is a suitable substitute.

To serve 4

1 lb.	whole lamb tenderloins	½ kg.
2 tbsp.	butter	30 ml.
½ lb.	fresh mushrooms, sliced (about 2½ cups [625 ml.])	¼ kg.
1	bouquet garni	1
2 tbsp.	flour	30 ml.
1 cup	meat stock *(recipe, page 164)*	¼ liter
3	egg yolks	3
½ cup	milk	125 ml.
	salt and pepper	
1 tbsp.	vinegar	15 ml.

Melt the butter in a saucepan and add the mushrooms and the bouquet garni. Mix the flour into the stock and pour the mixture into the pan. Cook over medium heat until the sauce is thickened and well reduced.

Grill the lamb tenderloins over hot coals for about 10 minutes, leaving them pink in the center. Slice them thin and add the slices to the sauce. Heat for a few minutes.

Mix the egg yolks with the milk. Off the heat, stir the yolk mixture into the sauce. Reheat it without letting the sauce boil. Season the sauce well. Immediately before serving, stir in the vinegar.

IL CUOCO PIEMONTESE RIDOTTO ALL'ULTIMO GUSTO

Mutton Stew from Ibiza
Estofado de Molto

Sobrasada, a specialty of the Balearic Islands in the Mediterranean near the coast of Spain, is a smooth-textured fresh pork sausage, spiced with cayenne pepper. If sobrasada is not available, another hot fresh sausage may be substituted.

To serve 8

6 to 9 lb.	leg of mutton, cut into serving pieces	3 to 4½ kg.
2 tbsp.	lard	30 ml.
	oil	
1 lb.	*sobrasada*, cut into small pieces	½ kg.
1	onion, sliced	1
1	tomato, peeled, seeded and sliced	1
1	garlic bulb, cloves separated and peeled	1
2 tbsp.	chopped fresh parsley	30 ml.
	salt and pepper	
	cayenne pepper	
8	medium-sized potatoes, quartered	8
4	artichoke bottoms or small artichokes	4
1 cup	freshly shelled peas	¼ liter

In a large fireproof casserole, preferably an earthenware one, brown the meat in the lard and oil. Add the sausage and brown it lightly; then add the onion, tomato, garlic and parsley. Season with the salt, pepper and cayenne pepper. Cover with water.

When the mixture begins to simmer, add the potatoes, artichokes and peas. Simmer uncovered for one to one and one half hours, or until the meat is tender, lowering the heat if necessary so the cooking liquid does not reduce too much.

JUAN CASTELLÓ GUASCH
¡BON PROFIT!

Russian Hot Pot

Tschanachi

To serve 4

1 lb.	boneless lean lamb, cut into serving pieces	½ kg.
1	onion, chopped	1
½ lb.	green beans, trimmed and sliced lengthwise	¼ kg.
5	medium-sized potatoes, peeled and sliced lengthwise	5
2	medium-sized tomatoes, halved	2
1	small eggplant, diced	1
2 tbsp.	chopped fresh coriander or parsley	30 ml.
	salt and pepper	
about 2 cups	hot water	about ½ liter

Place the meat in an earthenware casserole. Place the onion, beans and potatoes in layers over the meat. Add the tomatoes, eggplant and coriander or parsley. Season with salt and pepper, and add the hot water. Cover the casserole and bake in a preheated 350° F. [180° C.] oven for one and one half to two hours, or until tender. If necessary, add a little more hot water from time to time. Serve straight from the casserole.

KULINARISCHE GERICHTE

Lamb from the Stewpot

Agnello "a Cutturo"

The shepherds at Lucoli in central Italy, who live out in the open during the summertime, cook their lamb in a copper stewpot that is hung by an iron chain from three stakes driven into the ground.

To serve 4

2 lb.	boneless lamb shoulder or leg, cut into serving pieces	1 kg.
¼ cup	oil	50 ml.
2 tbsp.	lard	30 ml.
2	large onions, chopped	2
¼ cup	chopped fresh parsley	50 ml.
4	fresh sage leaves, chopped	4
	salt and pepper	
4	thick slices firm-textured white bread	4

Heat the oil and lard in a heavy enameled iron casserole. Place the meat in the casserole and add the onions, parsley

and sage. Season with salt and pepper. Cover and cook the mixture over low heat until the meat is tender, about one and one half hours. (Add water if the pieces dry up too much.)

Place the slices of bread in individual soup plates. When the meat is cooked, pour the broth and the meat over the bread, and serve.

NICE CORTELLI LUCREZI
LE RICETTE DELLA NONNA

Lamb Stew Sans Pareil

To serve 8

4 lb.	boneless leg of lamb, cut into 2-inch [5-cm.] pieces, all gristle and fat removed	2 kg.
¼ cup	olive oil	50 ml.
½ cup	Cognac	125 ml.
2	medium-sized onions, finely chopped	2
1	garlic clove, finely chopped	1
1 tsp.	finely chopped fresh tarragon or ½ tsp. [2 ml.] dried tarragon	5 ml.
1½ cups	white wine	375 ml.
3	medium-sized tomatoes, peeled, seeded and chopped	3
about 2 cups	meat stock (recipe, page 164)	about ½ liter
6	parsley sprigs, 4 tied together, 2 finely chopped	6
	salt and freshly ground pepper	
2	lemons, thinly sliced, slices quartered	2

In a heavy 5-quart [5-liter] casserole, brown the lamb pieces in the olive oil over brisk heat until colored on all sides. Add the Cognac and cook for another three minutes. Add the onions, garlic, tarragon, wine, tomatoes and stock. The lamb should be just covered with liquid; if it is not, add additional stock to cover. Tuck in the sprigs of parsley and season with salt and pepper.

Bring the mixture to a boil, stirring a bit. Reduce the heat, cover, and simmer for one and one half hours. Discard the parsley sprigs after one hour. Lift the lid now and then and skim off the fat that rises to the top. When the meat is tender, remove it with a slotted spoon and keep it warm.

Transfer the sauce to a small saucepan and cook over medium heat until reduced by about one third. This should take about 30 minutes. From time to time, skim off the skin that forms on the top of the sauce.

Return the meat to the casserole and lay the quartered lemon slices on top. Pour in the sauce and simmer, gently, over low heat for 15 to 20 minutes. Sprinkle with chopped parsley and serve.

DORIS TOBIAS AND MARY MERRIS
THE GOLDEN LEMON

Dutch Lamb Stew

Schaperagoût

To serve 6

2 lb.	boneless lean lamb, cubed	1 kg.
¼ lb.	lean salt pork with the rind removed, blanched for 5 minutes, drained and diced	125 g.
4 tbsp.	butter	60 ml.
3 or 4	onions, chopped	3 or 4
½ tsp.	grated nutmeg	2 ml.
2	carrots, diced	2
2	turnips, diced	2
1	bunch celery, separated into ribs, trimmed and sliced	1
1	head green cabbage, halved, cored and cut into thin shreds	1
1	leek, white part only, sliced	1
2½ cups	meat stock (recipe, page 164) or water	600 ml.
6	medium-sized potatoes, peeled and quartered	6

In a large pan, brown the lamb and salt pork in the butter. Remove the meats from the pan, pour off the excess fat, add the onions and cook for 10 minutes, or until golden. Return the meats to the pan with the nutmeg, carrots, turnips, celery, cabbage, leek, and the stock or water. Cover, and simmer over low heat for one hour, or until the meat is nearly tender. Arrange the potatoes in a layer on the meat, cover, and cook for 30 minutes, or until the potatoes are done.

ONS KOOKBOEK

Fricassee of Spring Lamb Valentine

Blanquette d'Agneau de Printemps à la Valentinoise

To serve 4

2 lb.	lamb breast and rib roast, cut into serving pieces	1 kg.
3 tbsp.	olive oil or butter	45 ml.
2 tbsp.	flour	30 ml.
	salt and pepper	
1 or 2	onions, each stuck with a whole clove	1 or 2
1	bouquet garni, including a garlic clove	1
3	egg yolks	3
3 tbsp.	fresh lemon juice	45 ml.
	chopped fresh parsley	

Put the lamb in a saucepan, cover with cold water and place over high heat. When the water comes to a boil, drain the lamb, plunge it into cold water and drain it again. Heat the oil or butter, add the lamb, cover and cook for about five minutes. Sprinkle with the flour and stir until all of the lamb pieces are coated with flour. Add enough hot water to cover the lamb completely. Add salt, pepper, the onions and the bouquet garni. Cover and cook over low heat for one and a half hours, or until the meat begins to fall off the bones.

Transfer the pieces of lamb to a deep, heated serving dish. Beat the egg yolks and lemon juice lightly with a few spoonfuls of the cooking liquid and, off the heat, gradually stir this mixture into the pan. Cook for a minute or two, without boiling, until the sauce thickens. Sieve the sauce onto the lamb, sprinkle with parsley and serve.

PAUL BOUILLARD
LA CUISINE AU COIN DU FEU

White Lamb Stew

Blanquette d'Agneau

To serve 6

4 to 6 lb.	lamb shoulder, cut into serving pieces without boning	2 to 3 kg.
	salt	
4	medium-sized carrots, cut into pieces	4
3	medium-sized turnips, cut into pieces	3
3	leeks, cut into ¾-inch [2-cm.] lengths	3
2	garlic cloves, crushed to a paste	2
3 tbsp.	butter	45 ml.
1 tbsp.	flour	15 ml.
2	sprigs thyme	2
1 tbsp.	fines herbes	15 ml.
2	egg yolks	2

Place the lamb in a saucepan and cover it with water. Salt the water lightly. Bring to a boil, skim, then add the carrots, turnips, leeks and garlic. Partially cover the pan and simmer the lamb for one and one half hours.

Remove the lamb and strain the cooking liquid, discarding the vegetables. In a clean pan, melt the butter, stir in the flour, then stir in 2 cups [½ liter] of the warm cooking liquid. Cook this sauce until it thickens to the consistency of light cream. Add the lamb and the thyme sprigs, and cook for 15 minutes. Add the fines herbes and cook for two minutes. Remove the thyme.

In a bowl, mix the egg yolks with a little of the sauce. Off the heat, gradually stir the yolk mixture into the pan. Return to the heat for 10 seconds, without letting the sauce boil. Serve in a deep serving dish.

ÉDOUARD DE POMIANE
LE CARNET D'ANNA

Lamb Breast Stew

Aricot de Poitrine de Mouton

To serve 4 to 6

4 to 6 lb.	lamb breast, trimmed of excess fat and cut into serving pieces	2 to 3 kg.
¼ lb.	salt pork with the rind removed, blanched in boiling water for 5 minutes, drained and cut into strips	125 g.
9	small turnips	9
1 tbsp.	flour	15 ml.
1 cup	meat stock (recipe, page 164)	¼ liter
1	bouquet garni	1
	salt and pepper	
1 tbsp.	vinegar	15 ml.
	croutons (recipe, page 167), fried in butter	

In a sauté pan, brown the lamb with the salt-pork strips and transfer the lamb to a saucepan. Brown the turnips lightly with the salt pork, sprinkle them with the flour and add them to the lamb. Deglaze the sauté pan with the stock and pour the liquid into the saucepan. Season with the bouquet garni, salt, pepper and vinegar. Cover the saucepan and simmer gently for one to one and one half hours, or until the meat is tender. Degrease the sauce and discard the bouquet garni. Serve the stew garnished with croutons.

PIERRE DE LUNE
LE NOUVEAU CUISINIER

Braised Lamb or Kid

Agneddu o Caprettu Agglassatu

To serve 8

4 lb.	boneless lamb or kid, trimmed of excess fat and cut into serving pieces	2 kg.
1	onion, thinly sliced	1
⅓ cup	olive oil	75 ml.
6 tbsp.	lard	90 ml.
¼ cup	chopped fresh parsley	50 ml.
6	garlic cloves, chopped	6
	salt and pepper	
¾ cup	red wine or 1 cup [¼ liter] chicken stock (recipe, page 164)	175 ml.
2 lb.	new potatoes, cut up (optional)	1 kg.
6 oz.	pecorino Romano or other firm sheep's-milk cheese	175 g.

Fry the onion in the oil in a deep pan and, when it begins to brown, add the lard, parsley, garlic and the pieces of meat.

Stirring continuously, continue cooking until all of the ingredients have browned all over.

For lamb in red wine, season with salt and pepper, pour in the red wine and cover the pan. Cook gently for one hour, or until the meat is tender. For lamb in stock, pour the stock over the meat, add the potatoes, season with salt and pepper, cover, and cook over gentle heat for about an hour, or until the meat is tender.

Cut about half of the cheese into small pieces and grate the rest. Five minutes before serving, add all of the cheese to the sauce to thicken it.

PINO CORRENTI
IL LIBRO D'ORO DELLA CUCINA E DEI VINI DI SICILIA

Tuscan Lamb Fricassee

Fricassée d'Agneau à la Toscane

In culinary terms, a liaison is any thickening agent for a sauce or broth. Here, the liaison is based on egg yolks.

To serve 8

4 lb.	boneless lean lamb, cubed	2 kg.
3½ oz.	lean salt pork with the rind removed, blanched in boiling water for 5 minutes, drained and chopped	100 g.
½ cup	oil	125 ml.
	salt and pepper	
1	onion, chopped	1
2	garlic cloves	2
1	bouquet garni	1
Egg liaison		
8	egg yolks	8
⅔ cup	freshly grated Parmesan cheese	150 ml.
½ cup	heavy cream	125 ml.
3 tbsp.	fresh lemon juice	45 ml.
1 tbsp.	flour	15 ml.

Put the salt pork into a skillet and set it over low heat until the fat begins to run. Add the oil and increase the heat. Season the lamb with salt and pepper. Brown it in the pork fat and oil, then add the onion, garlic cloves and bouquet garni. Cover, and cook over very low heat until the lamb is tender, about half an hour. Remove the pan from the heat. Drain off the excess oil from the pan and discard the garlic cloves and bouquet garni.

Beat together all of the ingredients for the liaison and stir this mixture into the pan containing the lamb. Return the pan to low heat and, stirring constantly, cook until the sauce thickens.

LOUIS MONOD
LA CUISINE FLORENTINE

Lamb with Artichokes and Broad Beans

Tajine de Viande aux Artichauts et Fèves (Mqualli)

To serve 6 to 8

3 lb.	lamb shoulder or rib roast, cut into serving pieces	1 ½ kg.
1 ½ tsp.	ground ginger	7 ml.
1 tsp.	ground saffron	5 ml.
1	garlic clove, lightly crushed	1
½ cup	oil	125 ml.
	salt	
6 to 8	medium-sized artichokes, leaves and chokes trimmed off, bottoms rubbed with lemon juice	6 to 8
2 lb.	broad beans, shelled	1 kg.
1	preserved lemon (recipe, page 166), quartered	1
10	ripe olives (preferably Mediterranean-style olives), pitted	10
3 tbsp.	fresh lemon juice	45 ml.

Place the lamb pieces, ginger, saffron, garlic, oil and salt in a large saucepan. Cover with water, bring to a boil, reduce the heat, cover and cook for two hours, or until the meat is tender. During cooking add boiling water, if necessary, to keep the meat immersed.

Remove the meat. Put the artichoke bottoms in another saucepan, pour in half of the lamb cooking liquid and enough additional water to cover the artichokes. Bring the liquid to a boil, then simmer the artichokes gently until tender, about 15 minutes. Remove the artichoke bottoms with a slotted spoon and boil the liquid to reduce it to a thick sauce, about 10 minutes. Check the seasoning.

Meanwhile, cook the beans in the remaining lamb cooking liquid and enough additional water to cover them, for five minutes, or until tender. Lift out the beans and boil the liquid to reduce it to a thick sauce.

Combine the lamb, artichoke bottoms, beans and reduced cooking liquids in the large saucepan. Add the preserved lemon and the olives. Simmer over low heat for about 15 minutes to reheat the meat and vegetables. Transfer the lamb to a round serving dish and cover it with the vegetables. Sprinkle with the lemon juice, pour the sauce over everything and serve very hot.

LATIFA BENNANI SMIRES
LA CUISINE MAROCAINE

Avignon-Style Lamb Stew

Daube de Mouton à l'Avignonnaise

Sliced salt pork, blanched for five minutes, can be used instead of pork fat to line the pot. Cepes and the vegetables from the marinade can be added to the stew with the onion and diced salt pork.

To serve 6 to 8

3 to 4 lb.	boneless leg or shoulder of lamb, cut into 2-inch [5-cm.] cubes	1 ½ to 2 kg.
¼ lb.	fresh pork fatback, half thinly sliced and half cut into lardons	125 g.
	mixed spices	
2 tbsp.	brandy	30 ml.
2 tbsp.	chopped fresh parsley	30 ml.
2 cups	red wine	½ liter
½ cup	olive oil	125 ml.
4	onions, finely chopped	4
2	carrots, chopped	2
2	garlic cloves, lightly crushed	2
2	sprigs thyme	2
1	bay leaf	1
1	sprig parsley	1
¼ lb.	lean salt pork with the rind removed, blanched in boiling water for 5 minutes, drained and diced	125 g.
¼ lb.	fresh pork rind, blanched in boiling water for 15 minutes, drained and cut into small pieces	125 g.
	salt	
1	bouquet garni, including a piece of dried orange peel	1
2 cups	meat stock (recipe, page 164), made with lamb bones	½ liter
⅔ cup	flour, mixed to a paste with about ⅓ cup [75 ml.] water	150 ml.

Toss the lardons of pork fatback in mixed spices, sprinkle them with brandy and coat them with chopped parsley. Lard each piece of lamb in the direction of the grain with a lardon.

Place the lamb in a bowl with the wine, oil, half the chopped onions and the carrots, garlic, thyme, bay leaf and parsley sprig.

After two hours, remove the lamb from the marinade and place it—in layers—in an earthenware pot that has been lined with slices of pork fat. Sprinkle each layer of lamb with the remaining chopped onions, diced salt pork and pork rind. Season each layer with salt and mixed spices. Put the bouquet garni in the center of the middle layer of meat. Pour the liquid from the marinade over the meat. Pour in the stock. Place the remaining slices of pork fat on top. Cover the pot tightly with its lid and seal on the lid with a strip of flour-and-water paste or with foil.

Place in a preheated 250° F. [120° C.] oven and cook for five hours. Serve the stew straight from the pot.

70 MÉDECINS DE FRANCE
LE TRÉSOR DE LA CUISINE DU BASSIN MÉDITERRANÉEN

Eggplant Royal-Style
Patlijan Hunkar

To serve 4

1 lb.	boneless lean lamb, cut into 1-inch [2½-cm.] cubes	½ kg.
1 tbsp.	butter	15 ml.
1	small onion, chopped	1
2 tbsp.	puréed tomato	30 ml.
1 cup	water	¼ liter
	salt and pepper	
2	large eggplants	2
⅓ cup	chopped celery	75 ml.

Cheese sauce

1 tbsp.	grated Gruyère cheese	15 ml.
2 tbsp.	butter	30 ml.
2 tbsp.	flour	30 ml.
1 cup	milk	¼ liter

Sauté the lamb in the butter and, when brown, add the onion and continue to sauté until the onion is golden in color. Add the puréed tomato, water, salt and pepper, and mix together. Cover the pan and cook over medium heat or bake in a preheated 350° F. [180° C.] oven for about one hour.

Meanwhile, broil the eggplants. Do not be alarmed when the skin gets black or burned. When the eggplants are soft, drop them into cold water to make them easier to handle. Peel off the skin and mash the flesh.

For the sauce, melt the butter in a saucepan, stir in the flour and brown lightly. Gradually add the milk, then cook, stirring, until a smooth, thick sauce is formed. Stir in the grated cheese.

Add this sauce to the mashed eggplant and beat well until the mixture is about the consistency of light, fluffy mashed potatoes. Reheat the mixture in the oven or in a steamer and pile on dinner plates with a ladleful of lamb sauté on top of each serving. Sprinkle the chopped celery on top of the meat.

GEORGE MARDIKIAN
DINNER AT OMAR KHAYYAM'S

Lamb Shoulder with Eggplant Purée
Épaule aux Aubergines

To serve 6

3 lb.	boneless lamb shoulder, cut into pieces	1½ kg.
½ tsp.	salt	2 ml.
1 tsp.	pepper	5 ml.
½ tsp.	ground saffron	2 ml.
2	onions, thinly sliced	2
2	garlic cloves, crushed to a paste	2
½ cup	oil	125 ml.
1½ quarts	water	1½ liters

Eggplant purée

4 lb.	eggplants, peeled, cut into slices ½ inch [1 cm.] thick	2 kg.
½ cup	oil	125 ml.
8	medium-sized tomatoes, peeled, seeded and chopped	8
4	garlic cloves, crushed to a paste	4
2 tbsp.	chopped fresh parsley	30 ml.
2 tbsp.	chopped fresh coriander leaves	30 ml.
½ tsp.	ground cumin	2 ml.
½ tsp.	salt	2 ml.

Put the lamb into a casserole with the salt and pepper, saffron, onions, garlic and oil. Add the water, bring to a boil, cover partially, and cook over medium heat for 45 minutes to an hour, or until the meat is very tender.

Meanwhile, fry the eggplant slices in the oil until golden brown on both sides, about five minutes. Drain the slices on paper towels and use a fork to mash them into a purée while they are still hot.

Put the tomatoes into a pan with the garlic, parsley, coriander, cumin and salt. Stirring frequently, cook uncovered over medium heat for 10 minutes, or until thick and pulpy. Add the eggplant purée and, stirring constantly, cook until all excess liquid has evaporated.

Serve the meat covered with the eggplant purée and sprinkled with the braising liquid.

FETTOUMA BENKIRANE
LA NOUVELLE CUISINE MAROCAINE

Braised Lamb with Vegetables

If rice wine is not available, a dry sherry can be substituted.

To serve 4

1 lb.	boneless lean lamb, thinly sliced	½ kg.
1 tbsp.	oil	15 ml.
1	garlic clove, finely chopped	1
3	green peppers, halved, seeded, deribbed and cut lengthwise into quarters or eighths	3
4	scallions, green tops included, cut diagonally into ½-inch [1-cm.] lengths	4
¼ cup	light soy sauce	50 ml.
2 tbsp.	Japanese rice wine	30 ml.
1 tbsp.	white wine vinegar	15 ml.
¼ tsp.	cayenne pepper	1 ml.
1 tsp.	grated lemon peel	5 ml.

Heat the oil in a skillet and add the garlic and lamb. Fry for a minute or two, then add the green peppers and scallions. Fry for another minute and add the soy sauce, rice wine, vinegar, cayenne pepper and lemon peel. Cook the mixture for three to four minutes longer, then transfer it to a warmed serving dish and serve immediately.

PETER AND JOAN MARTIN
JAPANESE COOKING

Lamb or Kid with Asparagus Tips

L'Agneau ou le Chevreau aux Pointes d'Asperges

To serve 4

2 lb.	boneless lamb or kid shoulder or rib roast, cut into 1½-inch [4-cm.] pieces	1 kg.
½ cup	oil or 4 tbsp. [60 ml.] lard and 4 tbsp. oil	125 ml.
	salt and pepper	
2 or 3	garlic cloves, unpeeled	2 or 3
	thyme	
	basil	
2 cups	dry white wine, or water mixed with 2 tbsp. [30 ml.] fresh lemon juice	½ liter
1 lb.	asparagus, tips broken off, stalks discarded	½ kg.
1 tbsp.	fresh lemon juice	15 ml.
2	egg yolks, lightly beaten	2

Sauté the pieces of meat in 4 tablespoons [60 ml.] of the oil or in the lard. Season with salt and pepper, add the garlic and a pinch each of thyme and basil, then pour in the wine or lemon water. Cover and cook over low heat for 45 minutes to one hour, until the meat is tender.

Meanwhile, cook the asparagus tips in a covered pan with the remaining oil until they are lightly glazed and barely tender, about two or three minutes.

Discard the garlic cloves and correct the seasoning of the meat. Add the asparagus tips in their oil and the lemon juice. Simmer for six minutes. Stir a spoonful of the sauce into the egg yolks, then remove the pan from the heat and gradually stir the yolk mixture into the sauce. Return the pan to the heat for a minute or two to thicken the sauce, without letting it come to a boil. Serve very hot.

ALBIN MARTY
FOURMIGUETTO: SOUVENIRS, CONTES ET RECETTES DU LANGUEDOC

Spring Lamb with Lettuce Leaves

Kapama

To serve 8

6 lb.	leg of lamb, sawed into 3-inch [8-cm.] chunks, including the bone	3 kg.
36	scallions, including the green tops, cut into 2-inch [5-cm.] lengths	36
1	onion, cut into 8 pieces	1
1	large carrot, cut into 2-inch [5-cm.] lengths	1
2	large heads Boston lettuce, cored and the leaves separated	2
2	large heads romaine lettuce, cored and the leaves separated	2
½	lemon	½
2 tbsp.	butter	30 ml.
½ tbsp.	sugar	7 ml.
	salt	
1 cup	water	¼ liter
¼ cup	finely cut fresh dill leaves	50 ml.

Spread the scallion, onion and carrot pieces on the bottom of a large heavy saucepan. Place the lettuce leaves evenly over the other vegetables. Do not be alarmed by the bulk; lettuce diminishes as it cooks. Trim all of the fat from the lamb and rub the chunks with lemon. Place the lamb on top of the lettuce leaves. Add the butter, sugar, a little salt and the water. Cover and cook over very low heat for about two and one half to three hours, or until the meat is tender and about 2 cups [½ liter] of liquid remain in the saucepan. Add the dill and cook for five minutes more.

Serve immediately, pouring one or two spoonfuls of the cooking liquid over each serving. Serve with warmed bread.

NEŞET EREN
THE ART OF TURKISH COOKING

Lamb with Vegetables
Hammelfleisch mit Gemüse

To serve 4

1 lb.	lamb including the bone, cut into large pieces	½ kg.
5	medium-sized potatoes, 2 or 3 whole and the others thickly sliced	5
	salt	
2	carrots, diced	2
1	onion, thinly sliced	1
1	kohlrabi, thickly sliced	1
1½ cups	shredded cabbage	375 ml.
2	bay leaves	2
	ground black pepper	
2	whole cloves	2
	chopped fresh parsley or dill	

Place the meat in a pan and cover with water. Cover the pan and bring to a boil. Add the whole potatoes. Add salt, reduce the heat, cover, and simmer for one hour, or until the meat is tender. If necessary, add water to keep the meat covered.

Remove the meat from the pan. Remove the bones. Slice or dice the meat and place it in another pan. Add the remaining vegetables in layers, including the sliced potatoes. Add the bay leaves, a pinch of pepper and the cloves.

Sieve the whole potatoes and stir them back into the cooking liquid. Pour the liquid over the meat and vegetables. Cover and simmer for 30 to 40 minutes, or until the vegetables are tender. Sprinkle with parsley or dill, and serve.

KULINARISCHE GERICHTE

Lamb Hungarian-Style
Agneau à la Hongroise

To serve 6 to 8

3 to 4 lb.	lamb breast, cut into oblong pieces	1½ to 2 kg.
12	medium-sized Spanish onions, sliced	12
7 tbsp.	butter	105 ml.
1 tbsp.	sugar	15 ml.
	salt, pepper and cayenne pepper	
1½ tbsp.	flour	22 ml.
1½ tbsp.	Hungarian paprika	22 ml.
1	bouquet garni	1
1 quart	beef stock *(recipe, page 164)*	1 liter

In a large, heavy pan, cook the onions in half of the butter, slowly at first, until they soften. Sprinkle on the sugar, increase the heat, and stir until the onions are lightly caramelized to an appetizing brown.

In another pan, at the same time, brown the pieces of lamb in the remaining butter. Season with salt, pepper and cayenne. When the onions are right, stir in the flour, paprika and bouquet garni. Cook for a few minutes, then add enough stock to make a creamy sauce. Put in the meat, and cover.

Simmer for at least one and one quarter hours, or until the meat begins to fall from the bones. Every quarter of an hour check on the liquid and thickness, adding a tumbler more of stock when necessary. This way of cooking means you have a sauce with a good strong flavor; if you take the lid off the pan after 30 minutes, the sauce will reduce even more, but you will have to add extra stock more frequently.

Before serving, check the seasoning, adding a little more cayenne if you like. Skim or blot away the surface fat.

JANE GRIGSON
FOOD WITH THE FAMOUS

Lamb Stew with Olives
Le Salabondin

To serve 4

2 lb.	lamb breast and shoulder or lamb rib roast, cut into serving pieces	1 kg.
¼ lb.	lean salt pork with the rind removed, blanched in boiling water for 5 minutes, drained and diced	125 g.
2 tbsp.	oil	30 ml.
2	onions, thinly sliced	2
6	tomatoes, peeled, seeded and diced	6
	salt and pepper	
about 4 cups	water	about 1 liter
4	medium-sized potatoes, peeled and quartered	4
1½ cups	ripe olives (preferably Mediterranean-style olives), blanched in boiling water for 10 minutes and pitted	375 ml.

Place the salt pork in a saucepan with the oil and cook over low heat until the fat runs. Increase the heat, add the lamb and brown the pieces on all sides. Stir in the onions, then the tomatoes, salt and pepper. Cover with water. Cover and bring to a boil, then reduce the heat and simmer for 30 minutes. Add the potatoes and olives. Cook for 30 minutes longer—adding more water if necessary—until the lamb and the potatoes are tender. Correct the seasoning, which should be rather peppery.

SUZANNE SIMONET
LE GRAND LIVRE DE LA CUISINE OCCITANE

Lamb and Potato Stew
Ragoût aux Pommes de Terre

To serve 4 to 6

2 to 3 lb.	lamb breast, cut into serving pieces	1 to 1½ kg.
4 tbsp.	butter	60 ml.
2	onions, 1 chopped, 1 left whole and stuck with 2 or 3 whole cloves	2
⅓ cup	flour	75 ml.
2 cups	meat stock *(recipe, page 164)*, heated	½ liter
	salt and pepper	
1	bouquet garni, including rosemary	1
3	carrots, sliced	3
1	turnip, diced	1
1	rutabaga, diced	1
6	potatoes	6

Melt the butter in a large cast-iron casserole. When it is hot, add the lamb and brown the pieces on all sides. Add the chopped onion and brown it. Sprinkle on the flour and, when it is absorbed, stir in the stock.

Season with salt and pepper, and add the bouquet garni, carrots, turnip, rutabaga and the whole onion. Cover and cook over low heat for one hour. Add the potatoes and continue to cook for a further one and a half hours. Remove the bouquet garni and the whole onion, and serve the stew.

LES PETITS PLATS ET LES GRANDS

Mutton Breast Baked with Rice and Potatoes

To serve 4

3 to 4 lb.	mutton breast, trimmed of fat and cut into serving pieces	1½ to 2 kg.
1	onion, sliced	1
	salt and pepper	
¼ tsp.	ground saffron	1 ml.
1 cup	raw unprocessed long-grain rice	¼ liter
4	medium-sized potatoes, thickly sliced	4
about 3 cups	water	about ¾ liter
1 tbsp.	chopped fresh parsley	15 ml.
1 tbsp.	chopped fresh marjoram or dried marjoram	15 ml.

Put the onion at the bottom of a deep baking dish; add salt, pepper and the saffron. Add the rice and potatoes to the dish, then put in the pieces of mutton. Fill the dish with the water,

add the herbs, cover the dish and put it in a preheated 325° F. [160° C.] oven. Bake for about one and one half hours, then uncover the dish and bake for a further 30 minutes, or until the mutton is tender and all of the water is absorbed.

MRS. J. ATRUTEL
AN EASY AND ECONOMICAL BOOK OF JEWISH COOKERY

Lamb Stew with Potatoes
Navarin de Mouton aux Pommes

The technique of preparing artichoke bottoms is demonstrated on page 57.

In addition to the boiling onions and new potatoes, you can add such vegetables as freshly shelled peas, blanched and lightly sautéed carrots and turnips, or blanched and drained lettuce heads, celery ribs or artichoke bottoms.

To serve 6

2½ lb.	boneless lamb shoulder, trimmed of fat and cut into 12 pieces	1¼ kg.
	salt and pepper	
1 tbsp.	lard or oil	15 ml.
1	large onion, stuck with 1 or 2 whole cloves	1
4	carrots, quartered	4
2	garlic cloves	2
1	whole clove	1
1	bouquet garni, including a celery rib	1
½ cup	flour	125 ml.
2	small tomatoes, coarsely chopped	2
⅔ cup	white wine (optional)	150 ml.
½ lb.	small boiling onions	¼ kg.
7 tbsp.	butter	105 ml.
	sugar	
2 lb.	small new potatoes, peeled to equal size	1 kg.

Salt and pepper the meat. Heat the lard or oil in a large saucepan. Put in the meat, the large onion, carrots, garlic, clove and bouquet garni. Sauté quickly until brown.

Sprinkle in the flour, stir, and transfer the mixture to a heavy casserole. Put the casserole, uncovered, into a preheated 400° F. [200° C.] oven and leave it for five minutes. Remove the casserole from the oven and spoon out all accumulated fat. Add the tomatoes and the wine, if using, and fill the casserole with water just to the top of its contents. Lightly salt the mixture, bring to a boil and skim it. Cover the casserole and return it to the oven, reducing the heat to 350° F. [180° C.]. Cook for one hour.

Meanwhile, place the small onions in a saucepan with the butter, salt and a pinch of sugar. Cook over low heat until the onions are golden brown and glazed—about 20 minutes.

Transfer the meat to a sauté pan and put the potatoes and onions on top. Strain and degrease the sauce and pour it into the pan, adding water if necessary to cover the vegetables. Cover the pan with buttered paper, put on the lid, and cook over medium heat until the potatoes and lamb are done, about 20 minutes. Correct the seasoning and serve.

H. HEYRAUD
LA CUISINE À NICE

Lamb Stew with Peas
Agneshkos Grah

To serve 5

1½ lb.	boneless lamb, cut into serving pieces	¾ kg.
5 tbsp.	rendered lamb fat or butter	75 ml.
1	large onion, finely chopped	1
¼ cup	flour	50 ml.
2	medium-sized tomatoes, peeled, seeded and chopped	2
1 tsp.	paprika	5 ml.
1 cup	warm water	¼ liter
2 cups	freshly shelled peas (about 2 lb. [1 kg.] before shelling)	½ liter
	salt	
	finely cut fresh dill	

Heat the fat or butter in a large saucepan; brown the meat pieces in it, then lift them out with a slotted spoon. In the same fat, fry the onions until they are translucent. Add the flour and fry until it turns gold. Add the tomatoes and, when the sauce has reduced, stir in the paprika. Return the meat to the pan and pour in the water. Cover and simmer for one hour. Add the peas and salt, and simmer until the meat and peas are tender. Serve hot, sprinkled with dill.

SONYA CHORTANOVA
NASHA KUCHNIYA

Lamb with Peas
Agneau Sauté aux Petits-Pois

To serve 6

4 to 6 lb.	lamb shoulder, cut into serving pieces	2 to 3 kg.
10 tbsp.	butter	150 ml.
3 cups	freshly shelled peas	¾ liter
1⅓ cups	meat stock *(recipe, page 164)*	325 ml.
1	sprig parsley	1
	salt	

Melt half of the butter in a sauté pan. Add the lamb and brown over high heat for five minutes, turning the pieces to brown them evenly. Cover the pan and cook over medium heat for 45 minutes to one hour, or until the lamb is tender.

Meanwhile, put the remaining butter into a saucepan, add the peas and place over high heat. When the butter has melted, add the stock and the parsley. Bring the stock to a boil, then reduce the heat and cook the peas over low heat for another 10 minutes, or until done.

When the lamb and peas are both cooked, mix the two together. Remove the parsley, add salt to taste and serve in a warmed, deep serving dish.

JEANNE SAVARIN (EDITOR)
LA CUISINE DES FAMILLES

Mutton with Pumpkin Sauce
Mderbel

To serve 2 or 3

1 lb.	boneless mutton, cut into 5 pieces	½ kg.
1	leek, cut into 5 pieces	1
2 tsp.	salt	10 ml.
1 tsp.	ground ginger	5 ml.
1 tsp.	ground saffron	5 ml.
1 cup	water	¼ liter
2 cups	olive oil	½ liter
1 lb.	peeled pumpkin, thinly sliced (about 3 cups [¾ liter])	½ kg.
2 tsp.	ground cinnamon	10 ml.
2 tbsp.	sugar	30 ml.

Mix in a cooking pot the mutton, leek, salt, ginger, saffron, water and half of the olive oil. Cover and simmer for about two hours, or until the mutton is tender.

In the meantime, put the rest of the olive oil in a frying pan to get smoking hot. Cook in it the pumpkin, turning the slices until well browned; this will take about 45 minutes. Then crush the pumpkin in a dish, and mix with it the cinnamon and sugar.

When the meat is cooked, take it out of the pot and put it in a deep plate. Mix the liquid from the pot with the pumpkin, put this over the mutton and so serve.

JOHN, FOURTH MARQUIS OF BUTE (EDITOR)
MOORISH RECIPES

POACHING, BRAISING AND STEWING

Tunisian Lamb Stew

Takfifa

To serve 6

6 to 8 lb.	lamb shoulder, boned and cut into serving pieces	3 to 4 kg.
½ lb.	pumpkin, halved, seeded, cut into pieces and peeled	¼ kg.
1	medium-sized cabbage, halved, cored and thickly sliced	1
½ cup	olive oil	125 ml.
	salt	
	ground coriander	
1 tbsp.	harissa sauce (recipe, page 165)	15 ml.

Sauté the pumpkin and cabbage in the oil for a few minutes. Add the lamb, and season with salt, a good pinch of coriander and the *harissa* sauce. Pour in enough water to come just to the top level of the meat. Cover, and cook over low heat for two hours, or until tender.

LÉON ISNARD
LA GASTRONOMIE AFRICAINE

Lamb Shoulder with Cauliflower

Épaule d'Agneau aux Choux-Fleurs

To serve 6

3 lb.	boneless lamb shoulder, cut into pieces	1½ kg.
½ cup	oil	125 ml.
3	onions, thinly sliced	3
3	garlic cloves, chopped	3
½ tsp.	ground ginger	2 ml.
½ tsp.	salt	2 ml.
¼ tsp.	ground saffron	1 ml.
1½ quarts	water	1½ liters
1	medium-sized cauliflower, cored and broken into florets	1
2 tbsp.	chopped fresh coriander leaves	30 ml.
2 tbsp.	chopped fresh parsley	30 ml.
1 tbsp.	paprika	15 ml.
½ tsp.	ground cumin	2 ml.

Put the lamb in a large pan with the oil, onions and garlic. Season with the ginger, salt and saffron, and add the water. Bring to a boil, cover the pan partially, and reduce the heat

to medium. Stirring occasionally, cook the lamb for one hour, or until tender.

Add the cauliflower, coriander, parsley, paprika and cumin. Simmer gently without stirring for 15 to 20 minutes, or until the cauliflower is just tender.

Serve the meat, surrounded by the cauliflower, on a round serving dish. Pour the sauce over all.

FETTOUMA BENKIRANE
LA NOUVELLE CUISINE MAROCAINE

Lamb Stew with Turnips

Haricot de Mouton

The name of this dish comes from the old French "halicoter," which means "to cut up finely."

To serve 4

4 to 6 lb.	lamb breast, trimmed of excess fat and cut into 12 or 16 equal-sized pieces	2 to 3 kg.
2	medium-sized onions, sliced	2
3	carrots, coarsely chopped	3
1	sprig thyme	1
1	bay leaf	1
2½ cups	meat stock (recipe, page 164)	625 ml.
	salt and pepper	
4 or 5	turnips, cut into pieces	4 or 5
4 tbsp.	butter	60 ml.

Cover the bottom of a heavy casserole with the onions, carrots, thyme and bay leaf. Lay the meat on top. Sprinkle with half of the stock. Cook uncovered over low heat for about 40 minutes, or until most of the liquid has evaporated. Add the remaining stock, season with salt and pepper, cover, and simmer for two hours over very low heat.

Meanwhile, fry the turnips in the butter for about 20 minutes, until they are browned and tender.

Take the pieces of lamb from the casserole and remove the largest bones. Strain the cooking liquid, degrease it carefully, and reduce it over high heat if necessary to achieve the desired consistency. Place the lamb and turnips in a warmed serving dish, pour the sauce over them, and serve very hot.

JULES BRETEUIL
LE CUISINIER EUROPÉEN

Algerian Lamb Couscous

Kesksou 'l-qbâyel

A version of ras el hanout, a Morrocan spice mixture, can be made by combining equal pinches of ground allspice, cinnamon, ginger, nutmeg, cardamom, black pepper and cloves.

If you do not have a couscoussier, you can use a steamer or a cheesecloth-lined colander set inside a pot that is large enough to hold it snugly.

To serve 6

2 lb.	lamb, cut into pieces	1 kg.
2	onions, sliced	2
3 or 4	ripe tomatoes, puréed through a food mill	3 or 4
¼ cup	oil	50 ml.
	salt and freshly ground black pepper	
2 tsp.	paprika	10 ml.
½ tsp.	ground cinnamon	2 ml.
½ cup	dried chick-peas, soaked overnight and drained	125 ml.
9 cups	couscous, spread on a tray and sprinkled with water	2¼ liters
3 or 4	carrots, cut into pieces	3 or 4
3 or 4	turnips, cut into pieces	3 or 4
3 or 4	potatoes, cut into pieces	3 or 4
1	dried chili	1
½ tsp.	*ras el hanout*	2 ml.
3 or 4	zucchini, thickly sliced	3 or 4
1 lb.	pumpkin or winter squash, cut into pieces, strings and seeds removed, and peeled (about 3 cups [¾ liter])	½ kg.
7 tbsp.	butter, cut into small pieces	105 ml.

Put the meat into the bottom of a *couscoussier* and add one of the sliced onions, the puréed tomatoes, oil, salt, black pepper, paprika and cinnamon. Cook gently over low heat until the mixture begins to stick. Add about 3 quarts [3 liters] of water and bring the mixture to a boil. Add the chick-peas and reduce the heat to maintain a light boil.

Fill the upper section of the *couscoussier* with the couscous and place it over the simmering liquid. About 15 to 20 minutes after steam has become visible above the surface of the couscous, remove the couscous and transfer it to a wide, shallow bowl. Break up the couscous pellets with a spoon, sprinkle them with cold water and crumble them lightly with your finger tips, tossing to separate the pellets and aerate the couscous.

Add the carrots, turnips, potatoes and chili to the meat and broth. Return the couscous to the upper section of the *couscoussier* and place it again over the simmering meat.

In a mortar, pound the *ras el hanout* with the remaining onion. Several minutes after steam has become visible above the surface of the couscous, return the couscous to the bowl and sprinkle it with about 1¼ cups [300 ml.] of salted water. Tilt the mortar to collect the onion juice, add the juice to the couscous and add the spice-and-onion paste to the meat. Aerate the couscous as before, let it absorb the liquid and return it to the heat.

After 15 minutes, add the zucchini and pumpkin to the meat and broth. Add a little boiling water if all of the vegetables are not covered.

About 15 minutes after steam is again visible above the couscous, transfer it to a large warmed bowl. Add the butter and two ladlefuls of the broth and mix well. Put the couscous in a mound on a warmed serving dish, place the meat and vegetables on top and pour in as much broth as the couscous can absorb. Serve the remaining broth separately.

FATIMA-ZOHRA BOUAYED
LA CUISINE ALGÉRIENNE

Breton Cassoulet

Cassoulet Breton

To serve 6

1 lb.	boneless lean lamb breast, cut into pieces	½ kg.
½ lb.	lean salt pork with the rind removed, blanched in boiling water for 5 minutes, drained and cut into large cubes	¼ kg.
10	small onions	10
5	large tomatoes, peeled, seeded and coarsely chopped	5
	salt and pepper	
1	bouquet garni	1
2	garlic cloves	2
2 cups	dried white beans, soaked overnight, cooked in water to cover for 1 hour and drained	½ liter
6	small *chipolata* sausages, pricked all over	6

Place the lamb and salt pork in a saucepan with the onions and tomatoes. Season, add the bouquet garni and garlic, and cover with water. Bring to a boil, skim, and simmer very gently for about one hour. Add the beans and sausages, and cook for 30 to 45 minutes more, or until the beans are tender.

Turn the cassoulet into an oval earthenware dish and place in a preheated 350° F. [180° C.] oven. Bake for 20 minutes, or until the surface is golden and bubbling. Serve in the earthenware dish.

ÉDOUARD NIGNON (EDITOR)
LE LIVRE DE CUISINE DE L'OUEST-ÉCLAIR

Lamb and Mixed Vegetable Casserole

Chanakhi

This is a Central Asian dish that has made its way to Russia.

	To serve 3 or 4	
1 lb.	boneless lean lamb, cubed	½ kg.
1	onion, finely chopped	1
4	medium-sized potatoes, sliced	4
2	medium-sized tomatoes, halved	2
½ lb.	green beans, cut into 1-inch [2½-cm.] pieces	¼ kg.
1	small eggplant, cubed (about 1½ cups [375 ml.])	1
1 tbsp.	finely chopped fresh parsley	15 ml.
	salt and pepper	
2 cups	water	½ liter

Place the cubes of lamb in a casserole, preferably earthenware. Add the onion, potatoes, tomatoes, beans and eggplant. Sprinkle with parsley, season with salt and pepper, and pour in the water. Cover and cook in a preheated 350° F. [180° C.] oven for one and one half to two hours, or until the meat is tender. Serve in the casserole.

THE ACADEMY OF MEDICAL SCIENCE OF THE U.S.S.R.
KNIGA O VKUSNOĬ I ZDOROVOĬ PISHCHE

Spinach Stew

Misov Spannak

	To serve 4	
1 lb.	boneless lamb shoulder, cubed	½ kg.
1 tbsp.	oil	15 ml.
1	large onion, sliced	1
2 lb.	spinach, the stems removed and the leaves cut into large pieces	1 kg.
1 cup	tomato juice or tomato sauce (recipe, page 165)	¼ liter
	salt and pepper	
1 cup	water	¼ liter

Sauté the meat in the oil until brown, add the onion, and cook slowly for 15 minutes so that the onion will cook but not brown. Add the spinach, tomato juice or sauce, salt and pepper, and water. Cover, and cook the stew until it is well blended, about one hour.

GEORGE MARDIKIAN
DINNER AT OMAR KHAYYAM'S

Lamb Braised with Vegetables

Agnello con Verdure

	To serve 4	
2 lb.	boneless lean lamb, cubed	1 kg.
4	large potatoes, sliced	4
4	carrots, sliced	4
½	Savoy cabbage, shredded (optional)	½
	salt	
	chopped fresh parsley	
1 tbsp.	flour	15 ml.
1 cup	meat stock (recipe, page 164)	¼ liter

Arrange the cubes of lamb in a saucepan and cover with layers of potato, carrot and cabbage, if using. Sprinkle each layer with a little salt, parsley and flour. Pour in the stock, cover and cook very slowly for about two hours, adding more hot stock if necessary.

LISA BIONDI (EDITOR)
350 RICETTE DI CUCINA LEGGERA

Lamb and Broccoli St. Francis

This stew is named for the St. Francis Hotel in San Francisco.

	To serve 4 to 6	
3 lb.	boneless lean lamb, trimmed of excess fat and cut into 1-inch [2½-cm.] cubes	1½ kg.
1 tsp.	salt	5 ml.
½ tsp.	freshly ground black pepper	2 ml.
6 tbsp.	vegetable oil	90 ml.
2 cups	finely chopped onions	½ liter
1 tsp.	finely chopped garlic	5 ml.
2 cups	water	½ liter
1 lb.	broccoli, stemmed and separated into florets	½ kg.
3	egg yolks	3
3 tbsp.	flour	45 ml.
½ cup	strained fresh lemon juice	125 ml.

Pat the lamb cubes dry with paper towels and season them with the salt and pepper. In a large heavy casserole, heat 4 tablespoons [60 ml.] of the oil over medium heat. Brown the lamb, seven or eight pieces at a time, turning the cubes frequently. As they brown, transfer the cubes to a plate.

Add the remaining 2 tablespoons [30 ml.] of oil to the casserole, then drop in the onions and garlic. Stirring frequently, cook over medium heat for about five minutes, or until the onions are soft and translucent but not brown. Pour in the water and bring the mixture to a boil over high heat, meanwhile scraping in the brown particles clinging to the bottom and sides of the casserole.

Return the lamb and the liquid that has accumulated around it to the casserole. Stir well, reduce the heat to low and simmer partially covered for 45 minutes. Stir in the broccoli, cover the casserole partially again and simmer for 15 minutes more, or until the lamb is tender. Reduce the heat to its lowest setting.

Combine the egg yolks and flour in a small bowl and whisk until the mixture is smooth. Whisk in the lemon juice, then beat in about ½ cup [125 ml.] of the lamb braising liquid. Stirring the lamb and broccoli constantly with a wooden spoon, pour in the egg-yolk mixture in a slow, thin stream and cook for two or three minutes, until the sauce thickens heavily and is smooth. Do not let the sauce come anywhere near a boil or the egg yolks will curdle. Taste for seasoning and serve at once, directly from the casserole or from a deep, heated platter.

FOODS OF THE WORLD/AMERICAN COOKING: THE GREAT WEST

Lamb Tajine with Fruit and Honey

To serve 4 to 6

2 lb.	boneless lean lamb, cut into 2-inch [5-cm.] cubes	1 kg.
¼ tsp.	ground ginger	1 ml.
¼ tsp.	ground saffron	1 ml.
¼ tsp.	salt	1 ml.
3 tbsp.	olive oil	45 ml.
1 tbsp.	crumbled dried coriander or 1 tsp. [5 ml.] ground coriander	15 ml.
1½-inch	stick cinnamon	4-cm.
	ground pepper	
1	small onion, chopped	1
1 lb.	dried prunes, pears or apples	½ kg.
¼ cup	honey	50 ml.
1 tsp.	orange-flower water (optional)	5 ml.
1 tbsp.	sesame seeds, toasted in the oven	15 ml.

Combine the lamb, ginger, saffron, salt, oil, coriander, cinnamon stick, pepper and onion. Cover the mixture with wa-

ter, set the lid ajar, and simmer for 30 minutes. Remove the lid, and continue to simmer until the lamb is cooked and the liquid reduced to a thick sauce, about 15 minutes. Remove the cinnamon stick.

Add the fruit and simmer slowly for about 15 minutes. Add the honey and cook for another 15 minutes. Add the orange-flower water and bring the mixture to a boil. Sprinkle with toasted sesame seeds and serve immediately.

HARVA HACHTEN
KITCHEN SAFARI

Lamb Stewed with Apricots

Mishmishiya

To serve 8

3 lb.	boneless lean lamb, cubed	1½ kg.
1 lb.	dried apricots	½ kg.
2	onions, chopped	2
	oil	
1 tbsp.	flour	15 ml.
1 tsp.	ground coriander	5 ml.
½ tsp.	ground ginger	2 ml.
¾ tsp.	ground cinnamon	4 ml.
⅛ tsp.	ground pepper	½ ml.
½ tsp.	salt	2 ml.
⅓ cup	almonds, ground in a nut grinder, or in a food processor operated at short spurts	75 ml.
½ tsp.	ground saffron	2 ml.
1 tbsp.	sugar	15 ml.
2 tsp.	rose water	10 ml.

Soak the apricots in water to cover overnight. Sauté the onions in the oil. Add the meat and stir to brown on all sides. Sprinkle with flour, coriander, ginger, cinnamon, pepper and salt. Stir. Add enough boiling water just to cover. Cover the pot and simmer for about 30 minutes. Add the almonds.

Remove the apricots from the water; reserve the water. Put half of the apricots into a blender, and blend at low speed for two or three seconds. Cut the remaining apricots into coarse pieces. Add all of the apricots to the meat.

Place the lid ajar and simmer the mixture until the meat is almost finished. Add the saffron and sugar. Add some of the apricot water, if more liquid is necessary. Cook until the meat is very tender. Stir in the rose water. Serve over rice.

MALVINA W. LIEBMAN
JEWISH COOKERY FROM BOSTON TO BAGHDAD

Lamb with Lemon and Olives
El Lahm El M'Qali

To serve 6

2½ lb.	boneless leg of lamb, trimmed of all fat and cut into 1-inch [2½-cm.] cubes	1¼ kg.
½ cup	corn oil	125 ml.
½ tsp.	ground ginger	2 ml.
½ tsp.	turmeric	2 ml.
1 tsp.	ground coriander	5 ml.
¼ tsp.	ground saffron	1 ml.
1 tsp.	finely chopped garlic	5 ml.
2 tsp.	salt	10 ml.
2 cups	finely chopped onions	½ liter
1 quart	water	1 liter
2 or 3	lemons, cut lengthwise into quarters	2 or 3
30 to 40	medium-sized green olives, pitted, rinsed under cold running water and drained	30 to 40
¼ cup	chopped fresh parsley	50 ml.

Pour the oil into a heavy 4-quart [4-liter] casserole, then mix into it until smooth the ginger, turmeric, coriander, saffron, garlic and salt. Turn on the heat and add the chopped onions, mixing thoroughly. Cover and simmer for a few minutes until the onions begin to soften, then add the lamb and water and bring to a boil. Reduce the heat and add the lemons; cover and simmer for about 45 minutes, or until the lamb is tender. With a skimmer, remove any foam that has risen to the top. Refrigerate the mixture overnight.

The next day remove all of the fat that has solidified on top of the liquid. Using a slotted spoon, transfer the lamb and lemons to a bowl. Boil the liquid briskly, uncovered, until it reduces and thickens slightly—about 10 to 15 minutes. Return the lamb and lemons to this sauce. Add the olives, cover, and simmer the stew for about three minutes. Taste for seasoning and correct if necessary. Just before serving, mix in the chopped parsley. Serve accompanied with boiled rice or with flat Arab bread.

CAROL CUTLER
HAUTE CUISINE FOR YOUR HEART'S DELIGHT

Lamb in Egg and Lemon
Abbacchio Brodettato

To serve 4

2 lb.	boneless shoulder or leg of lamb, cut into serving pieces	1 kg.
	flour	
1 tbsp.	lard	15 ml.
2½ oz.	prosciutto, diced	75 g.
1	small onion, sliced	1
	salt and pepper	
½ cup	dry white wine	125 ml.
about 2 cups	boiling water	about ½ liter
3	egg yolks	3
1½ tbsp.	fresh lemon juice	22 ml.
1 tbsp.	chopped fresh marjoram	15 ml.
2 tbsp.	chopped fresh parsley	30 ml.

Coat the lamb lightly with flour. Brown the lamb in the lard with the prosciutto and onion. Season with salt and pepper, and add the wine and boiling water to cover the lamb. Cover and cook slowly for one hour, or until the lamb is tender.

Beat the egg yolks with the lemon juice, marjoram and parsley. Stir this mixture gradually into the lamb mixture, keeping the pan warm, but not directly over the heat. Continue to stir until the egg yolks thicken the cooking liquid.

FRANCA FESLIKENIAN
CUCINA E VINI DEL LAZIO

Lamb with Apricots

To serve 4

1 lb.	boneless lean lamb, cut into ½-inch [1-cm.] cubes	½ kg.
3	onions, 2 thinly sliced, 1 chopped	3
¼ cup	oil or melted *ghee*	50 ml.
6	garlic cloves, pounded to a paste with ¾ inch [2 cm.] peeled fresh ginger	6
2-inch	stick cinnamon	5-cm.
1¼ tsp.	salt	6 ml.
3 cups	warm water	¾ liter
1 tbsp.	sugar	15 ml.
2 cups	dried apricots, soaked in 1 cup [¼ liter] water for at least 4 hours	½ liter

Fry the sliced onions in the oil or *ghee* until golden brown. Drain off excess oil, keeping only 1 tablespoon [15 ml.] in the pan. Add the garlic-and-ginger paste and cook for five minutes. Add the meat and chopped onion, and cook until all liquid has evaporated. Add the cinnamon, salt and ½ cup [125 ml.] of warm water, cover and simmer for 15 minutes. Add the remaining warm water and simmer, covered, until the meat is tender and only ½ cup of gravy remains, about one and one half hours.

Put the sugar in a small pan. Place over medium heat and let the sugar brown. Remove from the heat. Add the water in which the apricots were soaked. Stir over low heat until the caramelized sugar is dissolved. Add the apricots, cover and cook for 10 or 15 minutes until the apricots are soft. Add the apricots, together with their syrup, to the meat. Heat the mixture and serve.

JEROO MEHTA
101 PARSI RECIPES

Lamb or Kid in Caper Sauce

Le Sauté d'Agneau ou de Chevreau aux Câpres

To serve 10

6 to 8 lb.	baby lamb or kid shoulder with the rib attached, cut into serving pieces	3 to 4 kg.
2	shallots, finely chopped	2
7 tbsp.	rendered goose fat	105 ml.
8	garlic cloves, chopped	8
1 cup	finely chopped fresh parsley	¼ liter
3 tbsp.	flour	45 ml.
	salt and pepper	
2 cups	dry white wine	½ liter
¾ cup	sorrel leaves	175 ml.
¾ cup	spinach leaves	175 ml.
2 to 3 tbsp.	capers, rinsed and drained	30 to 45 ml.
2 tbsp.	butter	30 ml.

Sauté the shallots in the goose fat. When they are lightly browned, remove them and sauté the meat. Add the garlic, parsley and shallots, and sprinkle with flour. After two minutes, season with salt and pepper, and pour in the white wine. Cover and cook until tender—30 minutes to one hour, depending on the age of the meat. Transfer the meat to a serving dish and keep warm.

Cook the sorrel and spinach in the butter until they soften, then pass them through a fine sieve. Add this greenish brown purée to the cooking liquid with the capers, and simmer for 10 minutes, skimming. If the sauce is not thick enough, thicken it with a little butter worked with flour. Correct the seasoning, and serve in a gravy boat as an accompaniment to the meat.

ALBIN MARTY
FOURMIGUETTO: SOUVENIRS, CONTES ET RECETTES DU LANGUEDOC

Mint-flavored Lamb and Rice

Chorizo is a spicy pork sausage flavored with paprika and garlic. It is sold at Spanish or Latin American food stores.

To serve 4 to 6

1 lb.	boneless lean lamb, preferably shoulder, cut into 1-inch [2½-cm.] cubes	½ kg.
1	garlic clove, finely chopped	1
2 cups	fresh mint leaves, finely chopped	½ liter
¼ lb.	prosciutto or ham, finely chopped	125 g.
¼ lb.	chorizo or garlic sausage, finely chopped	125 g.
1½ cups	dry white wine	375 ml.
1 tsp.	salt	5 ml.
½ tsp.	freshly ground black pepper	2 ml.
1 tbsp.	olive oil	15 ml.
1¼ cups	raw unprocessed long-grain rice	300 ml.
1 cup	water	¼ liter

Mix the garlic, mint, ham and sausage. Add the lamb, wine, salt and pepper. Mix gently. Cover and place in the refrigerator overnight.

Drain the lamb, reserving the marinade. Heat the olive oil in a large skillet. Add the meat and lightly brown it over medium-high heat. Add the rice, marinade and water. Bring to a boil and remove from the heat.

Place the mixture in a greased, deep 2-quart [2-liter] baking dish. Cover with foil. Place the dish in a large saucepan or stockpot, and add enough water to reach two thirds of the way up the sides of the dish. Bring the water to a boil, reduce the heat, cover the pan, and simmer until the rice and meat are tender, about one and one half hours. Serve the dish immediately.

THE PLEASURES OF COOKING

Lamb with Tarragon

Lammfleisch mit Estragon

To serve 4

1½ lb.	lamb shoulder, cut into serving pieces	¾ kg.
4 tbsp.	butter, or 2 tbsp. [30 ml.] lard and 2 tbsp. butter	60 ml.
2¼ cups	boiling water	550 ml.
2 tbsp.	flour	30 ml.
15 to 20	tarragon leaves, finely chopped	15 to 20
1 tbsp.	strained fresh lemon juice (optional)	15 ml.
⅓ cup	sour cream (optional)	75 ml.

Brown the lamb in 2 tablespoons [30 ml.] of butter or lard. Pour in the water, cover, and simmer for 30 minutes, or until the lamb is tender. Put it into a dish and keep it warm.

In another pan, melt 2 tablespoons [30 ml.] of butter, stir in the flour and cook until well browned, about five minutes. Stir in the cooking liquid, add the tarragon, and simmer until thick and smooth, about 30 minutes. Add the optional lemon juice and sour cream. Pour this sauce over the lamb.

ELEK MAGYAR
KOCHBUCH FÜR FEINSCHMECKER

Lamb Fricassee with Capers and Anchovies

Lammfrikassee mit Kapern und Sardellen

To serve 4 to 6

1½ lb.	boneless lean lamb, cubed	¾ kg.
6 tbsp.	butter	90 ml.
2	whole cloves	2
2	bay leaves	2
¼ lb.	small boiling onions	125 g.
½ tsp.	ground mace	2 ml.
2 tbsp.	chopped basil	30 ml.
1¼ cups	boiling water	300 ml.
	salt	
¼ cup	flour	50 ml.
½	lemon, thinly sliced, seeds removed	½
2 tbsp.	capers, rinsed and drained	30 ml.
½ cup	white wine	125 ml.
4	oil-packed flat anchovy fillets, rinsed, patted dry and finely chopped	4

Melt 2 tablespoons [30 ml.] of the butter and add the lamb, cloves, bay leaves, onions, mace and basil. Sauté the lamb

mixture for two or three minutes, add the boiling water and salt, cover, and simmer gently for one hour, or until the lamb is tender. Remove the cloves and bay leaves.

In another pan, melt the remaining butter, stir in the flour, cook for one minute, and add ⅓ cup [75 ml.] of the cooking liquid from the lamb. When this sauce is smoothly mixed, stir it into the lamb mixture. Add the lemon slices, capers and wine, and simmer for about five minutes. Just before serving, stir in the anchovies.

HENRIETTE DAVIDIS
ILLUSTRIERTES PRAKTISCHES KOCHBUCH

Curried Goat

The volatile oils in hot chilies may make your skin sting; handle them carefully and wash your hands afterward.

This is almost a national Jamaican dish, eaten by many people at least once a week.

To serve 4

1½ lb.	boneless goat or mutton, trimmed of fat and cut into 1-inch [2½-cm.] cubes	¾ kg.
1 tsp.	salt	5 ml.
1 tsp.	freshly ground black pepper	5 ml.
1 tbsp.	curry powder	15 ml.
2 tbsp.	lard	30 ml.
1	onion, sliced	1
1¼ cups	meat stock *(recipe, page 164)* or water	300 ml.
2	fresh hot chilies, stemmed, halved, seeded and chopped	2
2	potatoes, diced	2
4 cups	boiled rice, made from 2 cups [½ liter] raw rice	1 liter

Sift together the salt, pepper and curry powder, and rub the mixture into the meat. Set aside for one hour.

Heat the lard in a saucepan, add the meat and onion, and brown them lightly. Add the stock or water and the chilies, cover, and simmer over low heat until the meat is tender. The timing varies with the meat; mutton takes less time (about one hour) than goat (about one and three quarters hours). Add the potatoes and continue cooking for another 20 minutes, or until the potatoes are soft and the gravy thickens. Serve on a bed of rice.

MARY SLATER
CARIBBEAN COOKING FOR PLEASURE

Colombo Curry

Colombo de Mouton ou de Cabri

The seeds from the long, narrow tamarind pods are obtainable in dried form where Indian or Latin American foods are sold. The brown fleshy pulp that covers the seeds is acidic and tart-flavored.

Curry was originally introduced to the West Indies by immigrant laborers from Ceylon; thus this dish is named after the capital of its country of origin. Curry powder is available ready-made, but you may make it yourself in a mortar or blender. Combine ½ teaspoon [2 ml.] each of coriander and cumin seeds, ground turmeric and whole black peppercorns with a small piece of peeled and grated fresh ginger and from one half to two fresh or dried chilies. Grind everything well.

To serve 4

2 lb.	boneless lamb or kid shoulder, cut into serving pieces	1 kg.
3 tbsp.	oil	45 ml.
2	onions, thinly sliced	2
1 cup	water	¼ liter
1 tbsp.	curry powder	15 ml.
3	tamarind seeds, covered with 1 tbsp. [15 ml.] boiling water, soaked for 1 hour, pulp rubbed through a sieve (optional)	3
	salt and pepper	
1	bouquet garni of thyme, scallion and parsley	1
1	chayote squash, diced	1
1	large zucchini, sliced into rounds	1
1	eggplant, sliced into rounds	1
2	potatoes, peeled and halved	2
2	garlic cloves, crushed to a paste	2
	cayenne pepper (optional)	

Lightly brown the pieces of meat in the oil with the onions. Add the water, curry powder and the tamarind pulp, if you are using it. Mix well and season with salt and pepper. When the mixture comes to a boil, put in the bouquet garni, vegetables, garlic and a pinch of cayenne pepper, if you wish. Cover and simmer gently for one hour, or until the meat is tender. Serve the curry hot.

CHRISTIANE ROY-CAMILLE AND ANNICK MARIE
LES MEILLEURES RECETTES DE LA CUISINE ANTILLAISE

Mutton Curry

Badshahi Gosht

To serve 4 to 6

1½ lb.	boneless mutton, cubed	¾ kg.
5 tbsp.	ghee	75 ml.
2	medium-sized onions, sliced	2
20	almonds, blanched, peeled, and sliced or chopped	20
20	pistachios, blanched and peeled (optional)	20
¼ cup	raisins, soaked in warm water for 15 minutes and drained	50 ml.
4 to 6	green cardamom pods	4 to 6
8 to 10	whole cloves	8 to 10
2 or 3	small pieces stick cinnamon	2 or 3
5 tbsp.	plain yogurt, mixed with a pinch of ground saffron	75 ml.
4	medium-sized potatoes, cut into pieces	4
¾ cup	freshly shelled peas	175 ml.
½ cup	heavy cream	125 ml.

Seasoning

8 to 10	garlic cloves, chopped	8 to 10
2-inch	piece fresh ginger, chopped	5-cm.
3	large onions, chopped	3
1½ tsp.	poppy seeds	7 ml.
2 tbsp.	dried grated coconut	30 ml.
3	dried red chilies, stemmed and seeded	3
1	handful fresh coriander leaves, coarsely chopped	1
	salt	

Pound the seasoning ingredients together to form a paste.

Brown the sliced onions in the *ghee*. Add the almonds, the pistachios, if using, and the raisins; cook for about five minutes. Remove the onions, nuts and raisins from the casserole. To the same *ghee*, add the cardamom pods, cloves, cinnamon pieces and the seasoning mixture, and fry for about five minutes. Then add the mutton and the saffron-flavored yogurt. Add enough water to cover the contents generously.

Cover and simmer for about 30 minutes. Then add the potatoes and peas, and simmer for a further 30 minutes, or until the mutton is tender. Just before removing the curry from the heat, add the cream and mix it in well. Serve garnished with the fried onion, nut and raisin mixture.

THE MAHARANI OF JAIPUR (EDITOR)
GOURMET'S GATEWAY

Shepherdess's Lamb

Cordero a la Pastora

Calf's liver and brains—although milder in flavor—can be substituted for the less available lamb liver and brains.

	To serve 8	
4 lb.	lamb shoulder, boned and cut into 2-inch [5-cm.] pieces	2 kg.
¼ lb.	lamb liver, chopped	125 g.
2 oz.	lamb brains	60 g.
1 cup	olive oil	¼ liter
1	onion, chopped	1
2 tbsp.	fresh bread crumbs	30 ml.
1 tbsp.	cayenne pepper	15 ml.
2 tbsp.	vinegar	30 ml.
4	garlic cloves, chopped	4
1	sprig thyme	1
	salt and freshly ground black pepper	

Put the oil and onion in a pot. Add the lamb shoulder and the liver, and stew for 10 minutes. Then add the bread crumbs, cayenne pepper and vinegar. In a mortar or food processor, grind together the garlic, thyme and brains, and add to the lamb. Season with salt and pepper. Pour in enough boiling water to cover the contents of the pot. Cover, and cook over low heat for 40 minutes, until the lamb is tender. Allow the stew to rest for one hour before reheating it to serve.

ANA MARÍA CALERA
COCINA CASTELLANA

Braised Lamb with Ham

Abbacchio alla Ciociara

	To serve 6	
3 lb.	boneless lamb shoulder, cut into 1-inch [2½-cm.] cubes	1½ kg.
2 tsp.	salt	10 ml.
½ tsp.	freshly ground black pepper	2 ml.
2 tbsp.	butter	30 ml.
¼ lb.	prosciutto or cooked ham, cut into julienne	125 g.
½ cup	brandy	125 ml.
¼ tsp.	rosemary	1 ml.
1	garlic clove, finely chopped	1

Season the lamb with the salt and pepper. Melt the butter in a deep skillet or casserole; brown the lamb in it. Add the ham; cook for five minutes. Mix in the brandy, rosemary and garlic; cover and cook over low heat for one hour, or until the lamb is tender. Watch carefully and add a little boiling water, if necessary, to keep the meat from burning. There should be very little gravy when the meat is finished.

ROMEO SALTA
THE PLEASURES OF ITALIAN COOKING

Lamb Hunter-Style

Abbacchio alla Cacciatora

Abbacchio is baby lamb, one to two months old. If you use an older lamb, allow a slightly longer cooking time.

	To serve 4	
2 lb.	baby lamb, cut into serving pieces	1 kg.
2	baby lamb kidneys, split and the fatty cores removed	2
½ cup	water	125 ml.
½ cup	white wine vinegar	125 ml.
3	garlic cloves, lightly crushed	3
3	sprigs rosemary	3
1	sprig sage	1
½ cup	olive oil	125 ml.
	salt and pepper	
3	salt anchovies, filleted, soaked in water for 30 minutes, drained and patted dry	3

Pour the water and vinegar into a glass. Add the garlic. Tie the rosemary and sage together with thread and add them. Let these ingredients soak for a few hours.

Brown the lamb and the kidneys in the oil and season with salt. Add the contents of the glass, cover and cook over medium heat for 45 minutes. Remove the garlic, rosemary and sage, season with pepper and add the anchovies. When the anchovies have been reduced to a pulp and the sauce has thickened—in about 30 minutes—serve.

STELLA DONATI (EDITOR)
IL GRANDE MANUALE DELLA CUCINA REGIONALE

Lamb Stew with Chicken and Potatoes

Tadjin Bel Batata

To serve 8

2 lb.	boneless lamb breast, cut into serving pieces	1 kg.
¼ cup	olive oil	50 ml.
1	large onion, thinly sliced	1
3 quarts	water	3 liters
	salt	
	mixed spices	
3 or 4	mint leaves	3 or 4
2 tsp.	paprika	10 ml.
one 3 lb.	roasting chicken, cut into 8 pieces	one 1½ kg.
4	medium sized potatoes, quartered	4

Heat the oil in a large saucepan. Add the pieces of lamb and let them brown lightly. Add the onion and water, bring to a boil and skim. Season with salt and a good pinch of mixed spices, and add the mint, paprika and the chicken. Cover and simmer for 30 minutes. Add the potatoes and continue to cook until the meat and potatoes are tender, about 30 minutes more. Serve straight from the pot.

LÉON ISNARD
LA GASTRONOMIE AFRICAINE

Bolton Hot Pot

To serve 4

2 lb.	boneless lamb shoulder, trimmed of excess fat and cut into serving pieces	1 kg.
2 tbsp.	lard	30 ml.
1	onion, thickly sliced	1
¼ cup	flour	50 ml.
3 cups	meat stock (recipe, page 164)	¾ liter
	salt and freshly ground pepper	
	sugar	
4	lamb kidneys, excess fat and outer membrane removed, halved, cored and sliced	4
¼ lb.	mushrooms, quartered (about 1½ cups [375 ml.])	125 g.
6	medium-sized potatoes, thinly sliced	6
1 tbsp.	butter, melted	15 ml.

Melt the lard in a skillet and brown the lamb pieces on all sides. Transfer the lamb pieces to a deep casserole, using a slotted spoon to drain them of their fat. Now gently fry the onion to a pale gold in the same fat. Stir in the flour and let it brown, then add the stock slowly, stirring all the time, to make smooth gravy. Season the gravy with salt and pepper and a pinch of sugar.

Spread the kidneys in a layer over the lamb pieces, then add the mushrooms in a layer. Season well with pepper and salt between each layer. Pour on the gravy. Arrange the potato slices on top, overlapping them like fish scales. Brush the top with the melted butter to keep the potatoes moist.

Cover the casserole and put it into a preheated 325° F. [160° C.] oven for two hours. For the last 30 minutes, remove the lid to brown the potatoes.

CAROLINE CONRAN
BRITISH COOKING

To Force a Leg of Mutton

In this 17th Century English recipe, the leg meat is chopped or ground to form the base of a stuffing.

To serve 8

one 6 to 9 lb.	leg of mutton, boned and the meat cut out, leaving the fell intact	one 3 to 4½ kg.
½ lb.	suet	¼ kg.
6 tbsp.	finely chopped mixed fresh sage, marjoram, thyme, sorrel and parsley	90 ml.
	salt and pepper	
	grated nutmeg	
4	eggs	4
Caper sauce		
2 tbsp.	chopped capers, rinsed and drained	30 ml.
2 tbsp.	butter	30 ml.
2 tbsp.	flour	30 ml.
1	anchovy fillet, finely chopped	1
1 tbsp.	white wine vinegar	15 ml.
2 tbsp.	chopped fresh parsley	30 ml.

Chop or grind the mutton very fine with the suet. Mix with the herbs, salt and pepper, nutmeg and eggs. When the mixture is smooth, fill the fell with the meat mixture, folding the fell over to enclose the stuffing completely. Tie the parcel up in a cloth.

Bring a large pan of lightly salted water to a boil, put in the mutton, and poach at a gentle simmer for about one and one half hours. Transfer the mutton to a platter to drain.

To make the sauce, melt the butter, stir in the flour, and slowly stir in 2 cups [½ liter] of the cooking liquid. Simmer for 40 minutes to make a thick, smooth sauce. Stir in the remaining ingredients.

Remove the stuffed mutton from its cloth and serve cut into slices, accompanied by the hot sauce.

THE RECEIPT BOOK OF ANN BLENCOWE

Leftovers and Mixed Methods

Broiled Morsels of Poached Lamb Breast

Épigrammes de Mouton (ou d'Agneau) à la Purée de Pommes de Terre

This recipe produces not only an appetizing dish, but a very good soup. The broth in which the lamb was cooked with its seasoning vegetables may be garnished with rice, barley or noodles. Serve the epigrams on a bed of puréed potatoes.

To serve 6 to 8

5 to 6 lb.	lamb breast, rolled and tied	2½ to 3 kg.
2 quarts	meat stock *(recipe, page 164)* or water	2 liters
2	carrots	2
2	onions	2
2	turnips	2
1	garlic clove	1
1	bouquet garni	1
	salt and pepper	
4 tbsp.	lard, softened	60 ml.
¼ cup	dry bread crumbs	50 ml.

Bring the stock or water to a boil with the vegetables, garlic, bouquet garni and salt. Add the lamb breast, cover, and simmer for about one and one half to two hours, or until the meat is tender. Drain the meat, bone it, and let it cool completely, under a weighted board. Cut the meat into neat squares. Spread the squares with lard, season them and coat them with bread crumbs. Broil the pieces until they are golden brown on both sides.

PROSPER MONTAGNÉ (EDITOR)
MANUEL DU BON CUISTOT ET DE LA BONNE MÉNAGÈRE

Epigrams of Lamb with Tartar Sauce

Épigrammes d'Agneau Sauce Tartare

An epigram of lamb consists of a piece of breast meat, a chop or a combination of the two, coated in bread crumbs, then fried or broiled. According to Larousse Gastronomique, the rather fanciful culinary meaning of the word dates back to 18th Century France, when a young lady overheard a man-about-town remarking on the feast of excellent epigrams that had been served up to him the previous evening. The lady, not realizing that he was referring to witty jokes told at a gathering, commanded her chef to duplicate the dish. At a loss, the chef simply breaded and fried some morsels of lamb; with a straight face he told his employer that they were Épigrammes d'Agneau, a name that survives to this day.

The stock in which the breasts of lamb were cooked may be made into an excellent soup. Remove the vegetables, cook some pearl barley in the stock, slice the vegetables and return them to the soup to serve.

To serve 8

two 3 to 5 lb.	lamb breasts	two 1½ to 2½ kg.
	salt	
2	onions	2
4	carrots	4
2	turnips	2
1	bouquet garni	1
2	garlic cloves	2
2	eggs, lightly beaten	2
1 tbsp.	olive oil	15 ml.
¾ cup	dry bread crumbs	175 ml.
4 tbsp.	clarified butter, melted	60 ml.
	Tartar sauce	
3	egg yolks	3
	salt and white pepper	
1 tbsp.	wine vinegar or fresh lemon juice	15 ml.
about 2 cups	olive oil	about ½ liter
1 tbsp.	Dijon mustard	15 ml.
2 tbsp.	finely chopped capers, rinsed and drained	30 ml.
2 tbsp.	finely chopped sour gherkins	30 ml.
2 tbsp.	finely chopped fresh parsley	30 ml.

Put the breasts of lamb in a suitably large cooking pot and cover with cold water. Add salt and the vegetables, bouquet garni and garlic. Bring slowly to a boil, skim carefully, cover, and simmer over low heat for about one and a quarter hours, until the meat pulls away from the bones easily.

Transfer the breasts to a dish and let them cool until lukewarm. Pull the bones out of the meat one by one. Place the meat between two cloths, put a weighted board on top and let the meat cool completely. Trim away any fat and cut the meat into lozenge shapes of equal size.

To make the sauce, season the egg yolks with a little salt and pepper, and whisk for about one minute, or until the yolks turn pale. Whisk in the vinegar or lemon juice. Whisking constantly, add the oil, drop by drop to begin with. When the sauce starts to thicken, pour in the remaining oil in a thin, steady stream, whisking rhythmically. When the mayonnaise has a soft but firm consistency, whisk in the mustard, capers, gherkins and parsley.

To finish the lamb, mix together the eggs and olive oil, dip the lozenges in the mixture and, when well covered, roll them in the bread crumbs. Place the lozenges side by side in a flat baking dish and sprinkle with the clarified butter.

Place the dish in a preheated 350° F. [180° C.] oven for 12 minutes, or until hot, then put it under a broiler for three minutes, or until golden. Serve accompanied with the sauce.

PAUL BOUILLARD
LA CUISINE AU COIN DU FEU

Coated Neck Slices

Cotelettes de Mouton en Robe-de-Chambre

This dish may be served with velouté sauce (recipe, page 164), tomato sauce (recipe, page 165) or another sauce you prefer.

	To serve 8	
8	lamb neck slices, trimmed of excess fat and cut through the bone into serving pieces 1½ inches [4 cm.] thick	8
about 2 cups	meat stock *(recipe, page 164)*, heated	about ½ liter
1	bouquet garni	1
½ lb.	finely ground veal	¼ kg.
¼ lb.	beef suet or marrow, chopped	125 g.
2	eggs	2
	salt and pepper	
3 tbsp.	chopped fresh parsley	45 ml.
2 or 3	scallions, chopped	2 or 3
¼ lb.	mushrooms, finely chopped (about 1½ cups [375 ml.])	125 g.
¼ cup	heavy cream	50 ml.
3 cups	fine fresh bread crumbs	¾ liter
	melted butter	

Arrange the neck slices side by side in a large sauté pan. Pour over enough hot stock to barely cover them, add the

bouquet garni, cover, and simmer for 30 to 40 minutes. Drain the neck slices, and degrease and strain the stock. Boil the stock until it is reduced to a thick, syrupy glaze. Turn the neck slices in the glaze to coat them. Cool them on a rack.

Mix the veal, suet or marrow, eggs, salt and pepper, parsley, scallions and mushrooms, and bind the mixture with the cream. Envelop the neck slices with this forcemeat, then coat them with bread crumbs. Place them on a buttered baking sheet, sprinkle with melted butter and bake in a preheated 400° F. [200° C.] oven until the coating is crisp and browned, about 15 minutes. Drain the neck slices on paper towels before serving.

MENON
LA CUISINIÈRE BOURGEOISE

Broiled Lamb Breast

Geröstete Lammbrust

The Hamburg parsley root called for in this 19th Century German recipe is the parsnip-sized root of a hardy variety of parsley. A parsnip or a celery heart makes a suitable substitute. For richer flavor, the poaching liquid may be enriched with garlic and such herbs as thyme and bay leaf.

	To serve 6	
4 to 6 lb.	lamb breast, trimmed of excess fat	2 to 3 kg.
1 cup	water	¼ liter
8 tbsp.	butter	120 ml.
1	carrot, diced	1
1	turnip, diced	1
1	Hamburg parsley root, diced	1
1	onion, finely chopped	1
	salt and pepper	
1 cup	fine dry bread crumbs	¼ liter

Place the lamb breast in a pan with the water, half of the butter, the vegetables and a little salt. Bring to a boil, cover and cook over low heat or in a preheated 375° F. [190° C.] oven until tender, about two hours. Let the breast cool in the cooking liquid.

When the breast is cool enough to handle, remove all of the bones and place the meat on a flat dish. Cover it with a lightly weighted board and let it cool to room temperature. Remove the vegetables from the liquid and keep them warm.

Cut the meat into square or triangular pieces. Melt the remaining butter. Sprinkle the meat with salt and pepper, dip it first in the melted butter, then in the bread crumbs, and broil it on both sides until it is golden brown. Serve with the vegetables.

SOPHIE WILHELMINE SCHEIBLER
ALLGEMEINES DEUTSCHES KOCHBUCH FÜR ALLE STÄNDE

Lamb Chops, Navarre-Style

Chuletas de Cordero a la Navarra

To serve 4

12 to 16	lamb rib chops, cut about ½ inch [1 cm.] thick, boned and slightly flattened	12 to 16
	salt	
4 tbsp.	lard	60 ml.
¼ cup	oil	50 ml.
¼ lb.	smoked ham, diced	125 g.
1	large onion, chopped	1
3	medium-sized tomatoes, peeled, seeded and finely chopped	3
1 tsp.	sugar	5 ml.
½ lb.	smoked *chorizo*, thinly sliced	¼ kg.

Sprinkle the chops with salt and fry them over high heat in the lard and oil. When browned on both sides, transfer the chops to an earthenware dish.

In the same fat, fry the ham and onion for about five minutes, or until they begin to brown. Add the tomatoes and let them cook until the mixture is thick, about 10 minutes. Season with salt and sugar. Cover the chops with the tomato mixture and place in a preheated 350° F. [180° C.] oven for about 30 minutes, or until the lamb is very tender. Cover with the slices of *chorizo*, increase the oven temperature to 450° F. [230° C.] and return the dish to the oven for about five minutes, or until the *chorizo* slices render some of their fat.

Bring to the table and serve from the cooking dish.

MARIA DOLORES COMAS
LO MEJOR DE LA COCINA ESPAÑOLA

Lamb and Potato Casserole in Spicy Sauce

To serve 4 to 6

2 cups	diced leftover lamb	½ liter
	butter	
½ tsp.	ground allspice	2 ml.
2	yellow onions, chopped	2
2 cups	meat stock *(recipe, page 164)*	½ liter
2 tbsp.	cornstarch	30 ml.
3 or 4	sweet gherkins, finely chopped	3 or 4
½ cup	currant jelly	125 ml.
3	potatoes, boiled, peeled and sliced	3
	salt and freshly ground pepper	

Combine the allspice and onions with the stock in a heavy saucepan, and simmer until the onions are very soft. Mix the

cornstarch with a little cold water to make a smooth paste. Stir the paste into the sauce and continue to simmer, stirring until the sauce has thickened slightly.

Arrange the lamb in a buttered 2-quart [2-liter] casserole, and cover it with the gherkins and jelly. Add the sliced potatoes. Sprinkle with salt and pepper to taste. Pour the onion sauce over all, and bake in a preheated 375° F. [190° C.] oven for about 30 minutes, or until piping hot.

HELEN MC CULLY
WASTE NOT WANT NOT

Fillets of Mutton

"Pickle" in this recipe is a 19th Century term for a marinade. The technique of larding is demonstrated on pages 58-59.

Dish up the fillets of mutton in a circle with any purée of vegetables or a white mushroom sauce in the center.

To serve 4

3 to 4 lb.	mutton loin roast, boned, halved crosswise, and each piece halved lengthwise to make 4 fillets in all	1½ to 2 kg.
3 oz.	salt pork with the rind removed, blanched in boiling water for 5 minutes, drained and cut into lardons	90 g.
8 tbsp.	butter	120 ml.
	Pickle	
5 cups	water	1¼ liters
2½ cups	vinegar	625 ml.
4	whole cloves	4
4	peppercorns	4
1	onion, sliced	1
1	carrot, sliced	1
½	bunch celery, sliced	½
10	sprigs parsley	10
5	sprigs thyme	5

Lard the fillets with the salt-pork lardons. Put all of the ingredients for the pickle into a bowl, lay the fillets in the pickle, cover them, and leave them for four hours.

Drain the fillets and lay them in a bright tin dish, with 1 tablespoon [15 ml.] of butter under each and ⅔ cup [150 ml.] of the strained pickle poured over them. Put them in a preheated 400° F. [200° C.] oven to bake for 15 minutes.

Put the fillets under a hot broiler for a minute or two, and serve.

COLONEL KENNEY-HERBERT
DAINTY DISHES FOR INDIAN TABLES

Lamb Rice Casserole

To serve 4

12 oz.	leftover roast lamb, cut into 1-inch [2½-cm.] cubes (2 cups [½ liter])	350 g.
1	large onion, finely chopped	1
1	garlic clove, finely chopped	1
2 tbsp.	butter	30 ml.
1 cup	lamb gravy or meat stock *(recipe, page 164)*	¼ liter
¼ cup	finely chopped fresh parsley	50 ml.
	salt and freshly ground pepper	
3 cups	cooked rice	¾ liter
¼ cup	dry bread crumbs	50 ml.

Sauté the onion and garlic in the butter. Combine them with the lamb, gravy or meat stock, and the parsley. Season to taste with salt and pepper.

Make a bed of rice in the bottom of a buttered 1½-quart [1½-liter] casserole or baking dish, then make alternate layers of the lamb mixture and rice, ending with a layer of rice. Top with bread crumbs; cover with a piece of well-buttered parchment paper. Bake in a preheated 350° F. [180° C.] oven for 35 to 40 minutes, or until heated through. Remove the paper cover for the last 10 minutes to color the top.

JAMES A. BEARD
JAMES BEARD'S AMERICAN COOKERY

Gratin of Ground Lamb

Qachchabiyet 's-sahrâwi

To serve 6

1 lb.	boneless lean lamb, cubed	½ kg.
10 oz.	ground lean lamb	300 g.
3	garlic cloves, coarsely chopped	3
1 tsp.	ground cinnamon	5 ml.
	salt and freshly ground black pepper	
2 tbsp.	water	30 ml.
2 tbsp.	oil	30 ml.
1 tbsp.	butter	15 ml.
¼ cup	dried chick-peas, soaked overnight and drained	50 ml.
4	eggs	4
3 or 4	sprigs parsley, finely chopped	3 or 4

Put the cubes of lamb into a casserole or saucepan. In a mortar, pound the garlic with half of the cinnamon and a pinch each of salt and pepper. Stir in the water. Add this mixture to the lamb cubes. Stir in the oil and butter, and sauté gently for about 10 minutes.

Add 2 cups [½ liter] of water and the chick-peas. Form the ground lamb into a large ball, add it to the pot and bring to a boil. Cover, simmer for one and a half hours, then remove the lid and simmer for 30 minutes to reduce the sauce.

Remove the ball of meat and crumble it into a bowl. Beat the eggs with the parsley, mix them into the crumbled meat and season with salt, pepper and the remaining cinnamon.

Transfer the lamb cubes and chick-peas to a greased shallow baking dish. Pour in half of the cooking liquid. Spread the egg-and-meat mixture over the top. Bake in a preheated 400° F. [200° C.] oven for 30 minutes, or until the top is golden brown. Heat the remaining cooking liquid and pour it over the finished dish before serving.

FATIMA-ZOHRA BOUAYED
LA CUISINE ALGÉRIENNE

Baked Mutton with Rice

Ovneshko s Oriz

To serve 5

1½ lb.	boneless mutton shoulder, cubed	¾ kg.
5 tbsp.	lard	75 ml.
1	medium-sized onion, finely chopped	1
2	medium-sized tomatoes, peeled, seeded and chopped	2
⅓ cup	water	75 ml.
	salt	
1 cup	raw short-grain rice	¼ liter
3 cups	boiling water	¾ liter
	freshly ground black pepper	
	chopped fresh parsley	

In a fireproof oven dish, melt the lard, then add the meat and brown the cubes on all sides. Add the onion and brown it too. Add the tomatoes and fry until most of their liquid has evaporated. Add the water, season with salt, cover tightly and bring to a boil. Simmer over low heat until the meat is tender and all of the liquid has evaporated, about 45 minutes. Stir in the rice, pour in the boiling water, cover again and return the mixture to a boil.

Remove the lid and place the dish in a preheated 350° F. [180° C.] oven. Bake for about 30 minutes, or until the rice is tender and has absorbed all of the liquid. Serve sprinkled with freshly ground pepper and chopped parsley.

SONYA CHORTANOVA
NASHA KUCHNIYA

Breast Ribs of Lamb with Chocolate

Costillas de Cordero con Chocolate

To serve 4

2 to 3 lb.	lamb breast, cut into individual ribs	1 to 1 ½ kg.
1 tbsp.	lard	15 ml.
3	small onions	3
⅔ cup	dried mushrooms (preferably cepes), soaked in warm water for 30 minutes, drained and chopped	150 ml.
1 tsp.	ground cinnamon	5 ml.
¼ tsp.	thyme	1 ml.
¼ tsp.	oregano	1 ml.
1	bay leaf	1
1 ½ cups	white wine	375 ml.
¼ cup	hazelnuts, ground in a nut grinder, or in a processor operated at short spurts	50 ml.
¼ cup	almonds, ground in a nut grinder, or in a processor operated at short spurts	50 ml.
2	garlic cloves, chopped	2
3 tbsp.	chopped fresh parsley	45 ml.
4 oz.	unsweetened baking chocolate, grated	125 g.
1 tbsp.	puréed tomato	15 ml.
	salt	
about 2 cups	water or meat stock (recipe, page 164)	about ½ liter

Grill the ribs over charcoal or under a hot broiler for about two minutes on each side, or until the fat begins to melt. Put the ribs into a heavy casserole with the lard, onions, mushrooms, cinnamon, thyme, oregano and bay leaf. Cover and cook over low heat for 10 minutes. Stir in the wine, hazelnuts, almonds, garlic, parsley, chocolate, tomato, salt and enough water or stock to cover the meat.

Cover the casserole with foil or a lid. Cook slowly for about one and one half hours, or until the meat is very tender and the liquid is reduced to a thick sauce.

ANA MARÍA CALERA
COCINA CATALANA

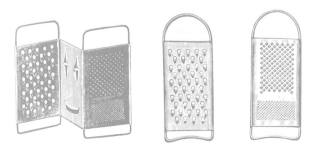

Baked Mutton Chops

This recipe was first published by Mrs. Mary Holland in The Economical Cook and Frugal Housewife in 1833.

To serve 6

12	mutton or lamb loin or rib chops, cut 1 inch [2½ cm.] thick	12
	salt and pepper	
¼ cup	flour	50 ml.
6	eggs, beaten	6
1 quart	milk	1 liter
½ tsp.	ground ginger	2 ml.
2½ cups	ale	625 ml.

Put salt and pepper over the chops, butter a baking dish and lay in the chops. Beat your flour and eggs into a little milk first, then put in the rest of the milk. Put in the ginger and ale. Pour this mixture over the chops and send the dish to a preheated 350° F. [180° C.] oven. After 30 minutes, lower the heat to 325° F. [160° C.]. An hour and a half will bake it.

SHEILA HUTCHINS
ENGLISH RECIPES AND OTHERS FROM SCOTLAND, WALES AND IRELAND

Kohlrabi Stuffed with Lamb

Kalarepa Nadziewana Mięsem

To serve 4

½ lb.	ground lean lamb	¼ kg.
⅓ cup	chopped onion	75 ml.
4 tbsp.	butter or lard	60 ml.
2	thick slices stale, firm-textured white bread, crusts removed, soaked in water and squeezed dry	2
	salt and pepper	
1	egg	1
12	kohlrabi, peeled, tops sliced off and reserved, centers scooped out	12
	boiling water	
¼ cup	flour	50 ml.
1 tbsp.	vinegar or fresh lemon juice	15 ml.
2 tsp.	sugar, cooked if desired with 3 tbsp. [45 ml.] of water until caramel brown	10 ml.
1 tbsp.	chopped fresh parsley	15 ml.

Brown the onion in 1 tablespoon [15 ml.] of the butter or lard. Mix the onion, meat and bread with salt and pepper, and work in the egg. Stuff the kohlrabi with this mixture and put the cut-off tops back on them. Place in one layer in a shallow pan and pour enough boiling water into the dish to come halfway up the sides of the kohlrabi.

Cover and cook over low heat or bake in a preheated 350° F. [180° C.] oven for 30 to 40 minutes. When they are tender, transfer the kohlrabi to an ovenproof platter. Add a little more boiling water to the reduced liquid in the pan. To make the sauce, brown the flour in the remaining butter or lard, add the liquid from the pan and bring to a boil. Cook until the sauce is smooth and thickened, and flavor it to taste with salt, vinegar or lemon juice and sugar, caramelized if desired. Pour the sauce over the kohlrabi, reheat briefly in the oven and serve sprinkled with chopped parsley.

HELENA HAWLICZKOWA
KUCHNIA POLSKA

Baked Lamb and Potato Moussaka

To serve 6 to 8

3½ lb.	lamb shoulder, boned, trimmed of fat and cut into ½-inch [1-cm.] cubes	1½ kg.
⅔ cup	puréed tomato	150 ml.
2	large onions, chopped	2
2	garlic cloves, finely chopped	2
1 tsp.	basil	5 ml.
2 tsp.	salt	10 ml.
	pepper	
½ cup	chopped fresh parsley	125 ml.
12	medium-sized potatoes, cut into thin matchsticks	12
¼ cup	olive oil	50 ml.

Combine all of the ingredients except the potatoes and the oil. Mix well with your hands, then place in a broad casserole (preferably one broader at the top than at the bottom). Press the mixture down firmly. Arrange the potatoes evenly on top of the meat, and sprinkle the potatoes with the oil.

Bake the casserole in a preheated 400° F. [200° C.] oven for about one and one half hours. Baste the potatoes occasionally with the meat juices from the casserole. The potatoes should be very crisp when the casserole is ready to eat. If the moussaka needs to be held over before serving, set the oven to very low and leave the casserole in the oven.

PAULA PECK
PAULA PECK'S ART OF GOOD COOKING

Vegetable Moussaka

If leftover lamb is used for this dish, the initial cooking time should be reduced from 30 minutes to 10 minutes. You may, if you wish, increase the quantity of zucchini and omit the eggplant and potatoes.

To serve 8

2 lb.	ground lean lamb	1 kg.
1 cup	olive oil	¼ liter
4	medium-sized zucchini, cut lengthwise into slices ⅓ inch [1 cm.] thick	4
1	large eggplant, cut crosswise into slices ½ inch [1 cm.] thick	1
1	large onion, finely chopped	1
1	garlic clove, finely chopped	1
4 tbsp.	butter	60 ml.
3	tomatoes, peeled, seeded and chopped	3
2 tsp.	salt	10 ml.
	pepper	
⅓ cup	dry bread crumbs	75 ml.
3	eggs, 1 beaten	3
¼ cup	chopped fresh parsley	50 ml.
1½ cups	béchamel sauce *(recipe, page 164)*	375 ml.
1 cup	ricotta or cottage cheese	¼ liter
⅔ cup	grated *kefalotiri* or Parmesan cheese	150 ml.
3	medium-sized potatoes, sliced	3

In a large skillet, fry the zucchini and eggplant slices—a few at a time—in the oil until the slices are lightly browned. Drain them on paper towels.

Sauté the lamb, onion and garlic in the butter. Add the tomatoes, salt and pepper. Cover and cook over low heat for 30 minutes. Remove the lamb mixture from the heat and add to it 3 tablespoons [45 ml.] of the bread crumbs, the beaten egg and the parsley. Prepare the béchamel sauce and beat into it the remaining eggs and the cheeses.

Butter a large baking dish and sprinkle it with the remaining bread crumbs. Put in the potato slices in one layer and cover them with half of the lamb mixture. Continue with a layer of the eggplant slices, the remaining lamb mixture and the zucchini slices. Top with the enriched béchamel sauce and bake the dish in a preheated 375° F. [190° C.] oven for about 45 minutes, or until golden brown.

CHRISSA PARADISSIS
THE BEST BOOK OF GREEK COOKERY

French Moussaka with Watercress

Moussaka à la Française, Vert-Pré

The technique of lining a mold with eggplant strips is shown on pages 78-79.

	To serve 6	
1 lb.	leftover boneless lean lamb, finely chopped (about 3 cups [¾ liter])	½ kg.
2	small eggplants, sliced lengthwise into slices ¼ inch [6 mm.] thick	2
	salt and pepper	
	olive oil	
1	onion, finely chopped	1
¼ lb.	fresh mushrooms, chopped (about 1½ cups [375 ml.])	125 g.
1	garlic clove, chopped	1
½ cup	puréed tomato	125 ml.
½ tsp.	ground mixed herbs	2 ml.
¼ cup	dry bread crumbs	50 ml.
1	egg	1
	watercress	

Sprinkle the eggplant slices with the salt and pepper. Heat about ½ inch [1 cm.] of olive oil in a skillet and fry the slices, in two or three batches, until golden on both sides. Drain them on paper towels.

Sprinkle the lamb with salt and cook in 2 tablespoons [30 ml.] of olive oil over medium to high heat, stirring regularly, for about 10 minutes. Meanwhile, cook the onion and mushrooms in 1 tablespoon [15 ml.] of olive oil until all of the liquid exuded by the mushrooms has evaporated. Add this mixture to the lamb, and continue cooking and stirring for a couple of minutes. Add the garlic, puréed tomato and herbs, turn the heat up as high as possible, and stir constantly until everything is well blended. Stir in the bread crumbs and let the meat mixture cool slightly while preparing the mold.

Using a 1½-quart [1½-liter] charlotte mold that is about 3 inches [7½ cm.] deep, line the bottom with eggplant slices laid next to one another. Then line the sides with slices positioned vertically and slightly overlapping; press them gently against the sides to be certain that they are firmly in place. Sprinkle the meat mixture with pepper, mix the egg into it and add it to the mold, a spoonful at a time, being careful not to displace any portions of the lining. Tap the bottom of the mold firmly several times against a wooden table or chopping board to be certain that the stuffing is well settled and that no air pockets remain. Press down more eggplant slices on the surface, carefully fold the overlapping ends of the side slices inward, one at a time, and press a buttered or oiled round of kitchen paper over the surface.

Place the mold in a larger pan, pour in enough boiling water to immerse the mold by two thirds, and poach in a preheated 350° F. [180° C.] oven or tightly covered over low heat for 40 minutes. Remove the mold from the water bath and let it settle for seven to eight minutes before unmolding.

Remove the round of paper, place a round serving platter upside down over the mold and, firmly holding the mold to the platter, turn them over together. Wait for a few seconds to be sure that the moussaka has unmolded and settled onto the platter, then gently lift off the mold. Surround with bouquets of watercress, the stem ends tucked underneath the edge of the moussaka.

RICHARD OLNEY
THE FRENCH MENU COOKBOOK

Lamb-stuffed Eggplant

	To serve 2	
1 cup	chopped leftover lamb	¼ liter
1	medium-sized eggplant (about 6 inches [15 cm.] long)	1
½ cup	chopped onion	125 ml.
¼ cup	finely chopped fresh parsley	50 ml.
¼ cup	olive oil	50 ml.
2	large tomatoes, peeled, seeded and chopped	2
1 or 2	garlic cloves, crushed to a paste	1 or 2
¾ tsp.	salt	4 ml.
½ tsp.	crushed dried mint	2 ml.
½ cup	fresh bread crumbs	125 ml.
2 tbsp.	butter, cut into small pieces	30 ml.

Cut the eggplant in half lengthwise, trim off the stem end, and scoop out the pulp, leaving a shell ½ inch [1 cm.] thick. Cover with boiling water for two minutes; drain, pat dry. Brush all over, inside and out, with olive oil. In a skillet cook the onion, parsley, tomatoes and garlic in olive oil until the onion is soft. Add the lamb, ½ teaspoon [2 ml.] of the salt, and the mint. Add some of the eggplant pulp, but none of the seedy part. Simmer for 10 minutes. Fill the two eggplant shells with this mixture. Top with the bread crumbs, sprinkle with the remaining salt and dot with the butter.

Bake the two eggplant halves in your roasting pan, which should first be well brushed with oil, in a preheated 350° F. [180° C.] oven for one hour, or until the eggplant skin is lightly wrinkled and softened, and the crumbs are golden.

BETTY WASON
BRIDE IN THE KITCHEN

❧

Baked Lamb Kebabs in Eggplant

Kebap v Patladzhani

Costmary is a flat, green-leafed herb of Oriental origin; it has a slightly bitter, minty flavor. If it is unavailable, substitute fresh mint leaves.

	To serve 6	
2 lb.	boneless lean lamb, cubed	1 kg.
3	small eggplants, halved lengthwise	3
	salt	
1 tbsp.	flour	15 ml.
7 tbsp.	butter	105 ml.
18	scallions, including 2 inches [5 cm.] of the green tops, finely chopped	18
7	medium-sized tomatoes, peeled, seeded and chopped	7
	freshly ground black pepper	
1 tsp.	paprika	5 ml.
¼ cup	white wine	50 ml.
1 cup	water	¼ liter
1 tbsp.	finely chopped fresh parsley	15 ml.
½ tbsp.	finely chopped costmary	7 ml.
3	eggs, beaten	3

Scoop out most of the flesh from the eggplant halves, leaving shells ¾ inch [2 cm.] thick. Chop the flesh, sprinkle the flesh and the shells liberally with salt, and put them in a bowl or on a kitchen towel to drain for at least two hours. Rinse thoroughly and drain again.

Combine the flour with a little salt and roll the meat cubes in the mixture. Heat the butter, and fry the meat in it until it is seared on all sides. Transfer the meat to a plate.

Using the same butter, fry the eggplant halves lightly on the outside to soften their skins. Place them in a well-greased rectangular baking dish that is just large enough to hold them snugly.

Transfer the butter from the frying pan to a large heavy saucepan. Heat the butter, slide in the scallions and let them brown. Add the tomatoes and the chopped eggplant, and cook over high heat until the mixture is fairly dry. Season

with salt and pepper, and add the paprika, wine and water. Bring to a boil, add the meat, cover, and simmer over very low heat until the meat is tender and the sauce considerably reduced, about 45 minutes. Stir in the parsley and costmary.

Fill the eggplant shells with the meat and pour the sauce over the top. Bake in a preheated 375° F. [190° C.] oven for about 30 minutes. Pour the eggs over the meat. Return to the oven and bake until the dish is golden brown on top.

GEORGI SHISHKOV AND STOIL VUCHKOV
BULGARSKI NATZIONALNI YASTIYA

❧

Cabbage Stuffed with Lamb

Baranina Duszona w Kapuście

Leftover roast lamb may be used for this dish, in which case the initial cooking of the meat is not necessary.

	To serve 4	
¾ to 1 lb.	shoulder or leg of lamb	350 to 500 g.
8	large cabbage leaves, carefully separated, or 16 small leaves	8
	salt and pepper	
1 tbsp.	finely chopped fresh rosemary	15 ml.
2 tbsp.	butter	30 ml.
¼ cup	flour	50 ml.
1 tbsp.	finely cut fresh dill	15 ml.

Bring a large pot of water to a boil, throw in the cabbage leaves and parboil for five minutes. Drain the leaves, reserving the cooking liquid. Rinse the leaves in cold water, drain them and let them cool. Cut into the thick central vein of each leaf, without cutting into the leaf itself, so that the leaf will lie flat.

Put the meat into the cabbage liquid and simmer for 30 minutes. Drain the meat, reserving the liquid. Bone the meat, cut it into eight rectangular pieces and season it with salt, pepper and rosemary.

Wrap each piece of meat carefully in one large or two small leaves. Roll up the leaves and arrange them in a single layer in an ovenproof dish just large enough to hold them, tucking under the end of each leaf. Pour in enough of the cooking liquid to come halfway up the rolls, and cover the dish with foil. Bake in a preheated 375° F. [190° C.] oven for one and one half hours or until tender, uncovering the dish for the last 30 minutes. Add more of the cooking liquid if necessary to keep the rolls moistened.

Meanwhile, melt the butter in a saucepan, stir in the flour and add enough cooking liquid to make a smooth sauce. Simmer for 30 minutes, or until thick and creamy. Season with salt, pepper and dill. Serve with the cabbage rolls.

HELENA HAWLICZKOWA
KUCHNIA POLSKA

Zucchini or Cucumbers Stuffed with Lamb

Kabaczki lub Ogórki Nadziewane Mięsem

The flesh scooped out of the vegetable shells may be sautéed with the onion and added to the stuffing. If leftover cooked meat is used, chop it fine, cook it in ½ cup [125 ml.] of meat stock for 15 minutes and combine it with the remaining stuffing ingredients.

To serve 6

10 oz.	boneless lean lamb, coarsely chopped	300 g.
2 lb.	zucchini or cucumbers, halved lengthwise if small, cut into 1½-inch [4-cm.] crosswise sections if large	1 kg.
1½ tbsp.	butter or olive oil	22 ml.
⅓ cup	chopped onion	75 ml.
7	slices stale, firm-textured white bread with the crusts removed, soaked in water and squeezed dry	7
1	egg, lightly beaten	1
	salt and pepper	
½ cup	water	125 ml.
½ cup	heavy cream	125 ml.
1 tbsp.	flour	15 ml.
1 tbsp.	finely cut fresh dill leaves	15 ml.
1 tbsp.	finely chopped fresh parsley	15 ml.

With a spoon, scoop out the seeds and flesh from the zucchini or cucumbers to form shells about ¼ inch [6 mm.] thick.

To make the stuffing, heat the butter or oil in a skillet and cook the onion for about five minutes, or until golden. Mix the onion with the meat and bread, and put the mixture through the fine disk of a food grinder. Add the egg, season with salt and pepper, and knead thoroughly until smooth.

Fill the zucchini or cucumber shells with the stuffing. Place the shells in one layer in a shallow baking dish and pour the water around them. Cover and bake in a preheated 350° F. [180° C.] oven for 20 to 30 minutes, or until the vegetable shells are tender. Add ½ teaspoon [2 ml.] of salt to the cream, mix in the flour and pour the mixture over the shells. Return them to the oven uncovered for 10 minutes.

Carefully transfer the stuffed vegetable shells to a serving dish. Pour the cooking juices over them and sprinkle with the dill and parsley. Serve with potatoes.

HELENA HAWLICZKOWA
KUCHNIA POLSKA

To Make a Delma

This recipe is adapted from a cookbook originally published in London in 1694.

To serve 8

1 lb.	lean lamb loin, ground in a food grinder or finely chopped	½ kg.
1 lb.	beef suet, finely chopped	½ kg.
1 cup	raw unprocessed rice, boiled until tender and drained	¼ liter
1 tbsp.	chopped fresh thyme	15 ml.
1 tbsp.	chopped fresh marjoram	15 ml.
1 tbsp.	chopped fresh savory	15 ml.
1 tbsp.	chopped fresh parsley	15 ml.
	salt and pepper	
	grated nutmeg	
2	eggs	2
about 30	cabbage or fresh grapevine leaves, blanched and drained	about 30
2 cups	meat stock *(recipe, page 164)*	½ liter
1	egg yolk	1

Mix the meat, suet and rice. Add the herbs, salt, pepper, nutmeg and eggs. Put a little of this mixture onto each leaf and roll it up, folding in the edges. Tie the rolls with coarse thread. Put them into a pot with the stock, cover, and simmer for 45 minutes. Lift them out and remove the threads.

Stir a spoonful of the stock into the egg yolk, then slowly pour the yolk mixture into the pot, stirring constantly. Heat the stock gently, without boiling, until it is slightly thickened. Pour this sauce over the rolls and serve.

THE RECEIPT BOOK OF ANN BLENCOWE

Old Cornish Pie

To serve 6 to 8

2 lb.	boneless lean lamb, cut into 1-inch [2½-cm.] cubes	1 kg.
1 cup	water	¼ liter
	salt and pepper	
1 tbsp.	flour	15 ml.
4 cups	finely chopped fresh parsley	1 liter
2	onions, finely chopped	2
½ lb.	short-crust dough *(recipe, page 167)*	¼ kg.
1 cup	lightly whipped heavy cream	¼ liter

Place the lamb and water in a stewpan, cover, bring to a boil, and simmer gently for 45 minutes to one hour. Remove the lamb pieces and season them with salt and pepper. Mix the flour with a little of the cooking liquid, then stir the mixture back into the pan and simmer for a minute or two until the stock is slightly thickened.

Place some of the lamb in a deep pie dish, then add a good layer of the chopped parsley and onion, then lamb, until the dish is full. See that the last layer is of the parsley and onion. Fill with the thickened stock. Roll out the dough ¼ inch [6 mm.] thick, cover the pie with it, slash the dough cover in several places to let steam escape, and bake in a preheated 375° F. [190° C.] oven for 45 minutes, or until the meat and pastry are nicely cooked.

Just before serving, remove the pastry cover by loosening its edges and sliding it off onto a plate. Spread the top of the pie liberally with the cream. Replace the pastry to serve.

THE DAILY TELEGRAPH
400 PRIZE RECIPES

Monckton Milnes Mutton Pie

To serve 10

2 lb.	boneless mutton loin, including the eye of loin and tenderloin, trimmed of excess fat and cut crosswise into slices ¼ inch [6 mm.] thick	1 kg.
	salt and pepper	
3 tbsp.	flour	45 ml.
4 tbsp.	butter, 2 tbsp. [30 ml.] cut into small pieces	60 ml.
48	live oysters, shucked, liquor reserved, beards trimmed off, trimmings reserved	48
	meat stock (recipe, page 164) or water	

Suet crust dough

½ lb.	beef suet, finely chopped	¼ kg.
4 cups	flour	1 liter
1 tsp.	salt	5 ml.
about 1 cup	cold water	about ¼ liter

For the dough, combine the suet, flour and salt. Stir in enough cold water to give a stiff, elastic consistency.

Roll out the dough and use about two thirds of it to line a large pudding basin. Place the loin slices in layers in the basin, leaving a hollow in the center and sprinkling each layer with pepper and salt. Sprinkle on 2 tablespoons [30 ml.] of the flour and dot the top layer with the small pieces of butter. Fill the hollow with the oysters. Sprinkle the oysters with pepper and salt, and cover them with the tenderloin slices. Moisten the ingredients with a little stock or water.

Now cover the basin with the remaining dough. Tie a cloth tightly over the basin and put it in a covered pot with water halfway up the sides of the basin. Boil slowly for four hours, replenishing the boiling water when necessary.

Meanwhile, simmer the trimmings of the oysters in the oyster liquor for about 15 minutes, then strain the liquor; add to it some stock or water and stir in the remaining butter—rolled in the remaining flour, mixed with a little pepper and salt. Bring the oyster-liquor mixture to a boil. Just before serving, make an opening in the crust and pour in this oyster-liquor mixture so that it can all incorporate a little and blend with the pudding. Serve the pudding very hot in the basin, with a napkin arranged around it.

SHEILA HUTCHINS
ENGLISH RECIPES AND OTHERS FROM SCOTLAND, WALES AND IRELAND

Shepherd's Pie

This recipe moistens the lamb by combining it with a milk-enriched velouté sauce. For a lighter filling, the lamb may be moistened with plain meat stock —about 2 cups [½ liter] will serve —as demonstrated on pages 74-75. With either moistener, the pie can be given a more complex flavor with the addition of vegetables: chopped and lightly sautéed onions; diced and parboiled carrots, turnips or parsnips; freshly shelled and parboiled peas.

To serve 4

5 to 6 cups	chopped leftover lamb or mutton, trimmed of all fat and gristle	1¼ to 1½ liters
6 tbsp.	butter, 3 tbsp. [45 ml.] cut into small pieces	90 ml.
¼ cup	flour	50 ml.
1 cup	milk	¼ liter
1¼ cups	meat stock (recipe, page 164)	300 ml.
	salt and pepper	
6	medium-sized potatoes, peeled, halved and boiled	6

Melt 3 tablespoons [45 ml.] of the butter in a saucepan and stir in the flour. Add the milk and meat stock slowly, stirring all the time. When the sauce is smooth, fairly thick and just begins to boil, stir in the chopped meat. Stir over very low heat for three minutes. Season to taste, pour into a shallow, buttered ovenproof dish and let the mixture cool.

Meanwhile, mash the potatoes. Season with salt and pepper, stir in 1 tablespooon [15 ml.] of the butter pieces and the remaining milk, and whisk until smooth.

When the meat is cold, spread the potatoes in a layer at least 1 inch [2½ cm.] thick over the top and mark like a plowed field with a fork. Dot with the remaining butter and cook in a preheated 350° F. [180° C.] oven for 40 minutes, by which time the top should be golden brown.

ELISABETH AYRTON
ENGLISH PROVINCIAL COOKING

Cephalonian Meat Pie

Kreatopita

Phyllo pastry sheets may be bought fresh or frozen from some supermarkets and from Middle Eastern or Greek grocery stores. If frozen, they should be defrosted overnight in the refrigerator—still in their package.

To serve 8 to 12

3 lb.	boneless lean lamb, diced	1½ kg.
24 tbsp.	butter (¾ lb. [⅓ kg.])	360 ml.
	salt and pepper	
2 cups	diced potatoes	½ liter
1½ cups	finely chopped onions	375 ml.
1 cup	finely chopped celery	¼ liter
½ cup	finely chopped fresh parsley	125 ml.
2	garlic cloves, finely chopped	2
1 tsp.	ground cinnamon	5 ml.
½ tsp.	crushed dried mint	2 ml.
4	eggs, hard-boiled and diced	4
½ cup	raw unprocessed long-grain rice	125 ml.
½ cup	olive oil	125 ml.
1 lb.	phyllo pastry sheets	½ kg.
1 cup	shredded Gruyère cheese or crumbled feta cheese	¼ liter

Sauté the lamb in 8 tablespoons [120 ml.] of the butter for 10 minutes or until well browned, and season to taste with salt and pepper.

In a small pan, melt the remaining 16 tablespoons [240 ml.] of butter. In a mixing bowl, combine the lamb with all of the other ingredients except the phyllo sheets, melted butter and cheese; mix well and season with salt and pepper.

Butter a 9-by-13-inch [23-by-33-cm.] baking pan and line the bottom with half of the phyllo sheets, brushing each sheet with melted butter. Spread the lamb mixture evenly over the phyllo sheets, sprinkle with the cheese and cover with the remaining phyllo sheets, brushing each leaf with melted butter. Brush the top leaf with butter and score it into squares with a sharp knife. Bake in a preheated 350° F. [180° C.] oven for one hour, or until the pastry is browned and flaky. Allow to cool slightly, cut and serve.

EVA ZANE
GREEK COOKING FOR THE GODS

Bidding Pie

Pastai Neithior

When bidding weddings were held on the Gower peninsula, this pie was specially prepared for the wedding feast held at the bride's home. The pie was served cold with beer. A bidder was appointed by the bride's family to invite the guests and, during the feast, to record the sum of money paid by each guest for a small piece of pie. The young couple were partly dependent on this gift money to set up their home.

To serve 4

½ lb.	boneless cooked mutton, diced	¼ kg.
3 cups	flour	¾ liter
1 tsp.	salt	5 ml.
10 tbsp.	lard	150 ml.
2 tbsp.	water	30 ml.
1	onion, finely chopped	1
1 tsp.	mixed herbs	5 ml.
about 1 cup	lamb stock *(recipe, page 164)*	about ¼ liter

Sift the flour and salt into a large bowl. In a small pan, melt the lard slowly in the water, bring to a boil and immediately pour the lard mixture into the flour. Work the lard into the flour and knead well to form a soft dough. Turn out the dough onto a floured board and roll it out until it is fairly thin. Grease a 7-inch [21-cm.] pie dish and line it with two thirds of the dough.

Fill the pie shell with the mutton and onion, add the herbs and enough stock to thoroughly moisten the ingredients. Cover with the rest of the dough, pressing the edges of both layers together to seal them. Cut a slit in the center and bake in a preheated 375° F. [190° C.] oven for about one hour, or until the pastry is golden.

S. MINWEL TIBBOTT
WELSH FARE

Mutton Pie and Tomatoes

To serve 4

1 lb.	boneless leftover roast mutton, thinly sliced	½ kg.
¾ cup	dry bread crumbs	175 ml.
6	medium-sized tomatoes, peeled and sliced	6
	salt and pepper	
4 tbsp.	butter, cut into small pieces	60 ml.

Spread the bottom of a buttered baking dish with bread crumbs, and fill with alternate layers of lamb and tomatoes; season each layer with pepper, salt and the butter. The last layer should be of tomatoes spread with bread crumbs.

Bake in a 350° F. [180° C.] oven for 45 minutes, or until the top coating of bread crumbs is well browned, and serve the pie immediately.

THE OHIO HOUSEWIVES COMPANION

Mutton Spicy Pie

To serve 4

1 lb.	boneless leftover mutton, cut into small pieces (about 2 cups [½ liter])	½ kg.
3	medium-sized apples, peeled, cored and chopped	3
	salt and pepper	
1 tbsp.	sugar	15 ml.
⅓ cup	dried currants, soaked in warm water for 15 minutes and drained	75 ml.
	freshly grated nutmeg	
2 tbsp.	butter, cut into small pieces	30 ml.
½ lb.	short-crust dough (recipe, page 167)	¼ kg.

In a deep baking dish, arrange the meat and apples in alternate layers. Season each layer well with salt and pepper, a little sugar, a few currants and a pinch of nutmeg. Complete the layers, top with the pieces of butter and cover with a lid of rolled dough. Make a hole in the center of the lid. Bake in a preheated 350° F. [180° C.] oven until the pastry is browned, about 40 minutes, and serve hot.

JOAN POULSON
OLD THAMES VALLEY RECIPES

Sliced Lamb with Chicory

Émincé de Mouton à la Chicorée

To serve 6

1½ lb.	leftover roast lamb, thinly sliced	¾ kg.
	salt	
3 or 4	heads chicory, cored	3 or 4
2 tbsp.	butter	30 ml.
1 tbsp.	flour	15 ml.
½ cup	white wine	125 ml.
½ cup	meat stock (recipe, page 164)	125 ml.
	croutons (recipe, page 167)	

Bring a large saucepan of lightly salted water to a boil, put in the chicory and cook for three minutes after the water returns to a boil. Drain the chicory, squeeze out as much moisture as possible and chop it fine.

In another saucepan, melt the butter over low heat, stir in the flour and cook for three or four minutes. Stir in the wine and stock, and simmer, stirring constantly, over low

heat until the sauce is smooth and thickened and no taste of uncooked flour remains. Add the chicory and continue to simmer the mixture until the sauce thickens again.

Place the lamb on top of the chicory mixture, cover, and heat the lamb without letting the sauce come to a boil. Arrange the meat and chicory on a warmed serving dish. At the moment of serving, surround the dish with fried croutons.

JULES BRETEUIL
LE CUISINIER EUROPÉEN

Suliman's Pilaf

To toast the nuts, put them on a baking sheet in a 400° F. [200° C.] oven for five minutes, or until lightly browned.

To serve 4

½ lb.	boneless leftover lamb or mutton, diced (about 1½ cups [375 ml.])	¼ kg.
½ cup	oil	125 ml.
2 cups	raw unprocessed long-grain rice	½ liter
8 cups	boiling water	2 liters
⅓ cup	chopped onion	75 ml.
¼ cup	raisins, soaked in warm water for 15 minutes and drained	50 ml.
¼ cup	dried currants, soaked in warm water for 15 minutes and drained	50 ml.
2	garlic cloves, chopped	2
2	tomatoes, peeled, seeded and chopped	2
2 tbsp.	pine nuts or blanched almonds, toasted	30 ml.
	salt and pepper	
	sour cream or plain yogurt	

Into a heavy pan put half of the oil and when it is warm, put in the rice and stir for a few minutes until the rice takes on a transparent look. Then pour in the boiling water and cook very fast for about 12 minutes. The time of cooking varies according to the rice, but it should be rather underdone than overdone. Drain the rice. In the meantime, heat the remaining oil and fry the onion until it is soft. Add the meat, raisins, currants, garlic, tomatoes, and pine nuts or almonds. Season well. Put the drained rice into a heavy pan and stir in the meat-and-onion mixture. Toss together for a few minutes over low heat before serving. Serve a bowl of sour cream or yogurt with the pilaf.

ELIZABETH DAVID
A BOOK OF MEDITERRANEAN FOOD

Very Special Lamb Hash

To serve 4

2 cups	diced leftover lamb	½ liter
3 tbsp.	butter	45 ml.
1 tbsp.	olive or vegetable oil	15 ml.
1	large onion, finely chopped	1
2	garlic cloves, finely chopped	2
3	large potatoes, peeled, boiled for 15 minutes and cut into ½-inch [1-cm.] dice	3
¼ cup	chopped ripe olives	50 ml.
1	small green pepper, stemmed, seeded, deribbed and coarsely chopped	1
1	small fresh jalapeño pepper, stemmed, seeded and chopped, or 2 tsp. [10 ml.] crushed dried hot chilies	1
2 tbsp.	chopped fresh mint leaves, or 2 tsp. [10 ml.] crumbled dried mint leaves	30 ml.
	salt and freshly ground black pepper	
2 tbsp.	soy sauce	30 ml.
¼ cup	beef stock *(recipe, page 164)*	50 ml.
3 tbsp.	freshly grated Parmesan cheese	45 ml.
	chili sauce (optional)	

Heat the butter and oil in a large, heavy ovenproof skillet. Sauté the onion and garlic until golden; push them to the edge of the skillet. Place the meat in the center of the skillet; cook and stir over medium heat until lightly browned.

Add the potatoes, olives, green pepper, jalapeño pepper or dried chilies, mint, salt, black pepper and soy sauce to the skillet; stir until well combined, and gently flatten the mixture against the bottom of the skillet. Stirring occasionally, cook over medium heat until the potatoes are brown but still slightly crunchy, about 10 minutes. Add the beef stock when the mixture begins to dry out.

Increase the heat under the skillet; without stirring, cook the hash for five minutes. Sprinkle the Parmesan cheese over the hash. Place the skillet under a preheated broiler until the top of the hash is brown and crisp. Serve with chili sauce, if desired.

BERT GREENE
BERT GREENE'S KITCHEN BOUQUETS

Hashed Lamb

To serve 6

½ lb.	leftover boneless lamb, finely chopped (about 2 cups [½ liter])	¼ kg.
2	onions, chopped	2
2 tbsp.	butter	30 ml.
2	medium-sized potatoes, boiled, peeled and chopped	2
1 tbsp.	salt	15 ml.
1 tsp.	pepper	5 ml.
½ tsp.	grated nutmeg	2 ml.
1 cup	meat stock *(recipe, page 164)*	¼ liter
6	eggs	6
	chopped fresh parsley	

In a large saucepan, fry the onions in the butter until golden. Add the potatoes and lamb, and season with the salt, pepper and nutmeg. Moisten with the stock and cook for 10 minutes.

Meanwhile, poach the eggs in a pan of simmering water for three minutes, or just until the whites have set.

Put the hash in a hot serving dish and arrange the poached eggs on top. Serve sprinkled with chopped parsley.

OSCAR TSCHIRKY
THE COOK BOOK BY "OSCAR" OF THE WALDORF

Mutton Hashed Venison-Fashion

To serve 4

1 lb.	leftover boneless mutton, sliced ⅓ inch [1 cm.] thick and trimmed of all fat and gristle	½ kg.
	salt and white pepper	
1 tbsp.	flour, browned in a 400° F. [200° C.] oven for 5 minutes	15 ml.
	mutton bones and trimmings	
1¼ cups	water	300 ml.
1	lamb kidney, halved, trimmed of all fat and coarsely chopped	1
1	shallot, chopped	1
½ cup	chopped carrot	125 ml.
2 oz.	lamb liver, chopped	60 g.
1 tbsp.	currant jelly	15 ml.
¼ cup	port	50 ml.

Season the slices of mutton with salt and pepper, and dip them in the browned flour. Place the slices in a small fireproof casserole. Put the bones and trimmings of the mutton in a saucepan with the water, kidney, shallot, carrot and liver. Simmer uncovered for 30 minutes. Strain this gravy and pour it over the mutton slices. Let the mutton mixture barely simmer for one and one half hours. Stir in the currant jelly, add the port and serve immediately.

COLONEL KENNEY-HERBERT
DAINTY DISHES FOR INDIAN TABLES

Southern Baked Lamb and Ham Hash

To serve 6

2 cups	diced leftover roast lamb	½ liter
½ cup	diced leftover baked or boiled ham	125 ml.
1	large onion, quartered	1
1	large green pepper, quartered, seeded and deribbed	1
2 or 3	sprigs parsley	2 or 3
1 tbsp.	butter	15 ml.
2 tbsp.	flour	30 ml.
2 cups	milk	½ liter
	salt and pepper	
	Tabasco sauce	
¼ cup	dry bread crumbs	50 ml.
3 tbsp.	melted butter	45 ml.

Put the lamb, ham, onion, green pepper and parsley through the coarse disk of a food grinder. Set the mixture aside.

In a heavy saucepan, melt the butter over low heat until it is bubbly. Using a wooden spoon, stir in the flour and cook, stirring constantly, until the mixture is light gold in color. Still stirring, slowly incorporate the milk. Stir until the mixture forms a thick smooth sauce. Season to taste with salt, pepper and Tabasco. Remove the sauce from the heat, add the ground meat mixture, and blend well. Pour into a well-greased, deep ovenproof casserole, sprinkle bread crumbs on top, and pour melted butter over the surface. Bake in a preheated 375° F. [190° C.] oven for 30 minutes.

BOB JEFFRIES
SOUL FOOD COOKBOOK

Bulgur and Meat

Kubbah Bulghur bis Siniyyah

Bulgur was the basic cereal for Middle Eastern people in ancient times. Later they used it in combination with meat, vegetables, fowl, herbs and spices as a versatile part of their colorful cuisine.

To serve 4

1½ lb.	ground lean lamb	¾ kg.
1 cup	very fine bulgur	¼ liter
1	onion, finely chopped	1
⅓ cup	olive oil	75 ml.
	salt and freshly ground pepper	
	ground turmeric	
½ cup	pine nuts	125 ml.
½ cup	dried currants, soaked in warm water for 15 minutes and drained (optional)	125 ml.
2 tbsp.	butter, cut into small pieces, plus (optional) 4 tbsp. [60 ml.] melted butter	30 ml.

Put the bulgur in a bowl and wash it in cold water. Skim off the film that rises to the top. Let the bulgur soak in 3 cups [¾ liter] of water for at least one hour.

In a large skillet, sauté the onion in 2 tablespoons [30 ml.] of the oil over medium-low heat. Add a dash of pepper and turmeric and stir occasionally until the onion is golden. Add 1 pound [½ kg.] of the meat to the onion and, stirring occasionally, cook over medium heat until all of the liquid is gone and the meat is cooked through. Add the pine nuts, currants, if using, and salt to taste; mix. Remove the mixture from the heat and let it stand.

Drain the soaked bulgur. Lift out a handful at a time, squeeze it dry and put it in a tray or a large bowl. Add the remaining meat, season with salt and pepper, and knead well—adding cold water or the melted butter, if necessary—to make a soft paste.

Grease an 11-by-7-inch [28-by-18-cm.] ovenproof pan generously with oil. Divide the paste in half. Put one half in the pan and, with a wet palm, flatten until the paste is about ⅓ inch [8 mm.] thick. Spread the cooked-meat mixture evenly on top. Spoon the remaining bulgur paste over the top and smooth it into an even layer. With a knife, cut a cross connecting the opposite corners of the pan, then make 2-inch [5-cm.] parallel cuts in both directions to form diamond-shaped portions. Place a piece of butter on each portion.

Bake on the bottom shelf of a preheated 400° F. [200° C.] oven for 40 minutes, then on the top shelf for 15 to 20 minutes, basting if necessary with a mixture of the remaining oil and 2 tablespoons of water to keep the meat moist. The top should be crisp. Serve hot with a salad.

DAISY INY
THE BEST OF BAGHDAD COOKING

Baked Lamb Curry

Once this baked lamb is cold, it cuts into nice neat wedges and makes perfect picnic fare. If you plan to serve the lamb cold, use a bit more curry because its flavor is weakened when it is chilled.

To serve 8

2 lb.	ground lamb shoulder	1 kg.
2 tbsp.	oil	30 ml.
2	apples, quartered, cored and sliced	2
2	medium-sized onions, sliced	2
4 tbsp.	butter	60 ml.
1½ tbsp.	curry powder	22 ml.
¼ cup	chopped almonds	50 ml.
¼ cup	seedless raisins	50 ml.
1 tbsp.	fresh lemon juice	15 ml.
	salt and pepper	
1	thick slice firm-textured white bread	1
1 cup	milk	¼ liter
2	eggs	2
	chutney	

Preheat the oven to 350° F. [180° C.]. Heat the oil in a large skillet and fry the lamb in it for about 10 minutes, stirring often. If the meat exudes a lot of liquid, drain most of it off before putting the meat into a mixing bowl.

After removing the meat, put the butter in the skillet and add the apples, onions, curry, almonds, raisins, lemon juice, salt and pepper. Mix these seasonings well, cover, and cook for about five minutes. Add the meat, cover, and cook for another five minutes.

While the meat is cooking, soak the bread in the milk, then squeeze the bread dry but reserve the milk. Break one egg into the softened bread and beat with a fork until light and frothy. Remove the meat from the stove and beat in the bread-egg combination.

Butter a 10-cup [2½-liter] baking dish and spoon in the meat mixture. Beat the other egg with the reserved milk, add salt and pepper, and spoon this custard mixture over the meat. Bake for 30 minutes, until the custard on top is set.

At the table cut the baked lamb curry into pie-shaped wedges and serve with chutney.

CAROL CUTLER
THE SIX-MINUTE SOUFFLÉ AND OTHER CULINARY DELIGHTS

Meatballs Cooked in Cream
Malai Kofta Curry

The volatile oils in chilies may make your skin smart or your eyes sting if you touch them after handling the chilies. Wear rubber gloves when handling the chilies or work carefully and wash your hands immediately afterward.

To serve 4

1 lb.	ground lean lamb	½ kg.
½ cup	ghee	125 ml.
⅓ cup	finely chopped onion	75 ml.
8	garlic cloves, finely chopped	8
2 tbsp.	finely shredded fresh ginger	30 ml.
2	fresh green chilies, stemmed, halved, seeded and chopped	2
½ tsp.	cayenne pepper	2 ml.
1½ tsp.	salt	7 ml.
1	egg, lightly beaten	1
1	egg yolk, lightly beaten	1
¼ tsp.	garam masala	1 ml.

Pistachio filling

32	pistachios	32
2	eggs, hard-boiled and chopped	2
¼ tsp.	salt	1 ml.
¼ tsp.	cayenne pepper	1 ml.
¼ tsp.	white pepper	1 ml.
16	white raisins, soaked in warm water for 15 minutes and drained	16
32	almonds, blanched	32

Cream gravy

1 cup	sour cream, or 2 tbsp. [30 ml.] farmer or pot cheese and ½ cup [125 ml.] light cream	¼ liter
¼ cup	ghee	50 ml.
1	medium-sized onion, grated	1
2	garlic cloves, finely chopped	2
½ tsp.	cayenne pepper	1 ml.
1 tbsp.	ground coriander	15 ml.
1 tbsp.	ground ginger	15 ml.
1 tsp.	salt	5 ml.
1	medium-sized tomato, peeled, seeded and sliced	1
1½ cups	water or meat stock *(recipe, page 164)*	375 ml.
½ tsp.	garam masala	2 ml.
1 tbsp.	finely chopped fresh coriander leaves	15 ml.

For the meatballs, heat ¼ cup [50 ml.] of the *ghee* and fry the onion and garlic until golden brown. Add the lamb, ginger, chilies, cayenne and salt. Cover the pan. Cook over low heat until the juices are reabsorbed by the lamb, about 15 minutes. Stir and remove from the heat. Cool.

In the meantime, prepare the gravy. Heat the *ghee,* and fry the onions and garlic until golden brown. Add the cayenne, coriander, ginger and salt; stir for five minutes. Add the tomato slices, mix thoroughly, and add the water or stock. Simmer over low heat for about 15 minutes, or until reduced by a third. For the filling, mix the chopped eggs with the salt, cayenne and white pepper.

Grind the cooled meat mixture, and blend in the beaten egg and egg yolk, and the *garam masala.* Divide the meat mixture into 16 equal portions. Flatten each portion, and put in its center 1½ tablespoons [22 ml.] of the chopped-egg mixture, two pistachios, one raisin and two almonds. Dipping your hands in cold water, shape each portion of meat into a ball enclosing the filling.

Heat the remaining *ghee* and fry the meatballs until golden. Add the fried meatballs to the gravy. Simmer for 15 minutes, or until they are soft and swollen and the gravy is reduced to half of its original volume. Beat the sour cream, or farmer or pot cheese and light cream, add it to the gravy, and sprinkle with ¼ teaspoon [1 ml.] of the *garam masala.* Place the pan in a preheated 250° F. [120° C.] oven for about 15 minutes. Turn off the heat and leave the mixture there until serving time, up to 15 minutes.

Sprinkle the coriander leaves and the remaining ¼ teaspoon of *garam masala* over the dish and serve.

MRS. BALBIR SINGH
MRS. BALBIR SINGH'S INDIAN COOKERY

Lamb Apples

Pommeaulx

To serve 8

1 lb.	boneless lean lamb, finely chopped	½ kg.
1 lb.	boneless lean pork, finely chopped	½ kg.
	salt and pepper	
1 tsp.	ground ginger	5 ml.
½ tsp.	ground cloves	2 ml.
3	egg whites	3
¼ lb.	parsley, stems removed, leaves chopped, ground to a paste in a mortar or processor and sieved	125 g.
¼ cup	flour	50 ml.
4 tbsp.	butter	60 ml.

In a bowl, thoroughly combine the lamb, pork, salt, pepper and spices. Knead the mixture with your hands, gradually adding the egg whites, until the mixture is smooth. Form it into eight balls the size and shape of apples.

Bring a large pot of salted water to a boil, put in the meatballs and return the water to a boil. After five minutes, drain the meatballs and thread them onto skewers. Grill the meatballs over hot coals or under a preheated broiler—turning them once—until they are lightly browned.

Work together the parsley, flour and butter until they form a smooth paste. Roll the meatballs in this paste, then return them to the grill or broiler. Repeat this operation several times, until the meatballs have a green coating and are cooked through.

LE MÉNAGIER DE PARIS

Lamb Sausage

Salame d'Agnello

To serve 4

14 oz.	ground lean lamb	400 g.
1	potato, boiled, peeled and mashed	1
½ cup	chopped spinach or chard, parboiled, drained, squeezed dry and puréed through a food mill	125 ml.
1	egg	1
2 tbsp.	freshly grated Parmesan cheese	30 ml.
	salt and pepper	
	bread crumbs (optional)	
¼ cup	flour, mixed with ¼ cup [50 ml.] dry bread crumbs	50 ml.
4 tbsp.	butter	60 ml.
1 tbsp.	olive oil	15 ml.
½ cup	white wine	125 ml.
2 cups	meat stock *(recipe, page 164)*	½ liter

In a bowl, mix the lamb, potato, spinach or chard, egg, Parmesan, and salt and pepper. Add bread crumbs, if necessary, to make a firm mixture. When thoroughly combined, form the lamb mixture into a ball and pound vigorously several times against the bottom of the bowl. Form a cylindrical sausage and coat it with the mixed flour and bread crumbs.

Heat the butter and oil, and brown the sausage on all sides. Add the white wine and cook until the wine evaporates. Add the stock, cover and simmer gently for one hour, turning the sausage occasionally.

Remove the sausage from the pan and keep it warm. Skim off the fat from the cooking liquid and reduce the liquid over high heat to the desired consistency. Correct the seasoning. Slice the sausage and serve it with the reduced liquid poured over it.

LISA BIONDI (EDITOR)
350 RICETTE DI CUCINA LEGGERA

Stuffed Meatballs

Harput Kufté

To serve 4 to 6

1 lb.	ground lean lamb	½ kg.
5 cups	meat stock *(recipe, page 164)*	1¼ liters
½ cup	chopped fresh parsley	125 ml.
⅓ cup	chopped onion	75 ml.
2	medium-sized tomatoes, peeled and chopped	2
1½ cups	very fine bulgur	375 ml.
	salt and pepper	
2 tbsp.	butter (optional)	30 ml.

Onion and pine nut stuffing

1	large onion, sliced	1
8 tbsp.	butter	120 ml.
2 tbsp.	pine nuts	30 ml.
2 tbsp.	chopped fresh parsley	30 ml.
¼ tsp.	ground allspice	1 ml.
¼ tsp.	ground cinnamon	1 ml.
2 tbsp.	dried currants, soaked in warm water for 15 minutes and drained (optional)	30 ml.

Bring the stock to a boil and add the chopped parsley, onion and tomatoes. Simmer for one hour.

Meanwhile, prepare the stuffing. Fry the sliced onion in the butter to the stage just before it turns pink. Add the remaining ingredients and cook for five minutes. Put the mixture in a dish, cover and refrigerate. When chilled, form the mixture into balls the size of large marbles.

For the meatballs, mix the lamb and bulgur with salt and pepper. Knead for 15 minutes, until blended into a gummy mixture. Shape into balls the size of walnuts. With your thumb, make a hollow in each ball to hold the stuffing, and press the side walls thin. Slip in a ball of stuffing and press the top of the hollow closed, smoothing and sealing it by rolling the meatball between your palms.

Drop the meatballs into the simmering stock. When they are cooked, they will rise to the surface. This will take about 20 minutes. Do not cook too many in the pot at one time, as they require room to rise. They may be served with the soup stock in deep bowls.

If they are to be served dry, remove the meatballs from the stock. Try not to break the surfaces of the balls, or you will lose some of the spicy juices that have been sealed inside. Melt the butter in a baking dish, roll the meatballs in the butter and place in a 375° F. [190° C.] oven until they have a crisp crust, about 10 minutes.

GEORGE MARDIKIAN
DINNER AT OMAR KHAYYAM'S

Lamb Burgers with Pine Nuts

Kafta Snoober

To serve 4

1 lb.	ground lean lamb	½ kg.
4 tbsp.	pine nuts	60 ml.
1 tbsp.	butter	15 ml.
¼ cup	chopped fresh parsley	50 ml.
1	onion, finely chopped	1
1 tsp.	dried mint	5 ml.
	salt and pepper	
1½ cups	puréed tomato	375 ml.

Brown the pine nuts in the butter; let the pine nuts cool slightly. Mix together the lamb, parsley, onion, mint, salt and pepper. Shape into four cylindrical rolls, filling each with 1 tablespoon [15 ml.] of the pine nuts. Place in an oiled baking pan and pour the puréed tomato over the rolls. Bake for 30 minutes in a preheated 350° F. [180° C.] oven.

HELEN COREY
THE ART OF SYRIAN COOKERY

Lamb Burgers Baked with Yogurt

Ćufteta od Jagnjećeg Mesa

To serve 4

1 lb.	ground lean lamb	½ kg.
	salt and freshly ground pepper	
	paprika	
1	garlic clove, crushed to a paste	1
½ cup	finely chopped onion, fried in 1 tbsp. [15 ml.] lard until soft	125 ml.
1 tbsp.	finely chopped flat-leafed parsley	15 ml.
1	thick slice firm-textured white bread with the crust removed, soaked in water and squeezed dry	1
4 tbsp.	lard or rendered fat	60 ml.
4 or 5	eggs, beaten	4 or 5
1 to 2 cups	plain yogurt	¼ to ½ liter

Season the meat generously with salt, pepper and paprika. Add the garlic, onion, parsley and bread. Mix thoroughly. Divide the mixture into eight equal portions and shape each portion into a neat patty.

In a frying pan, melt the lard and when it sizzles, put in the patties. Cook them over medium to high heat for about three minutes on each side. They should be well browned, but still pink inside. Remove them from the pan and arrange them in a single layer in a baking dish.

Whisk the eggs and yogurt together, season with salt and pepper, and stir in a spoonful of fat from the pan. Pour this mixture over the lamb burgers. Blend another spoonful of the fat with 1 teaspoon [5 ml.] of paprika and sprinkle this on top of the dish. Bake in a preheated 350° F. [180° C.] oven for one hour, or until the top is lightly browned. Serve at once.

SPASENIJA-PATA MARKOVIĆ (EDITOR)
VELIKI NARODNI KUVAR

Mutton Croquettes

To serve 4

1 lb.	boneless leftover roast mutton, very finely chopped	½ kg.
½ lb.	boneless leftover veal, beef or pork, very finely chopped	¼ kg.
12 tbsp.	butter, or 4 tbsp. [60 ml.] butter and 8 tbsp. [120 ml.] lard	180 ml.
	salt and pepper	
⅔ cup	meat stock (recipe, page 164)	150 ml.
1 tsp.	chopped fresh parsley	5 ml.
2	eggs, the yolks separated from the whites, and the whites lightly beaten	2
¾ cup	dry bread crumbs	175 ml.
1 tbsp.	olive oil	15 ml.
1 tbsp.	water	15 ml.
	Parsley garnish	
15	sprigs parsley	15
	oil for deep frying	

Mix the meats together. Melt 4 tablespoons [60 ml.] of the butter in a saucepan and add salt and pepper, the stock, chopped parsley and egg yolks. Stir in the meats and heat very briefly without letting the mixture boil. Spread it on a dish to cool.

When cold, divide the meat mixture into 12 equal portions. Form each portion into an egg-shaped croquette. Roll the croquettes in the bread crumbs. Mix the egg whites with salt and pepper, olive oil and water. Dip the croquettes in the egg-white mixture and roll them again in the crumbs.

Melt the remaining butter or the lard, if using, in a frying pan, and fry the croquettes over medium heat until they are a light brown on all sides, about 10 to 12 minutes. Drain them, sprinkle with salt, and pile them on a hot dish.

Deep fry the parsley sprigs in hot oil for one to two seconds, or until crisp. Garnish the croquettes with the parsley sprigs, and serve.

MYRA (EDITOR)
MYRA'S COOKERY BOOK

Spiced Lamb Patties

Shami Kabab

The volatile oils in chilies may irritate your skin: Wear rubber gloves when handling them.

To serve 6 to 8

2 lb.	lean ground lamb	1 kg.
2 cups	water	½ liter
1¼ cups	dried chick-peas (garbanzos), soaked in water overnight and drained	300 ml.
6	whole cloves	6
1-inch	stick cinnamon	2½-cm.
6	green cardamom pods	6
3	brown cardamom pods	3
1 tsp.	ground cumin	5 ml.
1 tsp.	cayenne pepper	5 ml.
1	garlic clove	1
8	peppercorns	8
	salt	
2 tsp.	garam masala	10 ml.
2-inch	slice fresh ginger, grated	5-cm.
3	onions, chopped and fried in butter until soft	3
2 tsp.	ground coriander	10 ml.
1 cup	chopped fresh coriander	¼ liter
2	fresh green chilies, stemmed, seeded and finely chopped	2
2	eggs (optional)	2
1	slice firm-textured bread with the crust removed, soaked in a little water, squeezed dry and crumbled (optional)	1
3 tbsp.	fresh lemon juice	45 ml.
1 cup	ghee or oil	¼ kg.

Place the meat in a heavy pan and add the water, chick-peas, cloves, cinnamon, cardamom, cumin, cayenne pepper, garlic, peppercorns and salt. Stirring frequently, boil for 45 minutes, or until the meat becomes soft and almost dry.

Put the mixture through a meat grinder and add the *garam masala,* ginger, onions, ground and fresh coriander, chilies and, if using, the eggs and bread. Mix well and add the lemon juice. Form the mixture into flat, round patties about ½ inch [1 cm.] thick and 3 inches [8 cm.] in diameter.

Heat the *ghee* or oil and, when really hot, fry the patties two or three at a time. Brown them well on both sides, and drain them on paper towels.

KRISHNA PRASAD DAR
KASHMIRI COOKING

Standard Preparations

Meat Stock

This general-purpose strong stock will keep for up to a week if refrigerated and brought to a boil every two days. Alternatively, it may be packed in freezer containers, tightly covered and stored in the freezer for up to six months.

To make about 3 quarts [3 liters] stock

2 lb.	meaty beef shank	1 kg.
2 lb.	meaty veal shank	1 kg.
2 lb.	chicken backs, necks, feet and wing tips	1 kg.
about 5 quarts	water	about 5 liters
1	bouquet garni, including leek and celery	1
1	garlic bulb, unpeeled	1
2	medium-sized onions, each stuck with 1 whole clove	2
4	carrots	4

Place a trivet or a rack in the bottom of a large stockpot to prevent the ingredients from sticking. Fit all of the meat, bones and chicken pieces into the pot, and add cold water to cover by about 2 inches [5 cm.]. Bring slowly to a boil, skimming off the scum that rises. Keep skimming, occasionally adding a glass of cold water, until no more scum rises. Do not stir, lest you cloud the stock.

Add the bouquet garni, garlic, onions and carrots, and skim once more as the liquid returns to a boil. Reduce the heat to very low, cover the pot with the lid ajar, and simmer for five hours. If the meat is to be eaten, remove the veal after one and one half hours, the beef after three hours.

Ladle the stock into a colander lined with dampened muslin or cheesecloth and placed over a large bowl. Let the strained stock cool completely, then remove the last traces of fat from the surface. If the stock has been refrigerated to cool, lift off the solidified fat.

Lamb stock. Omit the beef shank and chicken pieces, and substitute about 6 pounds [3 kg.] of lamb bones, including the shank and neck. Simmer for five hours.

Veal stock. Omit the beef shank and chicken pieces, and substitute about 4 pounds [2 kg.] of meaty veal trimmings (neck, shank or rib tips). For a richer, more gelatinous stock, add a calf's foot that has been cleaned, split and blanched for five minutes in boiling water. Simmer for five hours.

Beef stock. Substitute 4 pounds [2 kg.] of oxtail, beef shank or beef chuck for the veal shank and the chicken pieces, and simmer the stock for about five hours. A veal knuckle or calf's foot can be added to the pot if a more gelatinous stock is desired.

Chicken stock. Stewing chickens and roosters yield the richest stock. Omit the beef shank and veal shank, and use 5 pounds [2½ kg.] of chicken carcasses, necks, feet, wings, gizzards and hearts; simmer for two hours.

Basic White Sauce

Use this recipe whenever béchamel sauce is required.

To make about 1 ½ cups [375 ml.] sauce

2 tbsp.	butter	30 ml.
2 tbsp.	flour	30 ml.
2½ cups	milk	625 ml.
	salt	
	white pepper	
	freshly grated nutmeg (optional)	
	heavy cream (optional)	

Melt the butter in a heavy saucepan. Stir in the flour and cook, stirring, over low heat for two to five minutes. Pour in all of the milk at once, whisking constantly to blend the mixture smooth. Increase the heat and continue whisking while the sauce comes to a boil. Season with very little salt.

Reduce the heat to very low and simmer for about 40 minutes, stirring every so often to prevent the sauce from sticking to the bottom of the pan. When the sauce reaches the desired consistency, add white pepper and a pinch of nutmeg if desired. Taste for seasoning. Whisk again until the sauce is perfectly smooth, and add cream if you prefer a richer and whiter sauce.

Velouté Sauce

To make about 1 ½ cups [375 ml.] sauce

2 tbsp.	butter	30 ml.
2 tbsp.	flour	30 ml.
2 cups	meat stock *(recipe, left)*, or 1 cup [¼ liter] stock and 1 cup white wine	½ liter
	salt and pepper	

Melt the butter in a heavy saucepan over low heat and stir in the flour until this roux mixture is smooth. Cook, stirring constantly for two to three minutes. When the roux stops foaming and is a light golden color, pour in the stock, or stock and wine, whisking constantly to blend the mixture smooth. Increase the heat and continue whisking while the sauce comes to a boil. Reduce the heat to very low. Move the saucepan half off the heat so that the liquid on one side of the pan barely simmers. Skim off fat and impurities that form on the surface of the other, calm side of the liquid. From time to time spoon off the skin. Cook for 30 minutes, or until the sauce reaches the desired consistency. Season to taste with salt and pepper before serving.

Mint Sauce

To make about ⅓ cup [75 ml.] sauce

3 oz.	fresh mint leaves, finely chopped (about 3 cups [¾ liter])	90 g.
1 tbsp.	hot water	15 ml.
about ½ tbsp.	sugar	about 7 ml.
3 tbsp.	vinegar	45 ml.

Combine the mint leaves and hot water, and add sugar to taste. Let the mixture steep for at least 30 minutes. Stir in the vinegar and serve.

Harissa Sauce

The volatile oils in chilies may irritate your skin. Wear rubber gloves when handling them.

To make about ¼ cup [50 ml.] sauce

¼ cup	dried hot red chilies, split lengthwise, stemmed, seeded, soaked in water for 1 hour and drained	50 ml.
1	garlic clove, chopped	1
1 tsp.	coarse salt	5 ml.
½ tsp.	caraway seeds	2 ml.
¼ tsp.	ground cumin	1 ml.
	olive oil	

Cut the chilies into small pieces. In a mortar, food mill or food processor, pound or grind the chilies to a purée with the garlic, salt and spices. Mix in a spoonful or two of olive oil to give the paste a fluid consistency. Pack into a small jar and cover with a layer of olive oil. *Harissa* sauce will keep, refrigerated, for two to three months.

Tomato Sauce

When fresh ripe tomatoes are not available, use drained, canned Italian-style tomatoes or home-canned tomatoes.

To make about 1 ¼ cups [300 ml.] sauce

6	medium-sized very ripe tomatoes, quartered	6
1	bay leaf	1
1	large sprig dried thyme	1
	coarse salt	
1	onion, sliced	1
2	garlic cloves, lightly crushed (optional)	2
2 tbsp.	butter, cut into small pieces (optional)	30 ml.
	freshly ground black pepper	
1 to 2 tsp.	sugar (optional)	5 to 10 ml.
1 tbsp.	finely chopped fresh parsley (optional)	15 ml.
1 tbsp.	fresh basil leaves, torn into small pieces (optional)	15 ml.

Place the tomatoes in an enameled, tinned or stainless-steel saucepan with the bay leaf, thyme and a pinch of coarse salt. Add the onion and the garlic, if using. Bring to a boil, crushing the tomatoes lightly with a wooden spoon, and cook, uncovered, over a fairly brisk heat for 10 minutes, or until the tomatoes have disintegrated into a thick pulp. Tip the tomatoes into a plastic or stainless-steel sieve placed over a pan. Using a wooden pestle, press the tomatoes through the sieve. Cook, uncovered, over low heat until the sauce is reduced to the required consistency. Remove the pan from the heat. If you like, whisk in the pieces of butter to enrich the sauce. Season the sauce with pepper and, if desired, with sugar, chopped parsley and basil.

Chunky tomato sauce. Peel and seed the tomatoes, and cut them into chunks. Lightly sauté a finely chopped onion and a chopped garlic clove in a little oil and butter. Add the tomatoes and cook over a brisk heat, stirring occasionally, for 10 minutes, or until they are reduced to a pulp. Season and add herbs to taste. About 2 tablespoons [30 ml.] of butter can be added at the end of the cooking to enrich the sauce.

Ham and Cheese Stuffing

For added color and flavor, mix in 1 pound [½ kg.] of spinach that has been parboiled for 30 seconds, drained, squeezed and finely chopped.

To make about 5 cups [1 ¼ liters] stuffing

½ lb.	boiled ham, diced	¼ kg.
1	garlic clove, chopped	1
1 tsp.	coarse salt	5 ml.
2 tbsp.	finely chopped fresh parsley	30 ml.
1 cup	ricotta cheese	¼ liter
2 or 3	eggs	2 or 3
1 ½ cups	fresh bread crumbs	375 ml.
	pepper	
6 tbsp.	butter, softened	90 ml.
1 tsp.	mixed dried herbs	5 ml.
½ tsp.	grated nutmeg (optional)	2 ml.

In a mortar, pound the garlic and the salt to a paste. Mix in the parsley and transfer the mixture to a bowl. Add the remaining ingredients and work them all together with your hands until an evenly mixed, compact mass is formed.

Pork Stuffing

For added color and flavor, mix in about ¼ cup [50 ml.] of blanched and peeled pistachios or 1 pound [½ kg.] of spinach that has been parboiled for 30 seconds, drained, squeezed dry and finely chopped.

To make about 6 cups [1 ½ liters] stuffing

1 lb.	boneless lean pork, cubed and ground 3 times	½ kg.
½ lb.	fresh pork fatback or fatty pork belly, cubed and ground 3 times	¼ kg.
2 tbsp.	finely chopped fresh parsley	30 ml.
1	garlic clove, chopped and pounded to a paste	1
2 cups	fresh bread crumbs	½ liter
1	egg	1
2 tsp.	mixed dried herbs	10 ml.
1	onion, finely chopped and sautéed in 1 tbsp. [15 ml.] butter until soft	1
	salt and pepper	

Put all of the ingredients in a bowl and mix with your hands until thoroughly combined.

Preserved Lemons

To make 12 preserved lemons

12	lemons	12
1 lb.	coarse salt	½ kg.
1	cinnamon stick, halved (optional)	1
4	whole cloves (optional)	4
6	coriander seeds (optional)	6
4	black peppercorns (optional)	4
1	bay leaf, crumbled (optional)	1
	freshly squeezed lemon juice (optional)	

Quarter each lemon, starting at the top and cutting to within ½ inch [1 cm.] of the bottom, leaving the quarters attached at the base. Open out the lemons, stuff them with coarse salt, then reshape them.

Place a handful of salt in the bottom of each of two 1-quart [1-liter] canning jars. Pack in the lemons, adding more salt and distributing the spices, if used, between the layers. Press the lemons down to pack them tightly and squeeze out some of their juice. If the juice does not cover them, add more lemon juice. Seal the jars.

Leave the jars at room temperature for one month, inverting them briefly from time to time to redistribute the salt and spices. To use the lemons, rinse them and discard the pulp if you wish. Preserved lemons will keep for up to a year without refrigeration. Fresh lemons may be added to the pickling juice in the jars as the original lemons are used up, but must be covered completely by the juice.

Onion Purée

Soubise

To make about 3 cups [¾ liter] purée

6	very large onions	6
¼ cup	raw unprocessed long-grain rice, boiled until tender and drained	50 ml.
3 tbsp.	butter, diced	45 ml.
	salt	

Wrap the onions individually in foil and place them on a baking tray. Bake the onions in a preheated 350° F. [180° C.] oven for one and one half to two hours, or until they feel very tender when squeezed lightly. Unwrap the onions, discard the skins and chop the flesh coarse.

Place the chopped onions and the rice in a saucepan and, stirring occasionally, cook over very low heat for 10 minutes, or until the rice has absorbed any liquid from the onions. Purée the mixture in a food mill or processor, then pass it through a very fine sieve. Reheat the purée, beating constantly with a wooden spoon. Remove the purée from the heat, blend in the butter, and season to taste with salt.

Flageolets and Green Beans

If *flageolets* are not available, dried navy or pea beans may be substituted.

	To serve 6	
1 lb.	*flageolets*, soaked overnight and drained, or covered with water, brought to a boil, allowed to stand for 1 hour and drained	½ kg.
1 lb.	green beans	½ kg.
1	bouquet garni (optional)	1
1	carrot (optional)	1
1	onion, stuck with 2 whole cloves (optional)	1
7 tbsp.	butter, diced	105 ml.
	salt and pepper	
2 tbsp.	chopped fresh parsley (optional)	30 ml.

Place the soaked and drained *flageolets* in a pan with enough water to cover them by about 1½ inches [4 cm.]. Add the bouquet garni, carrot and onion, if using. Bring slowly to a boil. Reduce the heat, cover and simmer for one and one half hours, or until the beans are tender. Drain the beans, reserving the cooking liquid. Remove the bouquet garni, carrot and onion and discard them.

Top and tail the green beans, parboil them in salted water for five minutes and drain them. In a saucepan, combine the *flageolets* and the green beans. Toss for a minute or two over low heat to mix and reheat the beans, adding a little of the *flageolet* cooking liquid if the mixture seems too dry. Remove from the heat and toss in the butter, the parsley, if using, and salt and pepper to taste.

Croutons

You can substitute olive oil or clarified butter for the combination of butter and oil specified in this recipe.

	To make about 1 cup [¼ liter] croutons	
2	bread slices, ½ inch [1 cm.] thick, cut from a stale, firm-textured white loaf	2
4 tbsp.	butter	60 ml.
¼ to ½ cup	oil	50 to 125 ml.

Remove the crusts from the bread and cut the slices into cubes. Combine the butter and ¼ cup [50 ml.] of the oil in a large skillet. Melt the butter over medium heat and, as soon as the butter-and-oil mixture is hot, add the bread cubes and increase the heat to high. Turn the cubes frequently with a broad metal spatula so that they brown evenly on all sides, and add more oil as necessary to keep the cubes from burning. Before serving, drain the croutons on paper towels.

Short-Crust and Rough Puff Dough

One simple formula produces dough for both plain short-crust pastry and for rough puff pastry. The difference is in how you roll it out. For a two-crust pie, double the quantities of all of the ingredients.

	To make enough dough to line or cover a 7- to 8-inch [18- to 20-cm.] pie	
1 cup	flour	¼ liter
¼ tsp.	salt	1 ml.
8 tbsp.	cold unsalted butter, cut into small pieces	120 ml.
3 to 4 tbsp.	cold water	45 to 60 ml.

Mix the flour and salt in a mixing bowl. Add the butter and cut it into the flour rapidly, using two table knives, until the butter is in tiny pieces. Do not work it for more than a few minutes. Add about half of the water and, with a fork, quickly blend it into the flour-and-butter mixture. Add just enough of the rest of the water to allow you to gather the dough together with your hands into a firm ball. Wrap the ball in plastic wrap or wax paper and refrigerate it for two to three hours, or put it in the freezer for 20 minutes, until the outside surface is slightly frozen.

To roll out short-crust dough: Remove the ball of dough from the refrigerator or freezer and put it on a cool, floured surface (a marble slab is ideal). Press out the dough partially with your hand, then give it a few gentle smacks with the rolling pin to flatten it and render it more supple. Roll out the dough from the center until it forms a circle about ½ inch [1 cm.] thick. Turn the dough over so that both sides are floured, and continue rolling until the circle is about ⅛ inch [3 mm.] thick. Roll the dough onto the rolling pin, lift it up, and unroll it over the pie dish. If using the dough to line a piepan, press it firmly against all surfaces and trim the edges. If using the dough to cover a pie, trim the dough to within ½ inch of the rim. Turn under the edges of the dough around the rim to form a double layer, and press it firmly to the rim with thumb and forefinger to crimp the edges.

To roll out rough puff dough: Place the dough on a cool, floured surface and smack it flat with the rolling pin. Turn the dough over to make sure that both sides are well floured. Roll out the dough rapidly into a rectangle about 1 foot [30 cm.] long and 5 to 6 inches [13 to 15 cm.] wide. Fold the two short ends to meet each other in the center, then fold again to align the folded edges with each other. Following the direction of the fold lines, roll the dough into a rectangle again, fold again in the same way and refrigerate for at least 30 minutes. Repeat this process two or three times before using the dough. Always let the dough rest in the refrigerator between rollings.

Recipe Index

All recipes in the index that follows are listed by their English titles except in cases where a food of foreign origin, such as kebabs or moussaka, is universally recognized by its source name. Entries also are organized by the major ingredients specified in the recipe titles. Foreign recipes are listed by country or region of origin. Recipe credits appear on pages 174-176.

General Index/ Glossary

Included in the index to the cooking demonstrations are definitions, in italics, of special culinary terms not explained elsewhere in this volume. The Recipe Index begins on page 168.

Almonds: enclosing in meatballs, 86
Almonds, blanched: *peeled almonds. To make, pour shelled almonds into a pan of boiling water to loosen their skins. After a minute or so, drain the almonds, then slip off the skins with your fingers;* 86
Apron, 9; folding around a roasted saddle, 34, 35; wrapping around a loin chop, 18, 19
Aromatics: herbs, 14; in a hot pot, 64-65; in moussaka, 76; in pilaf, 74; spices, 80; in stew, 61-62; in stock, 52; vegetables, 7, 14, 48, 49, 50, 52, 58, 61, 62, 64, 65, 74, 76, 84
Artichoke bottoms: preparing, 57; in *tajine,* 56-57
Baby lamb: carving, 47; classed by age, 6; larding, 7; roasting whole in a home oven, 47; wine with, 7; wrapping in pork caul, 7, 47
Baron of lamb: carving, 46; deglazing juices, 46; ordering, 46; removing rib bones, 46; roasting, 46; stripping fell, 46; trimming fat, 46
Batter: coating meatballs with chick-pea flour, 86
Beans: broad, in *navarin printanier,* 61, 62; broad, in *tajine,* 56-57; combining *flageolets* with fresh green, 30; serving with roast lamb, 30; soaking dried, 63; stewing lamb with dried, 61, 63. *See also Flageolets*
Beef marrow: extracting and grinding, 23; flavoring lamb sausages, 22, 23
Bitter orange: *a tart-flavored orange used for its juice, also called a sour or Seville orange. Obtainable at fruit specialty stores and Latin American markets in winter. If not available, substitute the juice of a sweet orange mixed with 1 teaspoon [5 ml.] of fresh lemon juice;* 60
Black vinegar: *a black-colored vinegar with a distinctive mellow flavor. Also known as Chenkong rice vinegar, it is obtainable bottled at Oriental food stores.*
Bones: browning, 66; gelatin in, 80; making stock from, 52
Boning: breast, 10-11; chilling meat before boning, 10; removing the pelvic bone from a leg, 10-11; shoulder, 12-13
Bouquet garni: *a bunch of mixed herbs —the classic three being parsley, thyme and bay leaf —tied together or wrapped in cheesecloth and used for flavoring stocks, sauces, braises and*

stews; 51, 52, 53, 58, 59, 62, 63
Braising, 49; adding sugar to browning meat, 61; cooking leftovers, 69, 72, 76; cushion of lamb made with a pair of shoulders, 66-67; cuts for, 7, 49, 60; daube, 58-59; deglazing to make a sauce with liquid, 60; dried beans in a stew, 61, 63; rib chops cooked in a hot pot, 64-65; shanks with garlic, 60; shoulder stewed with spring vegetables, 61-62; using marinade as braising liquid, 14, 49. *See also Stewing*
Bread crumbs: coating rib chops for pan frying, 26, 27; coating wedges of breast meat for broiling, 80; in stuffings, 14, 15; topping moussaka, 77
Breast, 8; basting and glazing, 40, 41; boning, 10-11, 81; broiling pieces coated with bread crumbs and eggs, 80-81; chilling before boning, 10; cooking methods, 7; cooking in a stew, 52-53; diagram of bones, 10; fell, 40; flattening poached and boned meat, 81; poaching, 80; removing fell, 40, 52; roasting a stuffed, 40-41; rolled boneless, 8; shaping boned meat into wedges, 80; stuffing with ricotta cheese, ham and spinach, 40; trussing, 41
Broiling, 17; breast of lamb after poaching, 80-81; cooking leftovers, 69, 72, 74, 76; cuts for, 7; kebab sausages, 22-23; kebabs and zucchini on skewers, 22, 23; leg steaks, 20-21; marinade for, 20; oiling meat, 20; in oven, 20-21; on a ridged-griddle pan, 16, 20; searing meat, 17, 20, 21; thickness of meat for, 20
Bulgur: *a type of cracked wheat made from whole kernels partially cooked before cracking to speed their final cooking. It has a subtle, nutty flavor and is available —fine, medium or coarse —from markets that sell Middle Eastern foods and from health-food stores;* 82, 83. *See also Cracked wheat*
Butter: coating chops with Parmesan cheese and, 26; frying chops in butter and oil, 26-27
Cabbage: parboiling leaves, 72; wrapping and baking strips of leftover meat in, 72-73
Caper sauce: making, with poaching liquid, 51
Cardamom: *an East Indian spice consisting of a fibrous oval pod about 1/2 inch [1 cm.] long, containing 15 to 20 hard, brownish black seeds with a powerful, faintly lemon-like flavor. When dried in kilns, the pod remains green; when sun-dried, the pod bleaches to a cream color;* 86
Carrots: in a casserole with cushion shoulder, 66; in daube, 58; in hot pot, 64, 65; in marinade, 14; in navarin printanier, 61, 62; poached, 50-51; in shepherd's pie, 74-75; in stew, 52-54
Carving: attaching a *manche à gigot*

to the leg, 31, 32, 33; baby lamb, 47; baron of lamb, 46; boned rolled shoulder roast, 37; guard of honor, 39; leg of lamb, 31, 32-33; a leg of lamb with a short shank, 33; resting meat after cooking, 29; roast saddle, 34-35; stuffed and roasted foresaddle, 42-43
Caul: wrapping baby lamb in, 47
Celery: in a casserole with cushion shoulder, 66
Cepe: *an edible, wild mushroom, available dried at specialty markets;* 58
Chicory: parboiling, 70; preparing a bed of, to cook with leftover lamb, 70-71
Chine: *the backbone of an animal. Also, to cut through the backbone, or to scrape the meat off the bony tip of a rib;* 38
Chipolata: *a small, mildly seasoned fresh pork sausage available at French food markets. If not available, other small, mild fresh sausages may be substituted.*
Chops: blade, 8; cooking methods, 7; fried with a coating, 26-27; loin, 9; pan broiling, 20; rib, 8, 9; shoulder, 8; sirloin, 9
Chorizo: *a red and rough-textured smoked sausage made of pork seasoned with garlic and paprika or cayenne pepper. Chorizo is available where Spanish or Latin American foods are sold; if not obtainable, any other highly spiced smoked sausage may be substituted.*
Clarified butter: *butter with its easily burned milk solids removed. To make, melt butter over low heat; spoon off the foam; let stand off the heat until the milk solids settle; then decant the clear yellow liquid on top, discarding the milk solids;* 86
Coarse salt: pounding garlic with, 14; preparing lardons with, 58; preserving lemons in, 57; seasoning meat for stews, 55, 56; in tomato purée, 26
Coating: bread crumbs and egg, 26, 80; butter and Parmesan cheese, 26
Coconut, dried and grated: *sun-dried coconut flesh that is grated before being packaged —usually in cans labeled desiccated coconut. It should not be confused with the sweetened, shredded or flaked coconut known as baker's coconut. It may be used as is, or immersed in milk, refrigerated for several hours and drained before use. Obtainable at health-food stores and stores specializing in Indian foods.*
Cracked wheat: mixing with puréed and sautéed lamb to make kibbeh, 82-83; soaking and draining, 82, 83
Crème fraîche: *tart-flavored cream with the consistency of yogurt. Obtainable at French food markets and some specialty food stores. If not*

available, it can be made from the heavy —but not ultrapasteurized — cream usually sold in health-food stores. Add about 1 1/2 teaspoons [7 ml.] of buttermilk to 1 cup [1/4 liter] of cream. Stirring, heat to 85° F. [30° C.]. Pour the mixture into a crock, cover, and let it rest in a warm place for six to eight hours, or until it thickens. Refrigerate until ready to use.*
Croutons: sautéing bread cubes, 71
Crown roast: preparing, 38
Currants: in *kibbeh,* 83; in pilaf, 74-75
Curry sauce: serving with deep-fried meatballs, 86
Cushion, 66-67; assembling and cooking casserole, 66-67; browning bones, 66; pork stuffing, 66; sewing a pair of shoulders to make a cushion, 67
Custard: topping for gratin, 84-85
Daube, 48, 58-59; adding gelatinous cuts, 58; aromatic vegetables in, 49, 58; cooking pot, 58; herbs in, 58; larding meat, 58, 59; marinating, 59; serving *flageolets* with, 58; wine with, 7
Deep frying: meatballs served in a curry sauce, 86
Deglazing: adding sugar to deglazing liquid to darken color, 61; cooking garlic in deglazing liquid, 30; with lemon juice, 44, 45; making a sauce from pan juices, 24, 29, 32, 33, 36, 40, 42, 44, 45, 46, 60, 61, 64, 66, 84, 85; with wine, 24, 42, 44, 60, 61, 85
Degreasing: pan juices, 30, 36; stock, 52
Dijon mustard: *any mustard made in Dijon, France. Dijon mustards range from a smooth, dark, aromatic variety made from brown mustard seeds, to the very strong, pale-colored "blanc de Dijon" made from white mustard seeds. All are traditionally made with white wine and/or verjuice —the acid juice from unripe grapes —instead of with vinegar.*
Eggplant: in classic moussaka, 76-77; lining charlotte mold with slices of, for molded moussaka, 68, 78-79
Eggs: binding stuffing, 14, 15, 66, 72; coating chops for frying, 26, 27; thickening sauce with yolks, 50, 51; yolks as thickening agent for stew, 55
Eye of loin, 9; carving a roast saddle, 34, 35; pan frying, 24-25
Fell: cutting off a rack, 39; described, 7; on large cuts, 7; peeling from saddle, 34; on roasted breast, 40; stripping from baron, 46; stuffing a leg of lamb under the, 44-45
Fines herbes: *a mixture of finely chopped fresh herbs —the classic herbs being parsley, chives, tarragon and chervil.*
Flageolets: cooking and combining with fresh green beans, 30; cooking

Recipe Credits

The sources for the recipes in this volume are shown below. Page references in brackets indicate where the recipes appear in the anthology.

The Academy of Medicinal Science of the U.S.S.R., *Kniga o Vkusnoi i Zdorovoi Pishche.* Published by Izdatelstvo Pishchenaya Prornyshlennost (Publishing House for the Food Industry), Moscow, 1965. Translated by permission of Izdatelstvo Pishchenaya Prornyshlennost (Publishing House for the Food Industry)(138).
Ainé, Offray, *Le Cuisinier Méridional.* Offray Ainé, Imprimeur-Libraire, Avignon, 1855(92, 120).
Androuet, Pierre, *La Cuisine au Fromage.* © 1978. Éditions Stock. Published by Éditions Stock, Paris. Translated by permission of Éditions Stock, Paris(124).
Atrutel, Mrs. J., *An Easy and Economical Book of Jewish Cookery.* Printed by Alabaster & Passmore, London, 1874(120, 123, 134).
Aureden, Lilo, *Das Schmeckt so Gut.* © 1965 by Lichtenberg Verlag, München. Published by Lichtenberg Verlag, Munich. Translated by permission of Kindler Verlag GmbH, Munich(91, 117). *Was Männern so Gut Schmeckt.* Copyright 1953 Paul List Verlag, München. Published by Paul List Verlag, Munich. Translated by permission of Paul List Verlag GmbH & Co. KG(104).
Ayrton, Elisabeth, *English Provincial Cooking.* Copyright © 1980 by Elisabeth Ayrton. Reprinted by permission of Harper & Row, Publishers, Inc.(155).
Beard, James A., *James Beard's American Cookery.* Copyright © 1972 by James A. Beard. Published by Hart-Davis, MacGibbon Ltd./Granada Publishing Ltd., Hertfordshire. By permission of Hart-Davis, MacGibbon Ltd./Granada Publishing Ltd.(107, 149). *The Fireside Cook Book.* Copyright © 1949, 1976 by Simon & Schuster, Inc. Published by Simon & Schuster, Inc., New York. By permission of Simon & Schuster, Inc.(122).
Benkirane, Fettouma, *La Nouvelle Cuisine Marocaine.* © Fettouma Benkirane and SEFA, Paris. Published by J. P. Taillandier, Paris 1979. Translated by permission of SEFA Editions and the author(125, 131, 136).
Biondi, Lisa (Editor), *350 Ricette di Cucina Leggera.* Published by Edizioni Mondadori/Unil-It S.p.A., Milan. Translated by permission of Lisa Biondi(110, 138, 161).
Blake, Anthony and Quentin Crewe, *Great Chefs of France.* © 1978 Marshall Editions Limited. By permission of Marshall Editions Limited and Charles Barrier(96).
Blencowe, Anne, *The Receipt Book of Anne Blencowe.* (1694 A.D.). Published by Guy Chapman, The Adelphi, London, 1925(145, 154).
Bocuse, Paul, *The New Cuisine.* Copyright © Flammarion 1976. English translation, copyright © 1977 by Random House, Inc. Published by Hart-Davis, MacGibbon Ltd./Granada Publishing Ltd., Hertfordshire, 1978. By permission of Hart-Davis, MacGibbon Ltd./Granada Publishing Ltd.(119).
Bouayed, Fatima-Zohra, *La Cuisine Algérienne.* Published by S.N.E.D. (Société Nationale d'Édition et de Diffusion), Algiers, 1978. Translated by permission of the author(137, 149).
Bouillard, Paul, *La Gourmandise à Bon Marché.* Copyright 1925 by Albin Michel. Published by Éditions Albin Michel, Paris. Translated by permission of Éditions Albin Michel(104). *La Cuisine au Coin du Feu.* Copyright 1928 by Albin Michel. Published by Éditions Albin Michel, Paris. Translated by permission of Éditions Albin Michel(128, 146).
Breteuil, Jules, *Le Cuisinier Européen.* Published by Garnier Frères Libraires-Éditeurs, Paris, 1860(136, 157).
Bute, John, Fourth Marquis of (Editor), *Moorish Recipes.* Published by Oliver and Boyd, Edinburgh. By permission of the Sixth Marquess of Bute, Isle of Bute (90, 97, 135).
Calera, Ana-Maria, *Cocina Castellana.* © Ana-

Maria Calera 1974. Published by Editorial Bruguera S.A., Barcelona, 1974. Translated by permission of Editorial Bruguera S.A.(144). *Cocina Catalana.* © Ana-Maria Calera 1974. Published by Editorial Bruguera S.A., Barcelona, 1974. Translated by permission of Editorial Bruguera S.A.(150). *365 Recetas de Cocina Vasca.* © Ana-Maria Calera. © Editorial Everest. Published by Editorial Everest, S.A., Madrid. Translated by permission of Editorial Everest S.A.(112).
Carréras, Marie-Thérèse and Georges Lafforgue, *Les Bonnes Recettes du Pays Catalan.* © Presses de la Renaissance, 1979. Published by Presses de la Rennaissance, Paris. Translated by permission of Presses de la Renaissance(116).
Cavalcanti, Ippolito, Duca di Buonvicino, *Cucina Teorico-Pratica.* Sixth Edition. November 1849, Naples(111).
Chortanova, Sonya, *Nasha Kuchniya.* Published by Nauki i Izkustvo, Sofia, 1955. Translated by permission of Jusautor Copyright Agency, Sofia(135, 149).
Clark, Morton G., *French-American Cooking from New Orleans to Quebec.* Copyright © 1967 by Morton G. Clark. Published by J. B. Lippincott, New York. By permission of Harper & Row, Publishers, Inc., New York(88).
Comas, Maria Dolores, *Lo Mejor de la Cocina Española.* Copyright 1979 Geocolor S.A., Barcelona. Published by Geocolor, Barcelona. Translated by permission of Ediciones Grijalbo S.A., Barcelona(93, 148).
Conran, Caroline, *British Cooking.* © Caroline Conran Ink Ltd., 1978. Published by Park Lane Press, London. By permission of The Rainbird Publishing Group Ltd., London(145).
Corey, Helen, *The Art of Syrian Cookery.* Copyright © 1962 by Helen Corey. Published by Doubleday and Company, Inc., New York. By permission of Doubleday and Company, Inc.(162).
Correnti, Pino, *Il Libro d'Oro della Cucina e dei Vini di Sicilia.* Copyright © 1976 Ugo Mursia Editore, Milano. Published by Ugo Mursia Editore S.p.A., Milan. Translated by permission of Ugo Mursia Editore S.p.A.(89, 99, 110, 129).
Courtine, Robert (La Reynière), *Mes Repas les Plus Étonnants.* © 1973 by Éditions Robert Laffont. Published by Éditions Robert Laffont, Paris. Translated by permission of the author(93).
Il Cuoco Piemontese *(Che Insegna Facilmente a Cucinare Ogni Sorta di Vivande in Grasso ed in Magro).* Published by Le Livre Precieux, Turin, 1972, facsimile reprint(126).
Cutler, Carol, *Haute Cuisine for Your Heart's Delight.* Copyright © 1973 by Carol Cutler. By permission of Clarkson N. Potter, Inc.(140). *The Six-Minute Soufflé and Other Culinary Delights.* Copyright © 1976 by Carol Cutler. By permission of Clarkson N. Potter, Inc.(160).
The Daily Telegraph, *400 Prize Recipes for Practical Cookery.* © by The Daily Telegraph. Published by The Daily Telegraph, London, c. 1950. By permission of The Daily Telegraph(154).
Dar, Krishna Prasad, *Kashmiri Cooking.* © Krishna Prasad Dar, 1977. Published by Vikas Publishing House Pvt. Ltd., New Delhi. By permission of Vikas Publishing House Pvt. Ltd., Sahibabad(163).
David, Elizabeth, *A Book of Mediterranean Food.* © Elizabeth David, 1950, 1951, 1955, 1965, 1980. Published in 1980 under the title *Elizabeth David Classics,* comprising *A Book of Mediterranean Food, French Country Cooking* and *Summer Cooking,* by Jill Norman Ltd., London. By permission of Jill Norman Ltd.(157).
David, Josephine, *Every-Day Cookery for Families of Moderate Income.* © Copyright F. Warne (Publishers) Limited, London. Published by Frederick Warne and Co., London. By permission of Frederick Warne (Publishers) Ltd.(89).
Davidis, Henriette, *Henriette Davidis Illustriertes Praktisches Kochbuch.* Newly revised by Helene Faber. Published by Schreitersche Verlagsbuchhandlung, Berlin, W.35(142).
de Lune, Pierre, *Le Nouveau Cuisinier.* Paris, 1656 (115, 129).

de Pomiane, Edouard, *Le Carnet d'Anna.* Calmann-Levy, 1967. Translated by permission of Éditions Calmann-Levy, Paris(128).
Delfs, Robert A., *The Good Food of Szechwan.* Copyright © 1974 by Kodansha International Ltd. Reprinted by permission of Kodansha International(95).
Derys, Gaston, *Les Plats au Vin.* Copyright © 1937 by Albin Michel. Published by Éditions Albin Michel, Paris. Translated by permission of Éditions Albin Michel(99, 117).
Donati, Stella (Editor), *Il Grande Manuale della Cucina Regionale.* Copyright 1979 Euroclub Italia S.p.A., Bergamo. Published by Sugar Co. Edizioni S.r.l., Milan. Translated by permission of Euroclub(91, 102, 144).
Durand, Charles, *Le Cuisinier Durand (Cuisine du Midi et du Nord).* Newly revised eighth edition. Nîmes, 1863(103).
Elisabeth, Mme., *500 Nouvelles Recettes de Cuisine.* Published by Éditions Baudinière, Paris. Translated by permission of Nouvelles Éditions Baudinière(112).
Eren, Neşet, *The Art of Turkish Cooking.* Copyright © 1969 by Neşet Eren. Published by Doubleday & Company, Inc., New York. By permission of the author(89, 132).
Feslikenian, Franca, *Cucina e Vini del Lazio.* © copyright 1973 Ugo Mursia Editore, Milan, Italy. Published by Ugo Mursia Editore S.p.A. Translated by permission of Ugo Mursia Editore S.p.A.(105, 140).
Foods of the World, *American Cooking, The Great West; The Cooking of India.* Copyright © 1971 Time-Life Books Inc.; Copyright © 1975 Time Inc. Published by Time-Life Books, Alexandria(97, 139).
Greene, Bert, *Bert Greene's Kitchen Bouquets.* Copyright © 1979 by Bert Greene. Published by Contemporary Books, Inc., Chicago. By permission of the author and his agent, James Brown Associates, Inc., New York(102, 158).
Grigson, Jane, *English Food.* Copyright © 1974 Jane Grigson. Published by Macmillan London Limited, 1974. By permission of Macmillan, London and Basingstoke(106, 108). *Food with the Famous.* © 1979 by Jane Grigson. Published by Michael Joseph, London. By permission of David Higham Associates Limited, for the author(133).
Guasch, Juan Castello, *iBon Profit! (El Libro de la Cocina Ibicenca).* Copyright by the author. Published by Imprenta ALFA, Palma de Mallorca, 1971. Translated by permission of the author(126).
Guinaudeau-Franc, Zette, *Les Secrets des Fermes en Périgord Noir.* Published by Éditeur Berger-Levrault, Paris, 1980. Translated by permission of the author(112).
Hachten, Harva, *Kitchen Safari.* Copyright © 1970 by Harva Hachten. Reprinted by permission of Atheneum Publishers(139).
Hawliczkowa, Helena, *Kuchnia Polska.* Edited by Maria Librowska. Copyright by Helena Hawliczkowa. Published by Panstowe Wydawnictwo Edonomiczne, Warsaw, 1976. Translated by permission of Agencja Autorska, Warsaw, for the author(150, 153, 154).
Hayes, Babette, *Two Hundred Years of Australian Cooking.* Copyright © Thomas Nelson (Australia) 1970. Reprinted by permission of Thomas Nelson (Australia)(109).
Hellermann, Dorothee V., *Das Kochbuch aus Hamburg.* © Copyright 1975 by Verlagsteam Wolfgang Hölker. Published by Verlag Wolfgang Hölker, Münster. Translated by permission of Verlag Wolfgang Hölker(100).
Hewitt, Jean, *The New York Times Large Type Cookbook.* Copyright © 1969 by Jean Hewitt. By permission of Times Books, a division of Quadrangle/The New York Times Book Co.(122).
Heyraud, H., *La Cuisine à Nice.* Published by Imprimerie-Librairie-Papeterie, Nice, 1922(134).
House & Garden's New Cook Book. Copyright © 1967 by The Condé Nast Publications Inc. By permission of The Condé Nast Publications Inc.(111, 114).
Hutchins, Sheila, *English Recipes and Others from Scotland, Wales and Ireland.* © 1967 by Sheila Hutchins. Published by Methuen & Co. Ltd. By permission of the author(150, 155).
Iny, Daisy, *The Best of Baghdad Cooking.* Copyright © 1976 by Daisy Iny. Published by Saturday Review Press/E. P. Dutton & Co., Inc., New York. By permission of the Jean

V. Nagger Literary Agency, for the author(159).

Isnard, Léon, *La Gastronomie Africaine.* © Albin Michel 1930. Published by Éditions Albin Michel, Paris. Translated by permission of Éditions Albin Michel(136, 145).

Jans, Hugh, *Vrij Nederlands Kookboek.* © 1972, 1973, 1974, 1977 Unieboek BV/CAJ van Dishoeck, Bussum. Published by Unieboek BV/CAJ van Dishoeck. Translated by permission of Unieboek BV/CAJ van Dishoeck(108).

Jeffries, Bob, *Soul Food Cookbook.* Copyright © 1969 Bob Jeffries. Reprinted with permission of The Bobbs-Merrill Company, Inc.(159).

Karsenty, Irène and Lucienne, *La Cuisine Pied-Noir (Cuisines du Terroir).* © 1974, by Éditions Denoël, Paris. Published by Éditions Denoël. Translated by permission of Éditions Denoël(92).

Kenney-Herbert, Colonel, *Dainty Dishes for Indian Tables.* Second Edition. Published by W. Newman & Co., Calcutta, 1881(148, 158).

Keys, John D., *Japanese Cuisine.* Published by Charles E. Tuttle Co., Inc. 1966. By permission of Charles E. Tuttle Co., Inc.(95).

Kulinarische Gerichte: Zu Gast bei Freunden. Sixth Edition 1977. Copyright to German translation by Verlag für die Frau DDR Leipzig. Published by Verlag für die Frau and Verlag MIR, Moscow. Translated by permission of The Copyright Agency of the USSR-VAAP(127, 133).

La Chapelle, Vincent, *The Modern Cook,* Vol. 3. London, 1733(98).

Laasri, Ahmed, *240 Recettes de Cuisine Marocaine.* © 1978 Jacques Grancher, Éditeur. Published by Jacques Grancher, Éditeur, Paris. Translated by permission of Jacques Grancher, Éditeur(96, 118).

Labarre, Irène and Jean Mercier, *La Cuisine du Mouton.* © Solar, 1978. Published by Solar, Paris. Translated by permission of Solar(102, 121, 125).

Lagattolla, Franco, *The Recipes that Made a Million.* © Franco Lagattolla 1978. Published by Orbis Publishing Limited, London, 1978. By permission of Orbis Publishing Limited(123).

Lem, Arthur and Dan Morris, *The Hong Kong Cookbook.* Copyright © 1970 by Arthur Lem and Dan Morris. Published by Funk & Wagnalls, New York. By permission of Harper & Row, Publishers, New York(118).

Lemnis, Maria and Henryk Vitry, *W Staro Polskiej Kuchni I Przy Polskim Stole.* © Copyright by Polska Agencja Interpress. Published by Wydawnictwo Interpress, Warsaw, 1979. Translated by permission of Wydawnictwo Interpress(101, 105).

Liebman, Malvina, *Jewish Cookery from Boston to Baghdad.* © 1975, courtesy of E.A. Seemann Publishing, Inc., Miami, Florida(139).

London, Sheryl, *Eggplant and Squash: A Versatile Feast.* Copyright © 1976 by Sheryl London. Published by Atheneum Publishers, Inc., New York, 1976. By permission of Atheneum Publishers, Inc.(96, 122).

Lucrezi, Nice Cortelli, *Le Ricette della Nonna.* Published by Centro Editoriale Tipografico, Teramo, 1966, 1969, 1974. Translated by permission of the author(95, 127).

McCully, Helen, *Waste Not, Want Not.* Copyright © 1975 by Helen McCully. By permission of Random House, Inc.(148).

Magyar, Elek, *Kochbuch für Feinschmecker.* © Dr. Magyar Bálint, Dr. Magyar Pál. Published by Corvina, Budapest, 1979. Originally published in 1967 under the title *Az Inyesmester Szakacskonyve* by Corvina Verlag, Budapest. Translated by permission of Artisjus, Literary Agency, Budapest(142).

The Maharani of Jaipur (Editor), *Gourmet's Gateway.* Copyright by Her Highness Maharani Gayatri Devi of Jaipur. Published by Her Highness Maharani Gayatri Devi of Jaipur, 1969. By permission of Mrs. Vijay Singh, for the editor(143).

Le Manuel de la Friandise *(Ou les Talents de ma Cuisinière Isabeau Mis en Lumière.)* Attributed to author of *Le Petit Cuisinier Économe.* Published by Janet, Librairie rue Saint-Jacques, Paris, in 1796 and 1797(88, 113, 124).

Mardikian, George, *Dinner at Omar Khayyam's.* Copyright © 1945 by George Mardikian. Copyright renewed. Published by The Viking Press, New York. By permission of McIntosh and Otis, Inc., New York(131, 138, 162).

Markovic Spasenija-Pata (Editor), *Veliki Narodni Kuvar.* Copyright by the author. First Edition "Politika," Belgrade, 1938. Published by Narodna Knjiga, Belgrade, 1979. Translated by permission of Jogoslovenska Autorska Agencija, Belgrade, for the heir to the author(98, 162).

Martin, Peter and Joan, *Japanese Cooking.* Copyright © by Peter and Joan Martin. Reprinted by permission of Bobbs-Merrill Co. Inc., Indiana(132).

Marty, Albin, *Fourmiguetto: Souvenirs, Contes et Recettes du Languedoc.* Published by Éditions CREER, F63340 Nonette, 1978. Translated by permission of Éditions CREER(132, 141).

70 Médecins de France. *Le Trésor de la Cuisine du Bassin Méditerranéen.* Published by Les Laboratoires du Dr. Zizine(130).

Mehta, Jeroo, *101 Parsi Recipes.* Copyright © 1973 by Vakils, Feffer and Simons Private Ltd. Published by Vakils, Feffer and Simons Private Ltd., Bombay. By permission of the author(140).

Mei, Fu Pei, *Pei Mei's Chinese Cook Book,* Vol. 1. Published by T & S Industrial Co. Ltd., Taipei. By permission of T & S Industrial Co. Ltd.(94).

Le Ménagier de Paris, *(Traité de Morale et d'Economie Domestique par un Bourgeois Parisien),* Tome 2. Composed c. 1393. Reprinted by Slatkine Reprints, Geneva, 1967. Translated by permission of Slatkine Reprints(161).

Menon, *La Cuisinière Bourgeoise.* Paris, 1803(113, 147).

Metzler, Fred and Klaus Oster, *Aal Blau und Errö-thetes Mädchen.* © Walter Hädecke Verlag, Weil der Stadt, 1976. Published by Walter Hädecke Verlag. Translated by permission of Walter Hädecke Verlag(123).

Monod, Louis, *La Cuisine Florentine.* Published by Éditions Daniel Morcrette, 95270 Luzarches, 1977. Translated by permission of Éditions Daniel Morcrette(129).

Montagné, Prosper (Editor), *Manuel du Bon Cuistot et de la Bonne Ménagère.* Published by Librairie Chapelot, Paris, 1913. Translated by permission of Le Club Prosper Montagné, Paris(120, 146).

Myra (Editor), *Myra's Cookery Book.* Published by Goubaud and Son, London, 1883(163).

Nignon, Édouard (Editor), *Le Livre de Cuisine de L'Ouest-Éclair.* Published in 1941 by L'Ouest-Éclair, Rennes. Translated by permission of Société d'Éditions Ouest-France, Rennes(101, 137).

Ohio Housewives, *Ohio Housewives Companion,* 1876(156).

Olney, Judith, *Comforting Food.* Copyright © 1979 by Judith Olney. Published by Atheneum Publishers Inc., New York. By permission of Atheneum Publishers Inc.(114).

Olney, Richard, *The French Menu Cookbook.* Copyright © 1970 by Richard Olney. Published by Simon & Schuster, New York. By permission of John Schaffner, Literary Agent, New York(107, 152). *Simple French Food.* Copyright © 1974 by Richard Olney. Published by Atheneum Publishers, New York. By permission of Jill Norman Ltd., London(121).

Ons Kookboek. Published by Uitgever Belgische Boerenbond Economaat for Katholiek Vormingswerk van Landelijke Vrouwen, Leuven, 1977. Translated by permission of Katholiek Vormingswerk van Landelijke Vrouwen(103, 128).

Ortega, Simone, *Mil Ochenta Recetas de Cocina.* © Simone K. de Ortega, 1972. © Alianza Editorial, S.A., Madrid, 1972. Published by Alianza Editorial, S.A. Translated by permission of Alianza Editorial, S.A.(100).

Paradissis, Chrissa, *The Best Book of Greek Cookery.* Copyright © 1976 P. Efstathiadis & Sons. Published by Efstathiadis Group, Athens, 1976. By permission of P. Efstathiadis & Sons S.A.(151).

Peck, Paula, *Paula Peck's Art of Good Cooking.* Copyright © 1961, 1966 by Paula Peck. Published by Simon & Schuster, a division of Gulf & Western Corporation, New York. By permission of Simon & Schuster, a division of Gulf & Western Corporation(151).

Peter, Madeleine (Editor), *Favorite Recipes of the Great Women Chefs of France.* Translated and edited by Nancy Simmons. Copyright © 1977 by Éditions Robert Laffont S.A. Copyright © 1979 by Holt, Rinehart and Winston. By permission of Holt, Rinehart and Winston, publishers(94).

Petit, A., *La Gastronomie en Russie.* Published by the author and Émile Mellier, Paris, 1860(89).

Les Petits Plats et les Grands. © 1977 by Éditions Denoël, Paris. Published by Éditions Denoël Sarl, Paris. Translated by permission of Éditions Denoël Sarl(134).

The Pleasures of Cooking, Vol. 2 No. 1, May-June 1979. Bi-monthly publication. Copyright © 1979 by Cuisinart ® Cooking Club Inc. Published by Cuisinart ® Cooking Club Inc., Connecticut. By permission of Cuisinart ® Cooking Club Inc.(141).

Poulson, Joan, *Old Lancashire Recipes.* © Joan Poulson 1977. Published by Hendon Publishing Co., Ltd., Nelson. By permission of Hendon Publishing Co., Ltd.(124). *Old Thames Valley Recipes.* © Joan Poulson 1973. Published by Hendon Publishing Co., Ltd., Nelson. By permission of Hendon Publishing Co., Ltd.(157).

Roggero, Savina, *Come Scegliere e Cucinare le Carni.* © Arnoldo Mondadori Editore 1973. Published by Arnoldo Mondadori Editore, Milano. Translated by permission of the author(109).

Root, Waverley, *The Best of Italian Cooking.* Copyright © 1974 by Edita S.A. Published by André Deutsch Limited, London. By permission of André Deutsch Limited(93).

Rosa-Limpo, Bertha, *O Livro de Pantagruel.* Published by Sociedade National de Tipografia, Lisbon, 1952. Translated by permission of Sociedade Portuguesa de Autores, Lisbon, for the author(113).

Roy-Camille, Christiane and Annick Marie, *Les Meilleures Recettes de la Cuisine Antillaise.* © Jean-Pierre Delarge, Éditions Universitaires, 1978. Published by Jean-Pierre Delarge, Éditeur, Paris. Translated by permission of Jean-Pierre Delarge, Éditeur(92, 143).

Rundell, Mrs., *Modern Domestic Cookery.* Published by Milner and Company Limited, London(91).

Salta, Romeo, *The Pleasures of Italian Cooking.* Copyright © Romeo Salta 1962. Reprinted with permission of Macmillan Publishing Co., Inc.(109,144).

Savarin, Mme. Jeanne (Editor), *La Cuisine des Familles* (Weekly Magazine). May 24, 1908, June 28, 1908, July 2, 1905(115, 116, 135).

Scheibler, Sophie Wilhelmine, *Allgemeines Deutsches Kochbuch für alle Stände.* Published by C. J. Amelangs Berlag, Leipzig, 1896(147).

Sheridan, Monica, *My Irish Cook Book.* Copyright © 1965 by Monica Sheridan. Published by Frederick Muller Ltd., London, 1966. First published by Doubleday & Company, Inc., New York, under the title *The Art of Irish Cooking.* By permission of Frederick Muller Ltd.(125).

Schuler, Elizabeth, *Mein Kochbuch.* © Copyright 1948 by Schuler-Verlag, Stuttgart-N, Lenzhalde 28. Published by Schuler Verlagsgesellschaft mbH, Herrsching. Translated by permission of Schuler Verlagsgesellschaft mbH(116).

Schishkov, Dr. Georgi, and Stoil Vuchkov, *Bulgarski Natzionalni Yastiya.* © by the authors, 1978 c/o Jusautor, Sofia. First published by Projizdat, Sofia, 1959. Translated by permission of Jusautor Copyright Agency(153).

Simon, Nezih, *Turkish Cookery.* © Nezih Simon. Published by Tredolphin Press, London, 1968, 1970. By permission of the author(90).

Simonet, Suzanne, *Le Grand Livre de la Cuisine Occitane.* © Jean-Pierre Delarge, Éditions Universitaires, 1977. Published by Jean-Pierre Delarge, Éditeur, Paris. Translated by permission of Jean-Pierre Delarge, Éditeur(133).

Singh, Mrs. Balbir, *Mrs. Balbir Singh's Indian Cookery.* © Mrs. Balbir Singh, 1961. Published by Mills & Boon Limited, London. By permission of Mills & Boon Limited(160).

Slater, Mary, *Caribbean Cooking for Pleasure.* © Copyright Mary Slater 1970. Published by The Hamlyn Publishing Group Limited, London. By permission of The Hamlyn Publishing Group Limited(142).

Smires, Latifa Bennani, *La Cuisine Marocaine.* © Les Éditions Alpha. Published by Alpha G.E.A.M. Casablanca, 1974. Translated by permission of Société Nationale d'Édi-

tion et de Diffusion Al Madariss, Casablanca(91, 130).
Stuber, Hedwig Maria, *Ich Helf Dir Kochen.* © BLV Verlagsgesellschaft mbH, München, 1976. Published by BLV Verlagsgesellschaft mbH, Munich. Translated by permission of BLV Verlagsgesellschaft mbH(126).
Swedish Recipes (Publicity Booklet). Published by LT's Förlag for the Federation of Swedish Farmers (L.R.F.), Stockholm, 1975. By permission of Publicity Dept., Federation of Swedish Farmers (L.R.F.)(119).
Tibbott, S. Minwel, *Welsh Fare.* © National Museum of Wales (Welsh Folk Museum). Published by National Museum of Wales (Welsh Folk Museum), 1976. By permission of National Museum of Wales (Welsh Folk Museum) (156).
Tobias, Doris and Mary Merris, *The Golden Lemon.* Copyright © 1978 by Doris Tobias and Mary Merris. Published by Atheneum Publishers, New York, 1978. By per-

mission of Atheneum Publishers(127).
Tschirky, Oscar, *The Cook Book by "Oscar" of the Waldorf.* Copyright 1896 by Oscar Tschirky. Published by The Werner Company, Chicago and New York(158).
Urvater, Michèle and David Liederman, *Cooking the Nouvelle Cuisine in America.* Copyright © 1979 by Michèle Urvater and David Liederman. Published by the Workman Publishing Company, Inc., New York. By permission of the Workman Publishing Company, Inc. (108).
The Volunteers of the American Hospital of Paris and Elizabeth W. Esterling (Editors), *Le Cookbook.* © The American Hospital of Paris, 1978. Published by The American Hospital of Paris. Translated by permission of The American Hospital of Paris(100).
Vuyk, Beb, *Groot Indonesisch Kookboek.* Copyright © 1973 by Uitgeverij Luitingh B.V. Published by Uitgeverij Lui-

tingh B.V. Laren. Translated by permission of Uitgeverij Luitingh B.V.(90).
Wason, Betty, *Bride in the Kitchen.* Copyright © 1964 Elizabeth Wason Hall. Reprinted by permission of Doubleday & Company, Inc.(102, 152).
Women's Committee of The Walters Art Gallery, *Private Collections: A Culinary Treasure.* Copyright © 1973 by The Walters Art Gallery, Baltimore. By permission of The Walters Art Gallery, Baltimore(104).
Zane, Eva, *Greek Cooking for the Gods.* Copyright © 1970 by Eva Zane. Published by 101 Productions, San Francisco. By permission of 101 Productions(106, 110, 156).
Zelayeta, Elena, *Elena's Secrets of Mexican Cooking.* © 1958 by Prentice-Hall, Inc., Englewood Cliffs, N.J. Published by Prentice-Hall, Inc. By permission of Prentice-Hall, Inc.(103).

Acknowledgments

The indexes for this book were prepared by Louise W. Hedberg. The editors are particularly indebted to Dr. Bradford Berry, U.S. Department of Agriculture, Beltsville, Maryland; William A. Broscovak, American Sheep Producers Council, Inc., Denver, Colorado; John Davis, London; Gail Duff, Kent, England; Daniel L. Engeljohn, U.S. Department of Agriculture, Washington, D.C.; H. Kenneth Johnson, National Live Stock & Meat Board, Chicago, Illinois; Dr. Norman G. Marriott, Department of Food Science, Virginia Polytechnic Institute, Blacksburg; Ann O'Sullivan, Majorca, Spain; Dr. R. H. Smith, Aberdeen, Scotland; and Caroline Wood, Sussex, England.

The editors also wish to thank: Pat Alburey, Hertfordshire, England; R. Allen & Co., Ltd., London; Mary Attenborough, Essex, England; Sara Beck, U.S. Department of Agriculture, Washington, D.C.; Liz Clasen, London; Emma Codrington, Surrey, England; George M. Cooke, Department of Viticulture and Enology, University of California at Davis; Dr. Russell Cross, U.S. Department of Agriculture, Clay Center, Nebraska; Anne Dare, Meat Promotion Executive, London; W. J. Duncum, Hertfordshire, England; Mimi Errington, Nottingham, England; C. D. Figg, Meat & Livestock Commission, Milton Keynes, England; Dr. George Flick, Department of Food Science, Virginia Polytechnic Institute, Blacksburg; Frank Gerrard, M.B.E., London; Francisco Guillen, Giant Food Inc., Alexandria, Virginia; Annie Hall, London; Maggie

Heinz, London; Dr. Douglas E. Hogue, Cornell University, Ithaca, New York; Maria Johnson, Hertfordshire, England; Pippa Millard, London; Sonya Mills, Kent, England; Wendy Morris, London; Dilys Naylor, Surrey, England; LeAnn Nelson, American Sheep Producers Council, Inc., Denver, Colorado; Dr. Terry Roberts, Meat Research Institute, Bristol, England; Dr. John R. Romans, Department of Animal Science, University of Illinois, Urbana; Henry Sautter, Larimer's Market, Washington, D.C.; Cathy Sharpe, Annandale, Virginia; Dr. Gary C. Smith, Dr. James W. Bassett, Animal Science Department, Texas A. & M. University, College Station; Gay Starrack, National Live Stock & Meat Board, Chicago, Illinois; Stephanie Thompson, London; Fiona Tillett, London; Pat Tookey, London; Tina Walker, London.

Picture Credits

The sources for the pictures in this book are listed below. Credits for each of the photographers and illustrators are listed by page number in sequence with successive pages indicated by hyphens; where necessary, the locations of pictures within pages are also indicated —separated from page numbers by dashes.

Photographs by John Cook: 10 —bottom right, 11 —bottom, 14 —top right, 15 —left, 18 —top, 19 —top left, 22 —top right, 23 —bottom, 26-27, 30 —bottom, 32 —top right and bottom, 33, 40-41, 42-43 —top, 46, 50-51, 52 —top, bottom left, bottom center, 53-54, 56, 57 —top left (2) and bottom, 61-63, 64 —top right and bottom, 65, 68-74, 75 —top left, top center and bottom, 76-77, 78 —bottom,

79 —top center, top right and bottom, 84-85. Other photographs (alphabetically): Tom Belshaw, 14 —bottom, 15 —center, 18 —bottom, 19 —top center, top right and bottom, 75 —top right. Alan Duns, cover, 4, 15 —right, 16, 20 —bottom, 38-39, 44-45, 47, 57 —top right (2), 64 —top left, 78 —top, 79 —top left, 80-83. John Elliott, 10 —top right, 11 —top, 22 —top left and bottom, 23 —top, 24-25, 30 —top and center, 31, 32 —top left, top center, 48, 52 —bottom right, 59 —bottom right. Chris Harvey, 55, 58, 59 —except bottom right, 60. Louis Klein, 2. Bob Komar, 28, 42-43 —bottom. Aldo Tutino, 12 —except bottom left, 13, 14 —top left, 20 —top, 21, 34-37, 66-67, 86.

Illustrations (alphabetically): Biruta Akerbergs, 10 —top left and bottom left, 12 —bottom left. Richard Lovell, 8-9. From The Mary Evans Picture Library and private sources and

Food & Drink: A Pictorial Archive from Nineteenth Century Sources by Jim Harter, published by Dover Publications, Inc., 1979, 6-7, 91-151.

Library of Congress Cataloguing in Publication Data
Main entry under title:
Lamb.
    (The Good cook, techniques & recipes)
    Includes index.
    1. Cookery (Lamb and mutton) I. Time-Life Books.
II. Series: Good cook, techniques & recipes.
TX749.L228   1981   641.6'63   80-27942
ISBN 0-8094-2910-1
ISBN 0-8094-2909-8 (lib. bdg.)
ISBN 0-8094-2908-X (retail ed.)